VISUAL HABITS:
NUNS, FEMINISM, AND AMERICAN POSTWAR POPULAR CULTURE

The 1950s and 1960s were times of extraordinary social and political change that redrew the boundaries between traditional and progressive, conservative and liberal. Nowhere is this more apparent than in the history of Catholic nuns. During these two decades, nuns boldly experimented with their role in the church, removing their habits, rejecting the cloister, and fighting for social justice. The media quickly took to their cause and dubbed them 'the new nuns,' modern exemplars of liberated but sexually contained womanhood.

With *Visual Habits*, Rebecca Sullivan brings this unexamined history of nuns to the fore, revisiting the intersection of three distinct movements – the Second Vatican Council, the second wave of feminism, and the sexual revolution – to explore the pivotal role nuns played in revamping cultural expectations of femininity and feminism.

From *The Nun's Story* to *The Flying Nun* to *The Singing Nun*, nuns were a major presence in mainstream media and culture. Charting their evolving representation in film and television, popular music, magazines, and girls' literature, Sullivan discusses these images in the context of the period's seemingly unlimited potential for social change. In the process, she delivers a rich cultural analysis of a topic too long ignored.

REBECCA SULLIVAN is an assistant professor in the Faculty of Communication and Culture at the University of Calgary.

VISUAL HABITS

Nuns, Feminism, and American Postwar Popular Culture

Rebecca Sullivan

UNIVERSITY OF TORONTO PRESS
Toronto   Buffalo   London

© University of Toronto Press Incorporated 2005
Toronto Buffalo London
Printed in Canada

ISBN 0-8020-3935-9 (cloth)
ISBN 0-8020-3776-3 (paper)

Printed on acid-free paper

Library and Archives Canada Cataloguing in Publication

Sullivan, Rebecca, 1966–
 Visual habits : nuns and American postwar popular culture / Rebecca
 Sullivan

 Includes bibliographical references and index.
 ISBN 0-8020-3935-9 (bound)   ISBN 0-8020-3776-3 (pbk.)

 1. Nuns in mass media – United States.   2. Nuns in popular culture –
 United States.   3. Monasticism and religious orders for women – United
 States.   I. Title.

 BR115.A8S84 2005   305.43′282559′00973   C2004-906933-0

This book has been published with the help of a grant from the Canadian
Federation for the Humanities and Social Sciences, through the Aid to
Scholarly Publications Programme, using funds provided by the Social
Sciences and Humanities Research Council of Canada.

University of Toronto Press acknowledges the financial assistance to its
publishing program of the Canada Council for the Arts and the Ontario
Arts Council.

University of Toronto Press acknowledges the financial support for its
publishing activities of the Government of Canada through the Book
Publishing Industry Development Program (BPIDP).

For my husband, Bart Beaty

Contents

Acknowledgments

For the past ten years this book has been a personal passion, and I am very happy to take a moment to reflect on all the people who supported me and helped make it happen. Uncovering all the names will be a difficult task, as there were so many. Just thinking of the many individuals across North America who came to my aid with rare and invaluable sources, and who generously shared their memories with me, reminds me that research is not a solitary act but a process of community building itself. Detailing all their efforts on my behalf would be impossible here, but I hope I can convey something of their contribution.

This book began as my doctoral dissertation, therefore it is only right that I thank my supervisor, Dr Gertrude Robinson, first and foremost. She played a major role in the shaping of my career as a scholar, for which I am truly grateful. Other professors at McGill University whose guidance and advice were immeasurable include Dr Janine Marchessault and Dr William Straw. Without their insights, this project never would have gotten off the ground. Dr Priscilla Walton, of Carleton University, was a keen supporter and is in many ways responsible for the book being published with University of Toronto Press.

I could not have discovered much of the archival material presented here if I did not have access to a wonderful community of sisters and scholars. In particular, I would like to thank Margaret Susan Thompson of Syracuse University, who provided invaluable information on the social history of American sisters. Her expertise in this area is unparalleled, and I was very fortunate to have someone of her calibre available for crisis consultations whenever the complex web of church history overwhelmed me. I have also had the pleasure of meeting many women who lived through the cataclysmic reforms of the convent in the postwar era, thus enriching my research. Foremost in my mind is Sister Ritamary Bradley, a courageous activist and scholar who died before this book could be completed, but whose years of friendship I will cherish always. I want to also express my admiration and sincere gratitude to Sister Yvette Beaulieu, Mary Griffin (formerly Sister Mary Ignatia), Sister Mary Pat LeRoy, Sister Mary Lenore Martin, Sister Jean Meyer, Sister Rosalie Warpeha, and Sister Miriam Therese Winter. Others individuals provided me with archival materials during my research. For that I thank Jessica Matthews, Jeff Michaels, Terri Mitchell, Michelle Coyne, and Stephanie Morris.

There have been many friends and colleagues who spent long hours discussing the various nuances of my analysis and offering intriguing suggestions of their own. Carla Burks, Danielle Comeau, Joe Jackson, Keir Keightley, and Anne Whitelaw were there at the beginning of this project and continued their steady support through revisions. New colleagues at the University of Calgary made the daunting task of revision much more enjoyable. Warm thank yous to Heather Coleman, David Marshall, Annette Timm, and David Winter. In addition, the university provided encouragement by awarding me a Killam Resident Fellowship to assist in the completion of this book. At the dissertation stage I was financially supported by Fonds pour la Formation de Chercheurs et l'Aide à la Recherche (FCAR), the Teagle Foundation, and the McGill Major Scholarship Fund. I am grateful for their assistance.

I worked with a dedicated, professional, and above all enthusiastic group of people at the University of Toronto Press. Siobhan McMenemy was an expert guide through the treacherous terrain of academic publishing. This first-time author depended heavily on her and is glad that I can now call her a friend. I would also like to thank Frances Mundy and Ani Deyirmenjian who steered this book to completion. Charles Stuart provided an expert editing of the manuscript that only enhanced the final version. I would also like to extend my gratitude to the anonymous reviewers of the manuscript. Their positive reception and thoughtful critiques made this a much better book and challenged my own analysis in provocative and ultimately very productive ways that will affect future research as well. The Aid to Scholarly Publications Programme of the Canadian Federation for the Humanities and Social Sciences generously granted me a subvention for the publishing of the book.

Throughout all this, my family has been steadfast in their love and support. My parents, Bob and Alice Sullivan, have shown me by example that faith is a powerful force for change. Without them, I never would have realized the potential of this research. All my siblings – Cara, Kate, Jim, Diane, Louise, and David – have contributed to this project through our oftentimes absurd sense of humour, our delight in each other's accomplishments, and our easy-going acceptance of the indirect paths we have each taken to achieve our life goals. Without all of you, I doubt I would have made it this far. As I developed into a scholar, I also gained a new family. Harry and Dianne Beaty have given unwavering support to me and I thank them for welcoming me into their home. Don Beaty and Christine Beaty are also wonderful members of my extended family. Finally, I would like to thank the person with whom I am lucky to share all my good fortune. Bart Beaty has been with me since the very first day this project began, and will be with me forever. He has been my greatest colleague, staunchest supporter, and best friend. I dedicate this book to him with all my love.

VISUAL HABITS

Introduction: Gender, Religion, and Culture

When conjuring up images of postwar feminism, one rarely thinks to include nuns. Yet nuns played a key role in a period of great cultural anxiety over transitions in power relations between genders, institutions, and ideals. Their significance lies not merely in the representation of institutional religion but, more importantly, in popular culture mediations about gender roles. Names such as Sister Jacqueline Grennan or Sister Mary Joel Read don't appear alongside Betty Friedan or Gloria Steinem in the annals of women's history. Nonetheless, they were, along with many other nuns, key public voices in the dawning of second-wave feminism. They lent their religious status to social justice, women's rights, and a belief in the modernization of religion to meet the contemporary demands of everyday life. The presence of women religious (the canonical term that is generally preferred over the colloquial 'nuns') in the public sphere sparked intense media interest, resulting in a series of representations of convent life in film, television, music, journalism, and popular literature. After only a bit of reflection, the memories all begin to flood back. Audrey Hepburn as the impossibly glamorous Sister Luke in the box office smash *The Nun's Story*. The family television classic *The Flying Nun*, featuring a fresh-faced Sally Field. The kitsch novelty song 'Dominique' by The Singing Nun, which was finally dethroned from its number one position on the charts by the Beatles. These examples, among many others, speak to something more than quirky moments of camp culture.

This book examines many of the best-remembered and a few long-forgotten examples of nun culture. The selection is not comprehensive but, like many other studies concerned more with popular memory than with official history, follows an idiosyncratic path towards revealing sublimated meanings and alternative discourses (Douglas 1994, 19). It begins with representative or emblematic samples, based on their critical or popular success. In revealing the major themes and tropes evident in these cornerstone texts, other examples are incorporated to fill in some of the gaps, in conjunction with documents that describe the social milieu in which these popular culture artefacts circulated. For the first chapter, on film, the historical period covered by this book is charted by looking at representations before, during, and after the Second Vatican Council, a landmark event from 1962 to 1965 that completely overhauled Catholic life in a dramatic and unprecedented fashion. Two films from each of the three periods were selected, usually the two most popular or big budget. The decision to single out *The Nun's Story* in chapter 2 was based on its status as the most ambitious, serious-minded, and controversial attempt to build a narrative entirely from one nun's perspective. For the two chapters on nun-produced culture, the subject matter is not as well known. Producing vocation books and folk albums were distinct strategies by nuns to popularize the religious life and promote a modern vision of the convent. In both cases, I began with one or two primary examples that were the most ambitious or professional in their production, and explored outward based on the themes they presented. To those who remember poring over the pictures of nuns in these books or listening to the soft soprano voices of nun choirs, they may wonder why their favourite was left out. While it may not be mentioned by name, its ideas are likely central to the discussion. Finally, I return to a more widespread image with an exploration of *The Flying Nun*. As the only sitcom ever to be set in a missionary convent, this late-era example of nuns in popular culture shows how television responded to the new wave of spiritual and social experimentation. It was a decidedly conservative and nostalgic look back not at the way nuns were but at the way they were supposed to be. Taken together, these examinations, along with extratextual material from the news media and nuns' own reactions to their representations within a larger context of religious and social upheaval, illuminate aspects of the postwar era that challenge our easy stereotypes of nuns today.

The popularity of nuns in the fifties and sixties suggests that gender and religion were major and mutual concerns. Their rise to prominence came at a time when philosophers and sociologists were claiming that society was becoming more secularized. This pervasive sense of secular-ism had less to do with actual religious practices such as church atten-dance (which was rising) or personal belief in God than it did with the ways in which religion and religiosity were being defined. Religion in the Christian context had long been linked to church going and adher-ence to clerical leaders – priests, ministers, and elders. It was now shift-ing to occupy a space reserved for private feelings as an escape valve from the pressures of the secular world. The association of religion with the feminized private sphere was a source of consternation for the mas-culine religious leadership. Both religion and women were supposed to be committed to preserving a set of values that served little purpose in a rational, bureaucratic world but created a zone of comfort far from the realms of public decision making.

Ironically, at the same time that religion was being devalued through its association with femininity, women were organizing against these ideological constraints, especially traditional notions of bourgeois het-erosexual domesticity. Beginning with *The Feminine Mystique* and the rise of the sexual revolution in the early sixties, and extending to the radical women's liberation movement by the end of the decade, femi-nists rebelled against gender ideologies of the feminine as passive, nur-turing, and genteel. The conflicting attitudes towards cultural definitions of femininity and religiosity were manifested in widespread media attention on nuns and their potential to mediate between the two. However, many actual religious sisters refused that role and embarked on a path of unprecedented rebellion. They stood as a force of resistance not only to traditional Catholic doctrine, with its principles of triumphalism and ultramontanism, but also to popular configurations of 'the woman question' that became increasingly individualistic and consumerist in orientation.

In short, women and religious institutions were fighting similar bat-tles, but it is only through the example of nuns that this becomes appar-ent. Both were fighting a society that relegated them to the private sphere, assigned as the caretakers of society and defined as emotional, passive, and sentimental. However, feminism was looking forward, using progressive arguments of individualism and equality among per-sons. Religious institutions, in particular the Catholic Church, hark-ened to a corporatist tradition of communal responsibility, exemplified by family values. Between these seemingly incompatible cultural forces there was the nun. Neither wholly radical nor entirely traditional, the representation of nuns speaks to ongoing anxieties and contradictions between gender, religion, and culture.

This book is situated during a unique era, beginning in 1950 when the Vatican issued a Call for Renewal to religious sisters to modernize their way of life and make it more attractive to the general public, in particular teen girls, who were their target market. It closes in 1971, when sisters wrested control from the clerical hierarchy through a dramatic revamping of their Vatican-legislated association, the Conference of Major Superiors of Women. They dropped the habit and stepped up their fights for gender equality in the church and social justice in the streets. This twenty-year period coincides with an enormous amount of cultural activity by and about nuns, which just as quickly disappeared once the heady excitement of the new nuns began to wear off. It coincides not only with the revolutionary changes in the Catholic Church, brought on by the Second Vatican Council, but also with the re-emergence of the feminist movement. Also, crucially, the cultural presence of the nun comes into prominence at the same time as what is generally termed the sexual revolution. Why would the ultimate virgins become so popular at this time, vying for media space with the likes of Helen Gurley Brown? It is nothing so simple as suggesting that they were a reactionary force against such changes. Rather, incorporating nuns into the sexual-social ferment of the times sheds light on the way in which notions of the self, pleasure, consumption, and agency were being reimagined on the bodies of women. It is obvious that nuns were not key players in remapping the boundaries of feminine sexuality. Nonetheless, by their alternative, homosocial existence, their quasi-autonomy from men (but not patriarchy), and their promotion of a modern spirituality based on authenticity of the person, they stand as a bridge between two worlds that were soon to drift too far apart, leaving them stranded.

Most of the examples here come from Hollywood, because it was (and remains) the entertainment behemoth, churning out product at a pace that outstripped any competitors, adapting global commodities to suit its needs, and packaging its product for a worldwide market. Even when the source was from the old world of Europe, which was much more cautious in its religious reforms, the American media found ways to appropriate the story to fit nationalist ideals. Sister Luke of *The*

The Reverend Mother (Rosalind Russell) tries to fit in with her swinging students in *Where Angels Go, Trouble Follows.*

Nun's Story and The Singing Nun were both Belgian, but that did not stop them from becoming exemplary heroines of a new version of independent, authentic femininity according to American principles of individualism and freedom. Later, it was this freewheeling Americanism that helped to unravel the previously tight-knit relationship between the Vatican and the convent. Church officials began to take issue with the liberal or even radical experiments sisters undertook with their habits, cloister, and vows. When the exhilaration of the fifties and sixties turned into anger and disappointment, even sisters publicly doubted that Americanism held the promise in which they needed to believe. As media attention waned, their position at the centre of reform slipped away. Thus, while the American context is at the centre of my analysis, the point here is to at once identify the cultural specificity of this movement while still acknowledging the ability of the media and popular culture to extend past national barriers.

Nationalist ideals about social progress, democracy, and identity informed the representation of nuns across geographical boundaries and created a discursive link between modern Catholicism's process of *aggiornamento*, or updating, and America's postwar idealism. The experience of American nuns did not replicate itself exactly from country to country. Nevertheless, it took precedence first as the ideal and then as the cautionary tale. Nuns were appealing because in addition to their unassailable moral character, they were also attractive role models in gender debates from both a social and sexual standpoint. Their unique situation as highly educated and professionally adroit women in charge of their own vast institutions was mitigated by their devout, unproblematic (or so it seemed) chastity, keeping them bound to a patriarchal order that could contain their erotic power. Nuns, therefore, had a unique role to play in the embryonic stages of second-wave feminism because of their dual identities as both fiercely independent and devoutly chaste.

It is not a coincidence that at the time that nuns entered into the mainstream in the 1950s, the Catholic Church was undergoing a period of unprecedented modernization and was looking for a new public image. The triumphalist belief that Catholicism was the only path to salvation, necessitating strict adherence to the clerical hierarchy, was challenged at the grassroots level. Women religious became the hallmark of this modern Catholicism, appearing on the covers of major magazines including *Time, Ladies' Home Journal*, and *Harper's* and celebrated everywhere as 'the new nuns.' However, their religiosity soon became little more than a romantic backdrop, as audiences seemed more interested in their cachet as new prototypes for containable feminine independence. Hollywood and the rest of the entertainment industry quickly recognized the potential of the convent for the dramatization of women's conflicts. Their efforts were not without controversy. *The Nun's Story* created a transatlantic debate about using the convent to tell a story that was ultimately not about religion at all but about a strong-willed woman finding her independence. The apparently innocuous folk music of Soeur Luc-Gabrielle (aka 'The Singing

Nun') masked a lingering sense of anguish for those on a modern-day spiritual quest. Looking back at all these attempts to represent nuns raises a number of key questions. Why was there a seemingly sudden and expansive fascination with nuns? Who helped shape this fascination, and what were their vested interests? How did real sisters cope with their emergence onto the centre stage of popular culture after decades of rigorous cloister? When did this period of intense cultural activity end, and why? Finally, what can an examination of this phenomenon tell us today about changes in the definitions of women's roles and their links to religion in culture? Buried within the apparently trite and frivolous popular culture fare featuring nuns is a potentially exciting new line of inquiry.

We haven't forgotten about nuns in popular culture today. Every time a new character or image arises, the media latches on to it as a way of remembering something that now seems lost. However, these memories are in many ways turning nuns into kitsch, iconic representations of something self-evidently ironic and amusing without any historically grounded signifier. In a way, then, nuns are part of what Will Straw terms exhausted commodities, obsolete objects that still cycle through the informal economies of cultural fashion (2000, 176). Their role in popular culture has been one of displaced meaning. As Grant McCracken defines it, certain idealized desires that seemingly have no place in the reality of contemporary society are shifted onto particular objects in order that they may continue to thrive but not to actually engage or influence society directly (1988, 104). This is an intriguing idea, but it can be made all the more so when the issue of gender and its relation to value is considered. As scholars such as Ann Douglas (1977) and Colleen McDannell (1995a) argue, these strategies of displacement tend to feminize popular culture and reinforce patriarchal dominance over the public sphere. Nuns, because of their obvious affiliation to a whole other institutional order beyond the boundaries of secular society, were well suited to become the bearers of meanings about gender and religion that together held the possibility for a direct challenge to the status quo. They therefore needed to be quietly removed to the sidelines. What no one figured on was that sisters themselves would seek to transform this relationship between the real and the ideal and undermine both the romantic nostalgia for old world nuns and the strictly contained image of the progressive new nun. As a result, they no longer easily fit into any pre-arranged categories and forced a confrontation with the tenability of these ideals of gender and religion. Unfortunately, this did not lead to any radical revamping but to a redoubled effort to restabilize the work of displacement and remove real sisters from the representational strategies of the media. With declining numbers and a rising median age, sisters were at a disadvantage to stop this, and the popular culture of nuns was too easily reduced to a form of cultural waste, an icon that is no longer relevant to contemporary society but provides pleasure in the form of ironic or kitsch appropriation.

My goals are similar to those in other feminist cultural studies of the postwar era, by such scholars as Susan Douglas, Lynn Spigel, and Christine Geraghty. Through recapturing the lost stories behind these representations of nuns, we call into question our understanding of the relationship between gender, religion and popular culture and challenge our easy dismissal of nuns as irrelevant or outmoded. While they may not claim any attachment to 'real' nuns, their hold on us has more to do with the kinds of gender relations embedded in consumer-oriented popular culture. Colleen McDannell critiques the dismissal of Christian-themed objects like plaster statuary, Jesus or Mary portraits, rosaries and the like for the way that they are deemed overly feminine and domestic. Characterized as sentimental, superficial, or sweet, the popular representations of religious devotion helped to shift religious sensibility to a more privately oriented, feminized sphere (1995a, 164). Once removed as a force of public authority and decision making, religion became a question of personal belief and private solace.

This feminization of religion was especially true for postwar Catholicism, which was trying to overcome centuries of marginalization and suspicion and claim access to the suburbanized middle class. Thus, it is not surprising that nuns, as the only identifiable women in the elite ranks of Catholic celibates, became the hallmark of this new religiosity. However, this is not enough to explain why there was so much mass media attention on nuns during a particularly volatile time for women, when the ideologies of heterosexual domesticity conflicted with the sounds of protest on the streets. The figure of the nun acted as a kind of signifier of burgeoning yet manageable feminist consciousness. The convent operated in popular culture as a privileged symbolic space for women, somewhere between the private and the public sphere. Not solely an institution, it was also a discursive entity that mediated anxieties about women's roles, religious authority, and the space between the two. Thus, nuns and their relationship to the second-wave feminist movement is only one half of the argument here. The other challenge is to understand how religion as both hierarchical structure and cultural construct was assigned a gender that shifted its level of authority and power in postwar society.

Women and religion were locked into similar discursive space in postwar society through a complex network of social relations called feminization. As McDannell suggests, religion was assigned values and purposes that tended to be associated with women, such as docility, emotionalism, and nurturing. Iris Marion Young defines femininity as those structures and conditions that circumscribe a typical set of circumstances deemed appropriate to women, including but not limited to bodily comportment and social mobility. Such a definition does not suggest that femininity is necessarily a condition for all women, but that it is promoted as the ideal starting point for women to negotiate their identities (1989, 54). Like Young, Dorothy Smith argues that femininity is not an end-result in itself but refers to a network of social relations that assign a gender to objects, attitudes, beliefs, and even eras. It is not enough to identify the obvious conventions of women's representation in popular culture. A more interesting analysis identifies the organizing principles or doctrines – the context of social, economic, political, and historical factors – that coordinate audiences and shape their responses to the media according to typical gender stereotypes (1990, 170). Nun films, books, music, or television shows were almost always labelled as part of so-called women's culture, produced to appeal to female audiences by promoting lead female characters. They reasserted feminine values in ways that undermined a potentially radical message of feminist independence. As an almost perfect corollary, the convent was the setting for the nun-heroine's conflict. It was a locus of tradition, sexual inviolability, and institutionalism against which she was ostensibly rebelling. Yet even when it was the source of all the nun's problems, the convent was almost always represented as a beautiful and peaceful place for women to escape the crisis of modern liberalism. Thus, the subtext of the convent was always alluring and appealing, neutralizing any possibility of radical challenge to traditional femininity from the heroine.

The postwar era witnessed an increased emphasis on notions of personal liberty, fuelled by the success of the Second World War and by the economic boom that followed. However, women were exhorted by the media to dissociate their sense of identity from their own independence and define themselves through their relationships to others, preferably husbands and children. This double bind was reflected in a popular culture that promoted a traditional lifestyle of husband, children, and all-around domestic bliss while obliquely suggesting possibilities for controlled levels of independence through part-time employment or education that wouldn't interfere with women's conjugal responsibilities. On the one hand, such a contradictory culture increased women's confusion over their roles in society. On the other hand, as Wini Breines points out, it also gave women limited opportunities to pick and choose from the opposing values offered them and map out their own versions of appropriate femininity (1992, 125). This choice-based model meant that young women became full citizens only after their power as consumers was recognized and legitimated. Personal fulfilment and authority became hallmarks of youth-oriented popular culture as the fifties drifted into the sixties. In other words, the feminist maxim 'the personal is the political' was an acknowledgment that a new kind of feminine self was emerging that put women – not on relational terms of the family but as unique, autonomous subjects seeking pleasure for themselves – at the forefront (Radner 1999, 2). In the wide gulf between the sexually liberated single girl and the loving and lovable domestic goddess, nuns were a third option that fired up dreams of feminine independence while smothering any possibility that the flames might spread out of control.

As the boundaries of femininity were being tested in the relationship between media images and audiences, this double bind deepened a sense of dissatisfaction among women. It subsequently contributed to the re-emergence of the feminist movement in the mid-sixties alongside a more fun-filled image of the sexually aware single girl as the icon of the sexual revolution. These are the two most common tropes of postwar femininity, either recognized in histories of second-wave feminism by Jo Freeman and Alice Echols, or identified in representational analyses such as those by Susan Douglas on pregnancy melodramas and Hilary Radner on Helen Gurley Brown. The seemingly sudden contradictory status of nuns during this troubled era offers a different approach. Nuns held the promise of a strategic alternative to domesticity but still evoked a timeless femininity through the unspoken appeal of ancient tradition as vested in the habit. The regular appearance of nuns in popular culture also brings to light the increased scrutiny of religion in daily life. It suggests that while religion was losing its institutional, hierarchical control over the faithful, its role was being redefined according to feminine values of comfort, solace, and belonging. Its place was pushed further from the centres of public decision making into the private domain of familial relationships.

Not just people but institutions and traditions are organized according to gender stereotypes of masculinity versus femininity in a series of dichotomies such as rational/emotional, assertive/passive, or dominant/submissive. This idea draws attention to the problem of identity versus identification in cultural studies. As Celia Lury argues, there is a difference between identifying social networks and relations as feminine and analysing women's identity. While the former is largely concerned with representation, the latter draws analysis back to the social and political conditions of women's everyday lives (1995, 40–3). By linking one to the other, the processes of meaning making in popular culture can be examined in a social and historical context. In a feminist analysis, the context is the relationship of popular culture to the stratification of power and authority in a society that tends to privilege men over women. This particularly materialist approach to the question of gender and popular culture has the benefit of recognizing historical shifts in the identification processes of femininity and their connection to the social conditions of women's identity. Put another way, it recognizes not only that women's position in society is historically variant but also that it is dependent upon intellectual, cultural, and psychological factors as much as social, political, or economic ones (Hennessy and Ingraham 1997, 9).

Geraghty also insists upon the importance of history to feminist cultural studies. An emphasis on history can bring analyses of media texts away from formalism and into a relationship with other related social discourses that were simultaneously at work in the popular culture of the time (1996, 349). By integrating texts into their social context through the use of extratextual artefacts, a set of 'discursive rules,' as Lynn Spigel calls them (1989, 340), comes into light. Such a method can assist us in determining the way audiences were organized by popular culture without claiming to know precisely their perceptions at the time. Establishing an historical framework for a cultural analysis is a complicated task that brings to light the very problem of history in cultural studies. Since it is a field of study largely concerned with questions of meaning, identity, and representation, the difficulty of locating analysis in the past rests on the viability of conjuring up audiences who no longer exist. It also forces us to make value judgments on popular culture artefacts within a theoretical framework that claims their legitimacy a priori. Russell Berman argues that we can consider the question of significance not only through textual or aesthetic regimes but in terms of how these objects reflect particular moments in time and space (1995, 122). In this case, the goal is to confront the popular memory of nuns, what Lynn Spigel defines as a mode of historical consciousness that privileges contemporary needs or concerns (2001, 363).

The recognition that cultural history is not an exact science but an interpretative schema has been taken up by critics such as Hayden White (1978), Michel de Certeau (1988), and Dominick LaCapra (1983). They argue that the process of historical investigation is not simply that of documenting facts or giving one comprehensive account. Rather, it is bound to the discursive concerns of narrative and interpretation. White argues that a narrativist approach to history seeks to explain a historical moment by first unpacking key elements such as events and players and then arranging them on a timeline in a way that makes them appear coherent and logical in retrospect. This is not done so the historian can then argue that the past was always so neatly organized, but rather to make the formation of a historical moment a transparent part of the analysis (1978, 77). As de Certeau defines it, it is less about uncovering facts or getting to the real than it is about discovering the thinkable, creating narratives of significance (1988, 44). LaCapra also suggests two different approaches to history but believes, in contrast to White, that they are complementary aspects of the same project. He differentiates between the documentary aspects that trace accounts of dates, times, people, and places, and the dialogic aspects that compile documentary evidence into a coherent narrative with a specific point of view (1983, 27–30). By working with both, a historical investigation of nuns in popular culture is a valuable means of revealing evidence in new formulations to offer a kind of counter-memory that can in turn question our current sense of gender relations and feminized religiosity. It can never really be known what people thought as nuns began cropping up across the media landscape by asking those audience members today. Still, there are ways to at least come to terms with the way nun culture was shaped by media reception. With the benefit of hindsight, what begins to take shape is a triangulation between a fascination with nuns, apprehension over religious authority versus nationalist values, and the rebirth of feminism that was never clearly articulated at the time but remained a hidden subtext nonetheless. This subtext deserves careful attention to see what it reveals about the poorly understood relationship between gender and religion in popular culture.

Representations of the religious life for women were deeply enmeshed in the status of women in society and sisters' ambivalent relationship to dominant ideologies of femininity. At the same time, their religious appeal spurred a new level of romanticized, feminized piety, furthering that sense of ambivalence. The conjoining of predominantly Christian religious values with femininity had significant consequences for women and all Christian churches, not only Catholicism. However, while Protestant congregations were better equipped to adjust their doctrines to fit modern ideals of productivity and progress, Catholicism seemed at best a quaint throwback and at worst a threat to individual liberty. America had a long-standing suspicion of Catholicism, which stemmed from pre-Revolutionary border disputes and remained a part of its repressed 'other' through occasional spurts of nativism and outright public hostility. Catholics were frequently treated as a social problem because their urban, working-class immigrant culture centred so closely on the parish. Questions circulated in society about Catholic loyalty to their country over their fidelity to the Vatican. To be sure, an austere and secretive clerical hierarchy who preached isolationism and antimodernism bolstered this image. Gary Wills characterized such attitudes within the church as an 'untime capsule,' a strident belief that the Catholic Church does not change with time and whose teachings are eternal and universal (1972, 19).

By the 1950s, the Catholic Church was trying to soften its image by promoting a highly feminized kind of piety, based on intense emotional prayer, maternal or Marian imagery, and themes of consolation. A sea change in attitudes towards Catholicism occurred when John F. Kennedy was elected president, after a gruelling campaign in which he had to answers questions about his religious affiliation and his loyalty to his country. His insistence that religion was a private and personal matter not only helped to bring Catholicism into the mainstream but also emphasized this creeping feminization of religion. As the counterculture of the sixties emerged, activists responded with a new form of Catholic piety called personalism that married personal faith to social justice issues. Nuns were leaders in this movement, often called to the front of the protest lines at civil rights marches or antiwar demonstrations to act as signifiers of moral certainty in the face of social unrest. However, their status had already changed dramatically. No longer were nuns considered the exemplars of Catholic piety, to be imitated by laywomen, but the opposite relationship had taken hold (McDannell 1995b, 299). By the fifties maternal imagery was so prevalent that nuns were exhorted to be the 'lovers and mothers of the whole world.' The Second Vatican Council sealed this hierarchy of femininity by altering doctrine that had placed vowed religious on a higher plane than the laity. In effect, nuns were demoted in favour of a more maternal image. Thus, the relationship between religion and women and their cultural value was further cemented, but not necessarily in progressive ways.

Today, sisters generally agree that they're caught in a chasm between the reality of their lives now and representations of the religious life available in the contemporary media that remain stuck in the past. My task is to help repair that fracture in order to expose the anxieties and confusions that lie beneath the surface. However, I am not as concerned with uncovering some hidden truths about women religious as I am with revealing the negotiations at work in producing a dominant set of meanings in popular culture about the identity of a group of women who don't quite fit any particular mould. This cultural study isn't simply about giving credit to the enormous accomplishments of sisters during a volatile period of social change. By examining nuns in the context of postwar popular culture, what becomes apparent is the way that the media responds to and establishes conventions for the representations of women's struggles for equality and independence. As the example of nuns shows, this was not some hermetically sealed system but one that was schizophrenic in its openness to double meanings, to an ambiguous or even contradictory sense of closure, and to the psychic tension of the lead character, who was torn between two competing worlds of nostalgia and progress.

The circular relationship between cultural producers, special interest groups, and audiences led to representations of nuns that on the surface seemed to be offering new and exciting variations on the discourses of femininity and their value to women and religion alike. Yet when placed in the context of women's access to education and professional development at this time, their ability to live independently and define their sexual liberty, these representations suggest something far more ambivalent. The religiosity of nuns was not incidental to their cultural significance. Rather, it actually extended the scope of their influence to reflect widespread misgivings about the negative consequences of scientific and technical progress and industrial modernization. Religious salvation in this context confronted such issues as the sovereignty of the individual, community and belonging, and bureaucratic authority. The debates that ensued reflected a larger process of cultural value in the postwar era that assigned feminine characteristics to religion. Thus, its power was curtailed, leaving it only as an outlet for vague feelings of concern about the lonely crowd, the organization man, or any of the other popular terms used to describe postwar society. This form of feminized religiosity maintained a link to a nostalgic but rarely accurate sense of the way things used to be and promoted values that seemed outmoded or old fashioned without actually insisting on their prominence. Understood in this way, feminization does not occur at a conscious level but is the accumulation of attitudes, behaviours, and dispositions that have been associated with femininity for so long that they are taken for granted as natural or common sense. The feminization of an institution manages to diminish both its authority and that of women simultaneously through persistent and circuitous appeals to the doctrines of femininity. Such was the case with religion during the postwar era at the same time that women were actively rebelling against the confines of suburban domesticity.

A feminist analysis, therefore, does not have to limit itself to studies about women but can also examine the gender of institutions, systems, and structures and their association with women through similar cultural discourses. At its most basic level, critiquing religion in this way removes it from a privileged status as Truth and reveals it as ideology. Examining religion as ideology does not necessarily mean taking up Marx's maxim that 'religion ... is the opium of the people,' or that to critique religion is to bring individuals out of intellectual darkness and into reason and action. Rather, it means to open up the study of religion to its historical, social, and political contexts. Such an investigation reveals how religion operates in relation to other factors in culture, including but not limited to those factors that interest me: gender relations, social institutions, value systems, and power networks. In recent years, the question of religion has been recognized by cultural studies, after a lengthy and inexcusable absence. Researchers attempt to address this failing by offering analyses of religion in popular culture, as popular culture or vice versa (Forbes and Mahan 2000). What is missing in much of the literature is a way of integrating religion to stand alongside other issues pertinent in a critical analysis of culture, such as gender. Researchers also tend to perpetuate an ahistoric understanding of religion even while claiming its particularity, by ignoring the institutional and organizational aspects in favour of the representational. Religion needs to be viewed as something that manifests itself in society both institutionally and symbolically.

Some, like Robert Wuthnow and Stewart Hoover, have gone so far as to argue for an understanding of religion as a cultural industry. They claim that religion 'sells' the means for adducing the moral and aesthetic purposes of popular culture (Wuthnow 1994, 31; Hoover 1997, 293). Situating religion as part of a marketplace of ideas, jostling for primacy with other interpretative schemes – sacred or otherwise – was first suggested by Andrew Greeley. As the Catholic Church threw itself into turmoil, it was confronted with the need to acknowledge its historical status as an institution that must assert and justify its relevance for successive generations. This was a radically different concept than the triumphalist notion of eternal and unwavering righteousness. Suddenly, it was the church that had to follow its people and respond to their needs through new strategies of ecumenism, personalism, and pastoralism. It was a distinctly consumer-oriented approach that fit neatly with a society concerned with the self, personal fulfilment and authority, and the power of pleasure. Greeley offers the marketplace analogy as an effective way to understand why religious institutions like the convent undergo intensive structural and symbolic change despite claims to universality and eternalism (1971, 58). It also helps us to understand why nuns and the convent became so crucial to the public imagination in the fifties and sixties for reasons that ultimately had very little to do with Catholicism. They were crucial icons within ongoing debates about women's roles in a society that claimed progressivism and modernism as its hallmarks while seeking to maintain a place for tradition in ways that perpetuated an unequal distribution of power and access across the sexes. Of course, the irony here is that religious reformers and feminist activists alike were using these ideologies of gender to assert a different kind of authority. As the counterculture gained momentum they both turned these feminine values into positions of strength. In strategically different ways they positioned femininity as a cogent alternative to a bureaucratic, technologically driven, and alienating mass society.

The nun as a symbol of sentimentalized traditionalism at first caused much consternation for many real sisters fighting for change. One sister noted in 1965 that 'within strains of our Catholic sub-culture we have strong "Victorian lady" concepts of the sister' (Seng 1965, 253). Another complained that 'the church looks upon [sisters] as minors and defines their conduct as though they were Victorian ladies designed for Victorian drawing rooms' (Novak 1966, 23). Clearly, the nineteenth-century association of femininity with passivity and submissiveness had been anything but dispelled by the postwar era. In a unique twist, it had been recast through the figure of the nun to provide a counter-discourse to modern, bureaucratic ideals of rational economic progress and social democracy. To mitigate its conservative effects, from the ashes of bourgeois femininity rose personalism, with its own soundtrack from the folk scene. It preached against institutional authority or tradition in favour of a personal journey of self-discovery towards a more authentic way of life. Many sisters found something attractive in personalism and began producing music, publishing essays, and instigating community activism according to its values. For a time it seemed as if they had found a third way between the rising voice of the feminist movement and the panicked voice of the clergy who felt church reform had gone too far. Yet it eventually revealed itself as unsustainable, and sisters were forced to begin their search for a new sense of identity all over again. It didn't help that the media had begun to lose interest in the new nuns, whose controversial positions at the beginning of the sixties now seemed antiquated. What had begun in the fifties as a concerted effort by the mass media to affirmatively portray the modern religious life and the independent women within it had devolved by the end of the sixties into a reification of the traditional convent, where nuns were instantly identifiable, sexually unassailable, and assuredly non-confrontational. The warm relationship between sisters and the media

The Medical Mission Sisters were among the first to embrace personalism and folk music.

cooled off quickly in the seventies and interest in their stories plummeted. Sisters themselves retreated from the centre stage of Catholic life to reassess the changes wrought over twenty years and plan for the next phase in their own personal liberation movement.

Becoming a sister may seem like an anachronism now, but it was once viewed as a path to an enlightened, empowering way of life. The many depictions of the religious life during the fifties and sixties cannot be dismissed as a mere historical curiosity but ought to be seen as a missing link in the long-standing but largely unrecognized relationship between gender and religion in popular culture. As the examinations of film, vocation books, folk music, and television that follow show, each new nun character that entered into popular culture offered another piece to a highly complex and troubling puzzle about gender, tradition, and religion. That the sexual revolution coincided with a spiritual revolution is not coincidental but speaks crucially to the formation of new sets of discourses about the role of women and religion in a society that was moving away from family and towards the individual as the central focus of society. Through a three-pronged approach between analysis of the nun as a public personification of an acceptable alternative to domestic femininity, religious life as it related to questions of authority and public accountability, and the cultural currency of the nun as a popular icon, the largely overlooked yet highly significant relationship between gender and religion can begin to be explored.

1

Cracks in the Cloister:
The Changing Cultural Role of Nuns

The fifties and sixties were a time of tumultuous change for everyone, including women religious. In the wake of such revolutionary moments as the civil rights movement, the re-emergence of feminism, and the sexual revolution, the dramatic reappraisal of the religious life for women has received little consideration. Yet what may appear at first to have been a small, self-enclosed effort among religious sisters to reassess their lifestyle did play an integral role in the larger forces of change that swirled around them. This is evident in the number of magazine articles on the convent and so-called new nuns that were published during the 1950s and 1960s. Approximately fifty articles appeared dealing with subjects ranging from the trivial to the political. These include cover stories in such premier magazines as *Time*, *Newsweek*, and *Harper's*, among others. Taken as a whole, they present a picture of convent reforms that have less to do with historical accuracy than with representational strategies and the cultural currency of the nun. Relying primarily on these articles, augmented by writings from women religious on their reforms and social histories about the era from Catholic scholars, I map out the revolutionary changes that occurred in the convent during this time with at least two goals in mind. The first is to develop a conjunctural analysis that positions the symbolic value of women religious within a larger context of social unrest. Recognizing and reaffirming heretofore forgotten voices in the cacophony of postwar culture will help us to discover the identity of others who lurk in the shadows of postwar history. The second and more important goal is to demonstrate the centrality of questions about meaning and identity in postwar America, particularly as they concerned the ambivalent relationship between gender and religion.

The keen interest in the religious life for women demonstrated by the mass media during this time cannot simply be ascribed to the sisters who were taking actions that would be considered of public interest. Such an account does not explain why interest in sisters dropped precipitously in the seventies despite their continued political and social justice activities and their challenges to the Catholic hierarchy's conservative attitude towards women. Clearly the image of the liberated woman religious resonated beyond the confines of the convent and touched upon other issues that were accruing intense public interest at the same time. Scholars such as Jo Ann McNamara (1996), Pat Wittberg (1994), and Lora Ann Quiñonez and Mary Daniel Turner (1992) have explored in detail the transformation of the religious life during the postwar era. What matters more to me, however, is understanding the way in which those changes were represented and how those representations contributed to a symbolic regime that curtailed the potential for a major revision of the relationship between gender and religion in popular culture. This era of dramatic reform in the convent is not a well-known aspect of women's history. Yet, ironically, by telling their story not so much from their own experiences as from the standpoint of audiences and interested bystanders, nuns become better integrated into the larger picture of social change and are less likely to be sidelined as a historical or sociological curiosity. Thus, this exploration into the symbolic capital of nuns seeks to re-evaluate definitions of femininity and religiosity in the wake of social and sexual politics that ultimately ruled nuns out of feminist history and theory until only recently.

In the specific case of women religious, two major movements inform my narrative. First, there was the massive overhauling of Catholic doctrine, parochial organization, and relationships with lay society that has been termed the 'Americanization' of the Catholic Church. Second was the re-emergence of feminism in two stages from a liberal to a radical movement. The attempts of sisters to position themselves somewhere within this triangulation of Americanism, Catholicism, and feminism generated much debate over the identity, meaning, and purpose of the religious life for women that had repercussions far beyond the confines of the convent. The shift in the Catholic Church from an autocratic and staunchly anti-American hierarchy to a more open-minded and affectual religion, and the foregrounding of women religious as exemplars of progressive, pious femininity all spoke to a complex tension going on as the roles of both women and religion were increasingly under reappraisal. At a time when women had few opportunities for emancipated lifestyles, the Catholic Church seemed to offer them a unique and highly visible role. They were in charge of schools, hospitals, and other social institutions that interacted freely with lay society. The radical potential of the revitalized religious life for women seemed to have captivated the media. Women religious acted as a kind of figurehead for the new spirit of independence sweeping across the Catholic Church, not to mention religion's role in society as a whole. Their image also served to channel anxieties about women's roles and independence. What the public saw were educated, professional women unencumbered by husbands or children but still sexually contained and subservient to male authority figures.

At stake in the religious politics of the postwar era was a reconsideration of triumphalism, a fervently held belief that only through strict adherence to Catholic doctrine could anyone achieve salvation. One of the key tenets of triumphalism was that the Catholic Church was a fixed point in the universe, essentially unchanging in its righteousness and therefore justified in any actions it may take to protect the faithful that would otherwise seem repressive. A strictly isolationist subculture of parochialism was established to keep the modernizing and liberalizing influences of America from infiltrating the faith. It could be argued, of course, that such anti-Americanism was forged out of necessity, to protect Catholics from the vitriolic nativist sympathies of some extremist Protestant groups who wanted to keep America pure from the corrupting influences of Old World clericalism. Even into the postwar era, there were still inklings of a vitriolic disdain for Catholicism. Paul Blanshard's *American Freedom and Catholic Power* was first published in 1949, became a major best-seller, and went through twenty-six printings before a second edition was published in 1958, again to great success. In contrast to the strategy of nineteenth-century nativism, it was not a hysterical screed accusing Catholics in general of all kinds of lascivious and lustful behaviour. Rather, its main target was the Catholic hierarchy and a concern that the parochial structure of the church, if allowed to progress unchecked, would undermine the American democratic process (1958, 306).

To counteract the effects of a hostile Protestant society, the Catholic

Church turned increasingly inwards and cautioned its members to limit their interaction with non-Catholics as much as possible (Greeley 1971, 116–21). This separatist mentality defined itself in contradiction to perceived American values. Whereas Americans were thought to revere such values as freedom, egalitarianism, and personal accountability, Catholics were trained to spurn materialism and orient their culture according to otherworldly aspirations of hierarchical authority, elitism, and communal responsibility (Wakin and Scheuer 1966, 285–8). What makes this particular era of Catholicism interesting is the way in which this highly autocratic ecclesiology meshed with an intense devotionalism and renewed veneration of Mary. As Thomas O'Dea noted, 'It is as if the masculine behaviour of decision and combat and the dominance of the male authority structure of clergy and hierarchy required some fantasy compensations of a feminine character' (1968, 58). A renewed Mariology and the concomitant popularization of devotional activities such as pilgrimages or rosary circles operated in a similar manner to the Protestant cult of domesticity from the previous century. Catholic magazines extolled the virtues of self-abnegation to their predominantly female readership, nestled between articles on child rearing and beauty tips (Orsi 1997, 37). The idea that salvation ultimately lay in the hands of women was a common theme in popular writings on Catholicism during this time, in particular referencing their natural inclination towards suffering and sacrifice. Women were encouraged to explore a kind of mystical victimhood in which greater spiritual fulfilment could be achieved in direct relation to how far a woman was willing to humble and debase herself in the name of Mary (Fisher 1989, 94).

At first glance this servile feminine stance was supposed to mark the distinction between the American and the Catholic way of life. As Will Herberg argued in the mid-sixties, nationalist ideologies of individualism and freedom had taken on a near sacred sheen:

> American religiousness has been growing increasingly vacuous – a religiousness of belonging, without religious commitment, religious concern, or religious passion ... Consequently, religion enjoys a high place in the American scheme of things, higher today, perhaps, than at any time in the past century. But it is a religion thoroughly secularized and homogenized, a religion-in-general that is little more than a civic religion of democracy, the religionization of the American Way. (1964, 599)

Catholicism would be exempt from this trend, some hoped, through a thoroughly feminized – if not outright infantilized – slavish devotion to authority. However, the triumphant tone masked an anxiety that some identify as an admission of defeat to American values (Fisher 1989, 156). Relegating Catholic values to the level of the feminine in effect acknowledged that Catholicism was to be subservient to the dominant forces of Americanism. Furthermore, there was an implication that their maintenance was to be the responsibility of women, since men would be too preoccupied attaining the American goals of personal and financial success. Religion and women began to mutually support each other's secondary status as the keepers of those traditional values that posed difficulties for a progressive, technocratic society. It is hardly surprising, then, to discover that the most strenuous and even debilitating living conditions were imposed on women religious during the first half of the twentieth century, before they began to find their own voice and demand reforms.

In the first half of the twentieth century sisters were exhorted to restrict contact with the outside world as much as possible. The extent of this isolation was severe. Not only could they not speak freely with the laypeople they encountered in their work, including the parents of their students or the families of their patients, but they were also restricted from speaking with other members of their community. A ban on friendship in the convent was a common phenomenon at this time. A sister accused of a dreaded 'PF,' a particular or persistent friendship with another sister, could expect severe penance, and steps would be taken to see that the two women in question had as little contact with each other as possible. Homophobic fears of sexual expression were certainly a factor in this rule. However, this repression of intimate or erotic desire was also deemed necessary to train novices into childish dependence on their mother superior and priest (Glisky 1997, 159). A lack of any kind of friendship support, no time given to discuss ideas and concerns of one's own with like-minded individuals, highly restricted and monitored relaxation periods – all these were factors to ensure that a young sister-in-training would have no one to turn to for guidance except religious authority figures. To keep the outside world at bay, most congregations imposed bans on the mass media, as well as public meetings or special events that were not specifically related to the religious life (Ewens 1989, 33). In the first half of the twentieth century there could not possibly be women more isolated or more completely under the control of another than Catholic sisters.

These overbearing conditions persisted as obedience began to take precedence over every aspect of religious life and a personal sense of identity was considered anathema to the religious life. Was it any wonder, then, that enrolment in convents began to drop precipitously in the 1940s? The vocation crisis certainly alarmed Pope Pius XII enough to initiate the Call for Renewal and begin the slow process of dismantling the isolationist policies fostered by his predecessors and forge direct interactions with all members of society, Catholic and non-Catholic alike. Announcing this new initiative to the media, a Vatican spokesman noted: 'The present moment is of supreme importance in the development of the history of the religious institutes of women, especially in the field of their higher culture, intellectual or otherwise. In the course of the years and particularly in very recent years, Sisters have progressively assumed an ever-greater importance in all fields of the apostolate of the church' (Gallen 1955, 23).

All of this anxiety over the religious life for women had its foundation in some very basic concerns. Simply put, sisters were the grassroots labourers of the entire parochial system on which the Catholic Church depended. They were the ones who, for the most part, staffed and administered the network of Catholic schools, hospitals, and social welfare agencies at salaries substantially below the pay scale for lay workers. By sheer force of numbers they were viewed as the primary conduits to the religious life for young Catholics. In fact, according to the statistics compiled by the annual Official Catholic Directory, throughout the fifties and sixties sisters generally outnumbered priests by a three-to-one ratio. If the downward trend were to be turned around then the sisters themselves would have to make their way of life more appealing to the younger generation. As the New Yorker reported, it was clear that the pope was holding nuns responsible: 'Stating that "feminine religious life was in full flower twenty years ago but today its numbers are reduced by half," he counselled, as a remedy, that "the habits worn, the kind of life, and the seclusion of the religious sisterhoods should not constitute a barrier or a cause of unsuccess" in encouraging pious young girls to join' ('Letter from Rome' 1952, 124). One of the first steps the pope took was to create a Conference of Major Superiors of Women (CMSW) for each country to confront the vocation crisis on a national scale. Interestingly, while it wasn't established until 1956, American nuns appeared on the cutting edge by organizing their own grassroots coalition two years earlier. The Sister Formation Conference (SFC) laid the groundwork for a radical revitalization of the religious life that began in earnest by the next decade.

The goal of the CMSW was to seek innovative ways to reconcile the religious life, which had remained relatively unchanged since the medieval age, with the technology and bureaucracy of the modern world (Quiñonez and Turner 1992, 12). There were, unfortunately, few guidelines on how to initiate such reforms. In the meantime schools and hospitals were straining under the weight of an exhausted and demoralized staff. It is little wonder that the leaders of women's congregations were suspicious of any initiative that demanded even more of their time and scarce resources. With the Conference of Major Superiors of Women operating directly under the control of the Vatican, convent superiors really had no more authority over the shape and direction of the religious life than before. Sisters were working hard to improve the conditions of the religious life; however, they seemed to do better at arms-length from the Vatican.

Two years before the CMSW, the first organization for sisters was established that was neither directly affiliated with the Vatican nor under any jurisdiction but their own. The Sister Formation Conference was an American initiative to develop the spiritual, professional, and intellectual life of sisters that became a model for the revitalized religious life worldwide. The most important purpose for the Sister Formation Conference was to step back from a tradition in which young novices were sent into classrooms with only the bare minimum of training and education. The system in place up to that point was known colloquially as the 'Twenty Year Plan.' According to this, it could take a teaching sister up to twenty years to complete a university degree through a program of successive summer-school courses at Catholic universities and colleges across the country.

Despite its emphasis on professionalism, the Sister Formation Conference did not want to be seen as promoting the idea of the career woman. As one priest wrote: 'To be a "careerist" and to have a profession are not at all synonymous. Many women have a profession and still retain all their graceful womanliness within their nature. But a careerist is not a graceful woman. She is one whose nature has undergone some injurious fixation along the way' (McGoldrick 1963, 26).

In their rejection of careerism, sisters were echoing some of the criticisms about women that were current in the mainstream media. In a special issue entitled 'The American Woman,' published by *Life* magazine, a career-minded woman was branded as 'a very brisk, very terrifying, young Miss Efficiency, smugly competent, aloofly impersonal and about as compassionate as an armadillo' (Skinner 1956, 73). Another article called the career woman 'the fatal error that feminism propagated,' which mangled a girl's feminine traits and left both her and her husband-to-be in a state of emotional flux (Coughlan 1956, 110). It was into this gap between the positive ideal of a containable feminine independence based on love and sacrifice and the dark nightmare of desexed careerism that the religious life could be promoted as a viable option to any devout, dedicated young woman with ambition and a heroic sense of adventure.

Among the strategies of the CMSW and SFC was an effort to present a positive image of nuns in the mass media. At first, the result was a series of light-hearted articles on new habits along with indulgent photo essays of nuns on roller coasters, pursuing painting or music, or giggling away at new ventures in education. Even articles that attempted to show the real vigour of the religious life tended to back away from critical investigations, preferring a rather sentimentalized picture of feminine devotion as selfless service, in keeping with the Marian piety of the fifties. *Life* and *Look* magazines in particular seemed fascinated by this new access to the world of the convent and eager to publicize it through playful photo essays. As family-oriented lifestyle magazines, rather than hard news outlets, their stories focused far less on the complex political negotiations of reforms than on the whole beguiling newness of it all. *Life* was the first of these magazines to acknowledge the Call For Renewal by publishing a number of fanciful haute couture designs for modified habits by leading members of the Italian fashion world, including one with an elaborate turban that made the nun resemble Auntie Mame ('Speaking of Pictures' 1952, 16–17). Other stories included a glimpse into the 'walled-in world' of the cloister as one order arranged with the magazine to 'give outsiders a pictorial idea of the Carmelite nun's long, dedicated hours of fatiguing prayer, work and solitude' ('Walled in World' 1955, 12). The tone of ennobling yet humble sacrifice was very much in keeping with the triumphalist attitude of feminine servility. At the same time, the intention was to make this way of life appear to have greater rewards that far outweighed the sacrifices. Two months later, another picture of convent life appeared, this time emphasizing fun and excitement. A teaching congregation was profiled developing closed-circuit educational television. Behind a massive camera, two fully habited sisters giggled uncontrollably as they mounted a production of Snow White and the Seven Dwarfs ('Nuns Take on TV' 1955, 53–4).

Look also provided a rather conflicted if not outright contradictory image of the convent by emphasizing first pious self-denial and then following up later with a story that trivialized the religious life as one of unbridled gaiety. In 1955 it profiled a young woman from the Maryknoll community who was training to become a doctor. In the eight-page spread, the emphasis was on self-denial, service, and prayer (Berg 1955, 79–86). An unsmiling nun stared blankly out from the pages as the essay reported approvingly on her intense schedule and difficult task of meeting the demands of both medical school and the convent. The next time nuns appeared in the magazine was six years later, and the image was quite different. 'Spree for Sister Marie' showed an annual celebration in Pittsburgh in which the local amusement park was opened up to the nuns in the diocese for a free day in which they could 'ride coasters, shoot metal ducks and feast on pop and hot dogs' (1961, 85). Pictures showed them on the tilt-a-whirl or enjoying junk food, while captions like 'the nuns take a break for cotton candy, picking at the pink sticky stuff with their fingers. Later, they tried the ice cream' implied that such worldly treats were usually beyond their realm of comprehension. Even such trivial characterizations were couched in terms of devoted service. As the article concluded, 'The exhilarating but strenuous experience of teaching has always demanded the spirit of fun as a vital part of a teacher's training. Sister Marie Dominic has the capacity for fun required of an exceptional teacher' (1961, 90).

This delicate balancing act between ascetic, selfless service and innocent, childlike fun continued to weave itself into the media's accounts of the convent. Perhaps the most high-profile story of this first phase of reform was the 1955 cover story on the Maryknoll community in Time magazine. Celebrating sisters for being 'far from worldliness, close to the world,' the article veered wildly between admiration for their educational and professional accomplishments and a near patronizing regard for their theatrical skits and basketball games. In one passage, the article managed to combine both together:

The convent becomes news to a curious American public.

The Maryknoll sisters know how to drive jeeps (and repair them), how to administer hypodermics and do major surgery, how to teach Christian doctrine – and how to be gay. When they return from the missions to the motherhouse on the Hudson, they are received with laughter and merry chatter. And on the feast day of St. Teresa of Avila, Oct. 15, they celebrate by adding to their far from ascetic meals a special ice-cream soda. ('Laborare' 1955, 76)

The goal of this article, clearly stated, was to disavow long-standing suspicions towards the religious life in America and to promote a sense of booming vocations and renewed spiritual vigour. Acknowledging that few really knew or had seen what goes on in a convent and therefore viewed it as 'unnatural, unhealthy, a "waste,"' the article insisted that nuns most certainly had a role to play in the 'Age of Fission' and had begun 'to recapture the world's imagination' (81).

Of course, not all articles in this period were as admiring. The *New Yorker* published 'Portrait of a Nun,' about the author's visit to his aunt at the Convent of the Holy Blood (Von Weidinger 1957). There were no ice-cream sundaes or Sunday plays at this convent. His aunt wore a tattered habit, bathed in cold water, and worked long, hard hours in the laundry in order to earn her own dreary cell and not be farmed out to the dormitory. It was hard not to derive a sense of a miserable existence of drudgery and self-denial with little reward. However, this was not a contemporary American convent but a remembrance of a visit in 1925 to post–First World War Austria. Thus, this article, when taken into context with other stories being published at the time, was making an oblique claim that the path of modernization spearheaded by the Maryknollers and other Americans had begun just in time.

After centuries of anti-Catholicism in America, the approving tone of these articles alongside more critical takes on Old World convents hinted that it was finally possible to be both American and Catholic. Many liberal-minded reformers sought to marry what they saw as the best of both worlds. They explicitly viewed their task as bringing Catholic institutions and values in line with American values of personal liberty, progressivism, and industriousness (O'Brien 1972, 209). Critics like David Riesman remarked on the growing secularization of organized religion in general but singled out Catholicism in particular. With their rapid rise to the middle and upper classes, Catholics were now integrating their faith with notions of the 'good American' (1951, 272). However, in attempting to build a bridge between Americanism and Catholicism, the most prevalent images in the media seemed to sentimentalize and therefore, in effect, feminize the religion by relying heavily on a naïve representation of nuns. In this way, a three-way relationship of national, religious, and feminine cultures was forged to provide boundaries for women religious as they sought to establish a new sense of identity in keeping with the more open and approachable stance of the Catholic Church.

This enduring picture of religious life was far removed from the austerity of the previous era but still dedicated to the ideals of subservient womanly virtue. As one priest wrote in a book to young sisters: 'Let's get rid of the straitjackets and be done with the plaster casts and throw away the melancholy masks and be holy in a bright, warm, smiling, graceful manner. Let's be lovably holy, holy like the little Thérèse [de Liseaux], holy like Mary our *Mater Amabilis*, holy like Christ Himself, the all-holy, all-beautiful, infinitely lovable One' (Moffatt 1958, 13). This image of cheerful, charming self-immolation that predominated during the Call for Renewal was heartily encouraged in women but was met with grave concern when applied to men's culture and their institutions. Fears of emasculation lurked in the background of the new spiritual enthusiasm of the postwar era. In his anxiety-filled book *The Organization Man*, William Whyte blamed the demise of the Protestant ethic, the downgrading of institutional religion to a free-form spirituality, and the application of feminine values onto the masculine world of business and government for the moral and emotional confusion of Americans. Authority and individual responsibility had, in his mind, capitulated to an ethos of belonging and togetherness. Not even religion was safe from this new social pragmatic, as he complained: 'God likes regular people – people who play baseball, like movie nuns. He smiles on society, and his message is a relaxing one. He does not scold you; he does not demand of you. He is a gregarious God and he can be found in the smiling, happy people of the society about you. As the advertisements put it, religion can be fun' (1957, 282). By making the fun-loving nun the epitome of the new religious ethos, Whyte helped to cement in the public mind a thoroughly feminized image of religion, one that was frivolous, light-hearted, and always eager to be of service.

It wasn't just religion that was being sentimentalized in the fifties.

Women were also being pushed back into the domestic sphere, and idealism for the role of wife and mother ahead of personal identity began to take hold. The fifties were a conflicted time, especially for middle-class American women. While they were encouraged to make the home and family the centre of their life, at the same time women were entering the workforce in ever-higher numbers. Even the U.S. Department of Labor's Women's Bureau, charged with the task of defending women's right to work, promoted the idea that motherhood was the primary duty of the nation's women. Without it, they argued, the family might falter and citizens would be susceptible to Communist infiltration (Blackwelder 1997, 159). Yet, following a sharp drop in the number of women workers immediately after the war, by 1951 the percentage of women in the workforce had climbed to 30 per cent of total workers. This was just below the one-third mark reached in 1944 at the peak of the women-driven war economy (Samuels 1951, 13). So it appeared that more and more women were working outside the home at the same time that they were being encouraged to sacrifice career plans for the sake of their husbands and children. The positions available to women were not exactly on the same career track as those for men. Professional and highly skilled technical jobs remained out of reach for most women, who were clustered into routinized, low-skilled jobs in factories or clerical positions with little or no chance of on-the-job training or advancement. While the number of working women rose steadily throughout the fifties, the percentage of those women with jobs in the professional and technical fields actually dropped and did not check itself until the late sixties (Blackwelder 1997, 153; Freeman 1975, 31).

The pattern of low professional expectations for women was set while they were in high school. A study by the National Manpower Council in the mid-fifties found that adolescent girls were likely to be streamed out of college preparatory courses and into vocational subjects like typing or home economics (Blackwelder 1997, 171). In 1956 only 25 per cent of the women eligible for college enrolled, compared to 50 per cent of men. Only one-third of those women actually completed their degrees, compared with 55 per cent of men (Friedan 1963, 154, 368). Even if girls did go on to higher education, 60 per cent of them took courses in traditional feminine fields like secretarial skills, home economics, nursing, or education. Girls were encouraged to plan to work only temporarily and maybe part-time after marriage. As the U.S. Labor Department's Women's Bureau suggested in a 1954 leaflet, 'Prepare for both a job and marriage! You are right in thinking that you will probably marry ... The chances are you will [work] before marriage and perhaps for a few years afterward' (Blackwelder 1997, 159). With minimal education and training and no expectation of a full-time career, the jobs that women were likely to take were the low-paying, tedious ones that men had rejected – a trend that many news stories reported approvingly. One foreman even claimed that women were 'more valuable' in the fastidious, repetitive work on factory lines because the work was too unfulfilling to expect men to do it (Samuels 1951, 35).

There was no attempt to suggest that these jobs were to be a main source of satisfaction in themselves. Rather, fulfilment was to come through the sacrifice women workers were making to assist their family incomes and therefore the American economy as a whole. Thus, even as workers, their value was identified mainly as consumers. There was even a suggestion by members of the Rockefeller Foundation to create a National Women's Service Corps to organize women into service-area jobs. The argument put forward in *Harper's* was that the unemployed housewife was not contributing enough to the economy and therefore was failing in her citizenship duties (Sanders 1960, 45). There was, however, some slight acknowledgment that the pressure to marry and start a family right out of high school was a major factor in young women foregoing their civic responsibilities. The American Council on Education reported that 'Civic interest and ambition to serve the government are at a high level among adolescent girls ... but these hopes too often are overlaid during the subsequent years of emotional experience and early marriage' (Sanders 1960, 44). Thus, despite an affirmative stance in the media, the hidden subtext in many stories was that if a woman wanted meaningful work and the chance to contribute to the social welfare of the nation, marriage was a dead-end street. Nonetheless, according to *Newsweek*, 93 per cent of all women eventually married; clearly, the choice to remain single and independent did not yet appear acceptable as the fifties turned into the sixties ('The Women Have It' 1957, 94). There was one additional option for Catholic women in the years leading up to the sexual revolution: the convent. By joining a religious congregation, women could potentially reconcile the difficult relationship between Americanism, Catholicism, and femininity by sacrificing themselves to the ideals of all three. They would be simultaneously industrious workers in the underemployed social-services sector, sincere representatives of religious devotion, and the epitome of feminine sexual decorum and passivity.

By the end of the fifties American sisters had turned their fate around and were now the most educated and independent women in the Catholic Church and certainly among the most educated in their country. They had established a network of intercongregational communication and identified leaders to speak on their behalf to both the Catholic Church and the rest of the world. The incredible advances of American sisters prompted one Catholic scholar to later reflect that 'American religious women were thirty or forty years ahead of their sisters in Europe. Despite the similarity in their garb, they did not seem to belong to the same species at all – almost as if some mutation of feminine religious life had taken place during the Atlantic crossing' (Ellis 1969, 230). Their accomplishments were so impressive that they prompted Cardinal Suenens, the Archbishop of Malines-Brussels in Belgium, to write a book on the renewal of the religious life based upon the programs already in place in America. *The Nun in the World: New Dimensions in the Modern Apostolate* (1962) served as a kind of manifesto for the modernization of the religious life and the independence of sisters worldwide (Griffin 1975, 35). However, it was not viewed so much as a clarion call to American sisters as it was an affirmation of all the work they had done to date and an encouragement to press on with the renewal process. In fact, it was well known that the inspiration for the book came from the Maryknollers, the American-based community that had been so warmly portrayed on the cover of *Time*. The cardinal was so impressed with their activities that he wished to initiate similar reforms in the much more traditional convents of Europe (Ewens 1989, 38). Thus it was that by the 1960s the American model of religious life for women was considered by the church hierarchy to be the most effective and promising resolution to the problem of making Catholicism more relevant to the world.

One of the most striking features of the book was its explicit embrace of feminism and encouragement of women's independence both in the Catholic Church and in society. The book was published one year before *The Feminine Mystique* reignited the feminist movement. Yet, Suenens wrote, 'To revalue the religious life of today means, therefore, to bring the religious life into harmony with the evolutionary state of the world and womankind, to retain from the past everything of lasting value that can be adapted to circumstances, and to accept the positive contribution of feminism in order to improve the apostolic yield' (35). He went on to criticize the negative attitude of Catholic officials towards women and the unwritten rule of '*aut maritus aut murus* (a husband or a wall)' (48). However the general tone of the book maintained the prevalent belief that women were the keepers of moral fortitude and compassionate humanity in society. It is ironic that although he rebuked those congregations that were 'the last strongholds of the very studied manners of the middle-class woman of the nineteenth century' (20), Suenens nonetheless reiterated the cornerstone of that ideology with his persistent appeals to women's innate aptitude for suffering and atonement. Thus, while his book held the promise of a more commanding presence for women religious in the Catholic Church, it remained steadfastly grounded in traditional idealizations of gender. What Suenens could not have anticipated was the groundswell of protest against that last bastion of traditionalism, which began in the sixties but would take the remainder of the decade to reach full force.

The Feminine Mystique wasn't the only best-seller to claim new freedoms for women. The same year that Suenens outlined his model of modernized virginal womanhood, another book made the rather startling suggestion that virginity was not a feminine virtue after all. Helen Gurley Brown's *Sex and the Single Girl* heralded the sexual revolution, in which chastity would lose much of its value as the moral centre of femininity and sex would become a defining feature in the enlightened American goals of personal freedom and self-discovery (Ehrenreich 1986, 2). Like Friedan's call for a combination of work and family, this too was directed primarily at the middle class, as evidenced by the intense scrutiny the media placed on universities and the new co-ed campus. In 1961 *Harper's* featured a story by Milton Levine and Maya Pines titled 'Sex: The Problem Colleges Evade' that called on educators to come up with better policies and with sex education programs that encouraged sexual maturity rather than trying to legislate abstinence. Others appealed to the theories of social critic David Riesman to rearticulate a new sense of personhood for college women through their sexual experimentation. Riesman dismissed sex as 'a kind of defense against the threat of total apathy ... [the other-directed person] looks to it for reassurance that he is alive,' which, in a roundabout way, validated women's arguments for great sexual autonomy (Greene 1964, 38). Since women were supposed to be by nature 'other-directed,' that is, overly concerned with values of belonging, togetherness, and approval from others, sex replaced virginity as a kind of currency they could use to pay their way into a society that put individual desires and personal happiness ahead of family values (Radner 1999, 16). Brown, a successful businesswoman who didn't marry until her forties, urged girls not to waste their best years with some husband who wouldn't appreciate them or fulfil their needs. Better to move out on your own, find a job that will support a carefree lifestyle, and enjoy the company of many men, all of whom would be eager for the attentions of a sophisticated, intelligent woman of the world (Brown 1962).

How this was supposed to affect sisters was not explicitly dealt with, either in public through magazine reports on the religious life or, for that matter, in the convent itself. Even as congregations were opening their doors to let their members join in this co-ed campus culture, Catholic attitudes towards sex remained tightly guarded by centuries of repression and denial. Yet the sexual revolution was about more than just sex. That was only the most outward sign of a re-evaluation of morals that stressed the integrity of the person rather than the strictures of community. As many young college women told reporters, whether sexually active or not, the decision came down to individual choice ('Morals Revolution' 1964, 53; 'Second Sexual Revolution' 1964, 57). Such apparently progressive thinking could quickly turn into a smug conceit, supported by pop psychology that labelled virginity as sexual immaturity and queried the mental health of the girl who still said no ('Morals Revolution, 1964, 54; Steinem 1962, 156). It was also not without its own heterosexist biases. While the traditional ideals of marriage and motherhood may have been challenged, the sexual revolution still seemed very much caught up in notions of boy-girl relationships and the central importance of love in the feminine psyche. In her exposé *Sex and the College Girl*, Gael Greene noted that not one of her interview subjects mentioned lesbian desire and even the most promiscuous girls insisted that sex must come with love and at least some form of temporary fidelity (1964, 151).

Thus, this apparently new morality seems to have been not much more than a recasting of the doctrines of femininity under the mantle of the individualistic and democratic values that characterized American-ism. In that sense, there was a way for sisters to be a part of this move-ment, however tangentially. In the convent, the implications of the sexual revolution were not felt as much through the vow of celibacy as that of obedience. In questioning their identity as consecrated celibates within the cultural climate of the time, many sisters arrived at a posi-tion in which the rigid structures of the convent could no longer con-tain them. As Sandra Schneiders argues, this 'encounter between sexual naïveté on the one hand and cultural and personal sexual upheaval on the other' may have driven some women out of their vows, but it also drove many women religious straight into feminism and a renewed sense of moral accountability in the world (2001, 133). The result was personalism, a kind of hybrid spirituality somewhere between liberal individualism and conservative authoritarianism. Personalism formed the foundation of much radical social justice action prior to the advent of the New Left in the sixties. It combined liberal Catholic social theory with communitarianism, pacifism, and new aspects of humanist psychology in order to forge a more authentic way of life (Far-rell 1997, 6). The advent of personalism signalled a major shift in the role of religion from an autocratic, institutional system to a diffuse, pri-vate culture of feelings. Catholicism appeared to be leading the way towards a more romantic and compassionate role for religion in society through the image of women religious as the vanguard of personalist piety and politics. However, nothing could really change unless the Vatican willed it so.

The Vatican had begun to introduce significant doctrinal change in the fifties and encourage women religious to widen their perspective on the world, but only to a point. Continued acquiescence to an ideology of docile femininity minimized any potential for radicalism among sis-ters and continued to foster an image of women religious as 'obedient children of the church' (Quiñonez and Turner 1992, 17). Despite some faint rumblings over personal values and new morality, social and polit-ical consciousness for sisters seemed a long way off in 1962. Then Pope John XXIII convened the Second Vatican Council, initiating a cata-clysmic shift in the values and organizational structure of Catholicism.

While reaction to the Second Vatican Council was mixed in Europe, the American church was filled with enthusiasm for the possibility of *aggiornamento*, or modernization. Importantly, this interest was awash in a belief that Catholicism would be improved by a healthy injection of American pride, and definitely not the other way around. Some argued explicitly that the American way of life held the keys for religious renewal around the world (Parsons and Dunleavy 1967, 138). From 1962 to 1965, while Catholics and non-Catholics alike pored over daily reports from the council on the television networks and in the papers, an enthusiasm for Americanism crept into discussions about reforms. Sisters were especially happy to embrace any argument that would give them greater flexibility and autonomy. As one sister remembered, 'Finally, the struggle of sisters to reconcile religious life with American culture would be over. No longer would American freedom and independence be suspect' (Ewens 1989, 41). Her comments suggest that among women religious, raising questions of feminine independence could go a long way towards reconciling Catholic and American values. One of the most popular ways to do this was through increased participation in the mass media, a practice that Vatican II leaders endorsed and sisters readily embraced.

Since the 1930s with the Legion of Decency, and throughout the fifties and sixties, when an American held the presidency of the Pontifical Commission in charge of the mass media, the Vatican had looked to the American church for leadership in the area of social communication. However, the American flavour of these new media policies came with its own problems. If religious values were to adapt to the media, rather than vice versa, the particularly Catholic characteristics of authoritarianism and communal responsibility would be severely challenged. The democratization of Catholicism via the mass media in the sixties was seen to be chiefly the result of American cultural influence, leading to a blurring of Catholic distinctiveness and a general merging of religious values into a kind of civil religiosity.

Stewart Hoover notes that the rise of the mass media is responsible for at least three major factors in the democratization of religion. First, the media were able to mobilize the beliefs of different religions across a wide spectrum of society. Second, and related to the first, through such mass exposure the media introduced audiences to the possibility of choice and selection in religious practices. And finally, in representing religion, the media tended to commodify complex belief structures into simple formats, making it easier for audiences to assimilate them into their own religious perspectives (1997, 290–4). The debate over the democratization of religion and the media's role in it went to the heart of the personalist philosophy that had superseded Catholic triumphalism. It heightened the focus on the individual and recreated a sense of belonging based on a synthesis of private devotion and public action (Farrell 1997, 39). By making the mass media a priority, the Second Vatican Council had drawn up a new blueprint for the Catholic Church's relationship to the world that would influence all other council documents that came after. Questions of individual conscience and social communication became increasingly more significant, leading to massive changes in the very structure of the religious life and the relationship of the vowed religious to the laity.

These changes were laid out in the council decrees *Lumen Gentium*, the Dogmatic Constitution on the Church (1964), and *Perfectae Caritatis*, the Decree on the Up-to-date Renewal of the Religious Life (1965). Between them, these decrees completely transformed the theological justification for the religious life. *Lumen Gentium* changed a fundamental doctrine that suggested vowed religious were on a higher spiritual plane than the laity. Instead, the religious life was to be viewed more like a personal choice of service (Flannery 1975, 403). Similarly, *Perfectae Caritatis* stated explicitly that religious congregations were to consider themselves a part of the society around them and not set apart from the world (613). Between the exhortation to accelerate the pace of modernization in *Perfectae Caritatis* and the disavowal of their special status in *Lumen Gentium*, sisters were at a crossroads in defining the value of their vows. The Vatican wasn't in much better shape, and so left it to each congregation to redefine themselves according to their origins and the teachings of their founders. This devolution of power to the congregations was important for three reasons. First, it was an acknowledgment that the religious life was not some universal, eternally fixed entity but rather a corporate network with an identifiable history. Second, it promoted the role of the individual women who established congregations. Previously, much of the credit for the founding of women's congregations had been given to bishops, and the pioneer sisters were seen as merely servants to the Catholic hierarchy. Finally, it allowed for increased self-determination by congregations.

Charged with the power of these two documents, American sisters began to turn to overtly political action beyond narrow definitions of spiritual responsibility. They started to become directly involved in such causes as civil rights and the feminist movement. The Conference of Major Superiors of Women, which had squelched the Sister Formation Conference in a rather acrimonious battle in 1964 (Eby 2000), began to assert the power they had been given by the Vatican and use it to their advantage. In 1965 they sponsored the Sisters Survey, a survey of American sisters to help coordinate reforms nationwide. Importantly, they did this without the approval of the hierarchy. It wasn't that the pope rejected the idea but that he wasn't even consulted, which makes the survey an unprecedented act of anti-authoritianism (Quiñonez and Turner 1992, 83). The results, published in 1967, had some promising news in the form of rising educational levels for sisters and concomitant political consciousness. Two-thirds held at least a Bachelor of Arts degree, which was considerably higher than the national average of one person in five (Freeman 1975, 29). That same percentage also strongly supported the Second Vatican Council and its spirit of *aggiornamento*. However, the survey also uncovered the unpleasant reality that the number of women leaving the convent before taking their final vows was rising precipitously (Neal 1990, 32). What the survey was suggesting was that once young women received the chance through the sisterhood to explore their intellectual and professional potential they began to question their spiritual strength. In ever-growing numbers they quietly slipped away from the life that first gave them the opportunity to experiment with their identity. Rather than see that finding as a caution to slow down reforms, the CMSW instead decided that the problem was that reforms were going too slow. The pace needed to be accelerated to meet the expectations of younger sisters. The result was, in the immediate aftermath of the Second Vatican Council, an incredible period of boundless energy and enthusiasm for the modern religious life and a redefinition of the meaning and purpose of a sister in relation to the rest of society. This was reflected in articles that no longer chuckled indulgently at nuns on roller coasters or dressed up in fairy-tale costumes. Serious-minded current affairs magazines like *Harper's*, the *New York Times Magazine*, and the *Saturday Evening Post* presented hard-hitting accounts of nuns chafing under the confining rules of religious cloister and seeking exciting ways to express a revitalized, personalist form of worldly piety.

Unlike the generally affirmative and heart-warming tone of pre–Vatican II reports on women religious that seemed to affirm a sense of eternalism and tradition, magazine features now celebrated the 'new nun,' a thoroughly modern, confident woman on a journey of self-exploration but whose path was still clearly defined by religious duty. The excitement of the Second Vatican Council helped boost the number of vocations for the first half of the decade to an all-time high of 181,421 in 1966, one year after the council. Even better news was that the decline in ratio to the Catholic population seemed to be stabilizing, although still weak at approximately one sister for every two hundred lay members. This success in making the religious life more attractive was achieved with great effort by sisters who wanted more from the reform movement than a chance to shorten their veils and maybe attend a movie once in a while.

Armed with the Vatican's new emphasis on pastoral guidance and the democratic rights of the individual, sisters in the 1960s began to branch out into uncharted territory. They appeared at the front of civil rights protest marches and worked with explicitly feminist organizations like the National Organization for Women or the Planned Parenthood Federation. This spirit of civil activism caused some consternation among traditionalists, who complained that their behaviour was 'unladylike' (Griffin 1975, 40; Seng 1965, 253). Nonetheless, as long as the council continued to issue decrees that expressed openness to world affairs there seemed to be nothing to stop sisters from pressing on with a radical vision of reforms. This was the beginning of a long history of sister activism in America. The feeling was that if sisters were being asked to become more visible in the world as representatives of the Catholic faith then they should use that visibility to highlight social problems and give moral weight to demands for change. As one postulant told a reporter during Selma, 'This is really the first time I have ever appeared in public identified as a sister – what a wonderful way to begin the new life' (Cogley 1965, 46).

The media quickly picked up on the rather incongruous image of middle-aged white nuns linking arms with young radicals from the seamier sides of society. In many ways, the new nuns seemed to sum up the best of what the counterculture could offer by marrying it to the stabilizing influences of traditional, pious, bourgeois femininity. On a special two-part episode of the popular talk show *Open End with David Susskind*, television audiences were introduced to four women religious at the vanguard of convent reforms. It was early in 1966, just after the

Second Vatican Council. Into the forefront of this debate stepped sisters who were making the boldest strides towards modernization and challenging audiences to dispel old stereotypes. As one reviewer of the show noted, even the host proved badly in need of an attitude change:

> For the first few minutes of the program Mr. Susskind, observing all the 'good sisters' proprieties of an earlier era, attempted to say all the right things, as if he were recalling lines from an old Bing Crosby movie. But with this quartet, as he soon learned, the right things turned out to be largely wrong. Mr. Susskind was a quick student and soon learned they wanted to be treated with a little less reverence and somewhat more seriousness. As soon as he got that idea the 'Open End' man put aside the gee-whizzy attitude he began with. (Cogley 1966, E7)

The four sisters on *Open End* – Kristin Morrison, Jacqueline Grennan, Mary Charles Borromeo, and Mary Ignatia – were identified as leading examples of the 'new nuns.' They spoke about the changes they wanted to see and were clearly already influenced by *Lumen Gentium* and *Perfectae Caritatis* in their characterization of the modernized religious life for women. They said that they were no more holy than the laity, merely that they had chosen an alternative path. There were challenges to the old codes of obedience and withdrawal from the world. Most importantly, they emphasized their individuality and their right to be treated as mature, responsible women. It was clear by their presence on the show that sisters realized their reforms would remain incomplete until the public accepted their new image. As the reviewer concluded, 'Changing the image to fit the new nun's concept of her vocation will not be easy. But a few more programs like tonight's and next week's "Open End" will certainly help' (Cogley 1966, E7).

On this show and in the media blitz that followed the Second Vatican Council, sisters openly criticized their image and insisted on seeing it change. As one remarked, 'Some concepts about sisters come from movies, books and cartoons. Thus we learn that a sister is an incredibly naïve woman who grovels before a tyrannical superior and spends most of her time playing baseball or riding around in a jeep, smiling sweetly all the while and performing a few miracles everyday on the side' (Lexau 1964, xvi). It's not that there weren't some early warning signs that all was not well in the convent. *Look* featured a story titled 'The Vanishing Nun' that reported on the crisis in Catholic schools. They could no longer staff their classrooms exclusively with habited virgins and were, therefore, losing some of their unique, mystical sheen (Star 1963, 37–40). A *Harper's* cover story, 'The American Nun: Poor, Chaste and Restive,' recast the vows in a negative light at odds with modern psychology: 'Like the child whose interfering parent wants to govern every part of her life, the nun must fight for her own personal maturity' (Wakin and Scheuer 1965, 37). According to the authors, one of whom was a Jesuit priest, poverty was being realized through dangerous assaults on physical health. Chastity was equally neurotic, blending erotic imagery of Brides of Christ with a deep-seated fear of sexuality that led to advice such as 'put talcum powder in your bath, so your body won't be reflected in the water' (39). However, the vow most under siege was obedience as sisters began to realize the value of individual conscience 'in a world of outmoded regulations and worn-out attitudes which drown her involvement in the contemporary world' (40). It's important to note that the target of criticism was not women who enter into the religious life, but the rigid and uncompromising structures of the convent. For the most part, nuns themselves managed to escape the more scathing criticisms and were instead heralded for their willingness to confront the crisis, using their religious status as protective armour against both the forces of traditionalism and a sceptical counterculture.

In *Newsweek*, the idea of nuns 'going modern' was warmly received, and yet the sense of revolution was downplayed by frequent invocations to the traditions of feminine piety that framed sisters' political actions. This unspoken personalist edge mitigated their authority as threats to either Catholicism or society in general: 'As the cloister door swings open, there is a new sense of sisterhood – of feminine love – toward the human family. There is also a refreshing militancy. "When you take the vow of obedience," says a Poor Clare nun in New Orleans, "you don't abdicate your personality"' ('The Nun' 1967, 45). Claiming that women were somehow 'closer to the earth,' the article insisted that nuns would be the new face of a revitalized religious life, liberating the church from the 'intransigence of the male mystique.' However, its conclusion turned on that idea by suggesting that nuns 'are too busy and unself-conscious to press their own importance' (48). The contradic-

The new nun in transition: Corita Kent and Anita Caspary on the cover of *Newsweek*.

tory stance was perhaps best exemplified in a passage that praised one nun, the visual artist Sister Corita Kent, for wearing simple dresses. Yet on the cover her face loomed larger than life, most definitely swathed in a full veil and wimple. It appears, then, that the public weren't quite ready to give up on the old nuns, as hard as sisters tried.

The cover story on the 'new nuns' in the *Saturday Evening Post* was much more radical in tone than the one in *Newsweek*, opening with this challenge to both church and society: 'Breaking through the old rules that long imprisoned them, many liberated young religious women are boldly moving out into the streets to attack the major problems of American society' (Novak 1966, 21). The accompanying picture of a young nun in a modified habit walking through the slums of Chicago summed up the desire for some nuns to up the ante in this revolution of the convent: '"Too often," says Sister Mary Peter Traxler of Chicago, "sisters are considered a money-saving device for a middle-class society with middle-class values. And people want to keep them middle-class." People do so by treating nuns as "nice little things" – "the good sisters" – of no consequence to real adult life in America' (22). In this article, there was no mistaking that some sisters were planning a full-scale attack on conventional religious and feminine values that kept them trapped in 'our little nunny world' of bourgeois complacency. For that, they were still looking rather naïvely at America for their salvation. As one sister who was also a sociologist claimed,

'There are *two* cultures coexisting side by side in American life.' One of these cultures, the one in which the sisters had been happily and effec- tively living until the end of World War II, is 'family-centered, traditional, stable, sheltered, relatively changeless, often rural, proud.' The second culture, in whose anxieties the sisters have increasingly involved them- selves, is 'technical, swift, mobile, faceless, pragmatic, restless, pluralistic, urban.' The question the sisters ask is: 'Can our life retain its values in the new culture?' (24).

The answer seemed at this point to most assuredly be yes, especially as the effects of the sexual and social politics of second-wave feminism began to creep into the convent.

The dawning of feminist consciousness came slowly to sisters and did not really break into the open until the early seventies. However, there were signs that sisters were as tired of the Victorian lady stereotypes they laboured under as their secular counterparts were of the Occupation: Housewife syndrome identified by Friedan. In 1966, concerned that the government was not going to monitor the implementation of new legislation on employment equity for women, Friedan and others decided to found NOW, the National Organization for Women. What is not well known is that two of the original board members were sisters. Friedan recalled their particular conflicts:

> A young Catholic nun had been particularly eloquent and commonsensible, breaking through the quibbling over detail that could have kept [NOW] from getting born. Her name was Sister Mary Joel Read, later president of Alverno College in Milwaukee. I asked if I could nominate her for the NOW board. She was modest and suggested instead that she would nominate Sister Mary Austin Doherty of Chicago. Walking across the street to the hotel where we were going to have a drink before the election, I said I still wanted to nominate her. Would she join us? 'No, Betty,' she said regretfully, 'it wouldn't be right wearing this habit, but someday maybe.' In the years to come, Sister Joel, like so many of the militant nuns who have been at the heart of our movement while they were liberating themselves from the cloister, abandoned that habit, revolutionized the order and the college she now heads, and is now pioneering in 'relevant' education for women. (1985, 85)

Both Read and Doherty did eventually join the NOW board. Friedan recognized their participation as crucial in forging alliances across demographic lines and drawing attention to the different struggles women faced under the banner of the feminine mystique.

Sister Mary Aloysious Schaldenbrand took even more radical steps by publicly aligning herself with the Planned Parenthood Federation to improve women's access to birth control. In 1966, at their fiftieth anniversary conference in New York, she was a keynote speaker alongside other public figures such as Margaret Mead. Her argument for women's reproductive freedom was based on personalist values in 'the full scope and free exercise of their personal powers.' It was her belief that such rights were as important as the civil rights movement in the 'building up of a world of not merely masses, but persons' (Smith Collection). The individual actions of sisters like Read and Schaldenbrand were just the tip of the iceberg of a new sense of identity for many sisters. Not willing to leave this important issue to the media alone, they entered into the public debate with their own thoughtful accounts of the crisis in the convent and the growing need for modernization.

Sister Mary Charles Borromeo, who had been one of the guests on *Open End*, edited two anthologies sponsored by the CMSW. *The Changing Sister* (1965) blasted the regressive tendencies among congregations that continued to uphold customs and mentalities more in keeping with nineteenth-century parlours than contemporary urban life. Criticisms of family metaphors within the convent, a lack of artistic and intellectual development, and a need to bring a new attitude to nuns' psychosexual identity were the main themes of this book. Without these initiatives, cautioned Sister Mary Elena Malits, the convent 'will produce some tight-lipped sisters afraid of being women, not knowing how to be fully adult, and incapable of making their full contribution to modern society' (1965, 98). For many, the answer continued to reside within the sentimentally upbeat ethos of personalism. Yet the promise foretold by merging the best of Catholicism and Americanism within a resolutely feminine framework was starting to appear very shaky.

In 1967, in her follow-up book, *The New Nuns*, Borromeo referred to this unforgiving triangulation: 'The most popular referent is still the sister as teacher and nurse in turn-of-the-century immigrant institutions. However, a smaller group today tends to want all sisters to be on the front lines of social protest. This group is amply balanced by those who insist that sisters incarnate the eternal feminine, whatever that may be' (1967, 4). Once again, sisters were realizing that they were being asked to fulfil three roles in one. They were to be the guardians of the traditional church with its vast institutional network. They were also supposed to encapsulate the modern spirit of American freedom on the picket lines. And they were to stay true to an essential ideal of femininity while contending with overcrowded classrooms and mass demonstrations. With so many conflicting demands placed on them, it is little wonder that Borromeo asked not so rhetorically, 'can sisters be relevant?' (1967, 38). In 1965 Sister Marie Augusta Neal had claimed with confidence that 'the conscience of the American Catholic population is a reflection of the thinking, believing, and behaving of the American sisters' (1965, 42). Borromeo now countered that the pressure on sisters to be all things to all people had left them fumbling with a deep identity crisis. She said, 'We sisters insist that we have certain meanings and symbolic value. But we can hardly explain these to ourselves. And this inner uncertainty within sisters is the real drama of renewal for religious' (1967, 38). As the debate raged on it became clear, as Borromeo concluded, 'there is no viable middle ground in our day between the traditional monastic life and apostolic social action' (1967, 206). The results of the Sisters Survey suggested that the route was stretching forward, not back. However, the Catholic hierarchy was beginning to grow weary of reforms and wanted to put on the brakes if not turn right around. It is interesting that their primary targets were nuns and sexuality, although the two were kept distinctly apart.

Probably the only issue not covered by the Second Vatican Council in its total re-evaluation of Catholicism in the modern world was birth control. Realizing its potential for controversy, Pope Paul VI, who succeeded John XXIII after his death in 1963, appeared not to have as strong a stomach for reforms as his predecessor. He did make some bold steps by creating an advisory commission outside the jurisdiction of the council that included married couples as well as the usual members of the clerical hierarchy. Initially, excitement ran high that the church would finally acknowledge sexuality as an important aspect of personhood, and not merely a function of reproduction to repopulate the faithful. Even more, by doing so, some hoped it would mean that the church was living up to its promise to create a conscience-driven spirituality that placed more value on the authenticity of the self than subservience to hierarchy ('The Pope and the Pill' 1965, 66). The debate was likened to the Copernican Revolution in terms of doctrinal revision in light of incontrovertible new knowledge taken from the world ('Birth Control' 1964, 51). The majority opinion was that change was imminent, fuelled by leaked reports to the media from some of the more liberal members of the commission ('Time for a Change' 1967, 62). Their confidence was premature as a final decision from the pope was repeatedly stalled and, once the lay members of the commission returned home, the conservative clerical minority remained behind in Rome to step up the pressure to resist change. Less on the case of birth control itself and more on the dangers of undoing yet another mainstay of Catholic doctrine, the traditionalists ultimately won. *Humanae Vitae*, the Encyclical on the Regulation of Birth, was not released until 1968, and it conclusively reiterated a complete ban on all forms of birth control except for the rhythm method. The sense of betrayal and stunned disappointment reverberates in the church even today.

While this issue obviously had more direct relevance to secular Catholics than to vowed religious, the real lesson at stake was that the church was no longer willing to entertain progressive, modern values that infringed on its rights of authority. That was certainly bad news to those nuns who were the most radical reformers. The 'male mystique' identified by *Newsweek* was rearing its head and declaring war on the personalist, feminist approach to the religious life that was gaining ground in convents all over the world but primarily in America. Like with the issue of birth control, all the conservative clerics needed was a prime target to make their power known. They found it in the popular, progressive community of Corita Kent. The Immaculate Hearts of Mary (IHM) of Los Angeles were to be made examples of the limits of reform to the rest of the country.

The pretext for this confrontation was the habit. A signifier of timeless dedication to the eternal values of the church, it was also an effective container of feminine identity, smothering any suggestion of sexual self-awareness or any other outward sign of personal distinctiveness. When the IHMs decided to abandon the habit and their religious names, they knew it was a radical gesture, but it was not without precedent. Such action was taking place across the country with little fanfare; but the deeply conservative archbishop of the Los Angeles diocese, James Francis Cardinal McIntyre, decided it was not going to take place on his turf. Other issues soon arose, so they took their dispute first to Rome and then to the media, both sides pleading their case for the salvation of Catholic religious life. The controversy took four years to resolve, with the Sacred Congregation of Religious ultimately ruling in favour of the archbishop. His victory was a hollow one since 315 out of the 380 members quickly requested dispensation from their vows and left the canonical religious life. Some transferred to other communities, while others abandoned their vows altogether. The majority reconstituted themselves as an ecumenical lay community of devout persons called the Immaculate Heart Community (Caspary 2003, 209–17). After announcing their departure, Sister Anita Caspary, the former mother superior of the IHMs, suggested to *Time* that 'the religious life ... may not survive.' The Vatican spokesman countered that its decision to rule against the sisters was necessary to demonstrate the 'limits of its

From new nun to ex-nun: Anita Caspary.

toleration of innovation' ('Immaculate Heart Rebels' 1970, 50). However, it was clear that sisters were reaching their limits too. After 1966, the peak year for the total sister population, the number of women in congregations began to decline precipitously. By the late sixties celebrations of the new nuns in the media changed to agonizing over ex-nuns. Caspary, who had been on the cover of *Newsweek* as a new nun, was now on the cover of *Time* three years later as an ex-nun. As her own mother said to her, 'You've come a long way, Baby' ('Priests and Nuns' 1970, 55).

The turning point in the media came in 1967. While *Newsweek* was celebrating the nuns' 'joyous revolution,' *Ladies' Home Journal* asked a more direct question about 'why 3,600 [nuns] quit last year ... and what happened to them' (Kaiser 1967a). Many cited marriage and motherhood; however, that desire was not about changing one form of cloister for another, but about realizing their feminine identity more fully. Some marvelled at their sexual naïveté as they entered the dating world after years of being sexual 'neuters.' One admitted that she dated a different man every night and found herself getting too involved too fast, a hidden suggestion that she was a virgin no more. Others voiced anger at the convent for making virginity synonymous with perfection and leaving them in a state of psychological neurosis that led to physical health problems, particularly with their menstrual and menopausal cycles (137). As the author, Robert Kaiser, argued,

> It is precisely this unreal stance of the traditional convent toward sexuality that drives many sisters out. Mary McElroy of Antioch, Calif., now a pretty, vivacious mother of two baby girls, found that the 'sexlessness' of the convent life made her face up to her own conditioned Puritanism. 'When I did that,' she says, 'I knew that I wanted to be a wife and mother, and I saw that it was God who had given me those feelings.' In her case this realization proved to be the key to a happy marriage ... 'Larry [her husband] couldn't get over the fact that I had no inhibitions.' (137)

While stories of ex-nuns' sexual awakening almost always concluded with a happy heterosexual household, the main issue at stake wasn't so much promiscuity as the values of personal expression, experimentation, and self-realization, which underpinned the sexual revolution and had a spiritual twin in personalism. This was reflected in a brutally honest story in *Ebony* about one black nun who left her religious community after realizing that to remain in a predominantly white and middle-class cloister would mean 'forfeiting my birthright; selling my soul' (Willingham 1968, 74).

The warm and comforting image of nuns in civil rights protests took a serious hit as the movement evolved into Black Power. Complaining that events like Selma failed to resonate in her community, Saundra Willingham recalled her tears, which then were for herself but now were 'over the blindness of that group of Sisters who in failing me failed themselves' (68). She began to read voraciously about race relations in America. This so upset her mother superior that she was forbidden from continuing her reading so as not to unhinge her already 'hypersensitive ego.' Ironically, in the wake of such casual, paternalistic racism, it was the personalist writings of such Catholic activists as Harvey Cox and Philip and Daniel Berrigan that transformed her sense of personal redemption from her identity as a Catholic nun to that of a black woman: '[These authors] convinced me that the call to redemption is a constant call; a contemporary call. I began to believe then, as I do today, that the black man expresses that call in the 20th century, not only in America but all over the world. So I simply refused to argue about it; I became tight lipped and in some ways defensive – and progressively more lonely' (72).

Willingham's disillusionment with Catholicism was matched only by that with America and its double standard of democracy. First and foremost, her identity was tied to her race, not to any institutional or structural framework like religion or nationalism. This was characteristic of personalism, but it was also its weakness. It slowly dawned on sisters that by spurning attempts to coordinate individuals according to one value system, they were left in a state of cultural paralysis that was incompatible with any kind of coherent organization. Some made the painful decision to give up and turn their backs on the religious life. Among the sisters who left the convent for good were all four nuns profiled in *Open End* plus Corita Kent from *Newsweek*. When Sister Grennan departed in 1967, *Look* stated, 'Jacqueline was almost a model of a nun. Now unvowed, she can be herself' (Kaiser 1967b). The deepening crisis of structure revived the debate over values, leading to a creeping belief among those who stayed that perhaps Americanism was not the panacea that they had hoped it would be.

The alliances with Americanism failed to provide sisters with either alternative structures for the religious life or a morally righteous position like that which they enjoyed back in the fifties. After a decade of protests for justice, peace, and equality, the whole Americanizing project came under fire as the failures of the country became synonymous in sisters' eyes with the failures of the church (O'Brien 1972, 209). Rather than leaving, though, some sisters redoubled their efforts at reform, adopting an even more radical position. It is at the end of the decade that feminism became a crucial issue among sisters, a political factor that would help them to develop a more critical attitude in their relationship to both the Catholic Church and to American society. Unfortunately, it seemed that their moment had passed as the media lost interest and turned their attention to new models of feminine independence reflected in the radical, sexual women's liberation movement.

This decline in the social status of the nun was exacerbated by changes wrought from the dual forces of the sexual revolution and second-wave feminism. In vocation books from the fifties and early sixties there was much emphasis on the exciting, adventurous, fun-filled life of a sister. The educational and professional opportunities for women religious were unmatched in society and, coupled with a sense of heroic purpose, made a religious vocation appear especially romantic and enticing. By the late sixties, however, the convent was no longer the only option for women who were not eager to embrace marriage and motherhood. In a 1971 study on the changing status of women, researchers noted a marked increase in single women. During the 1960s the percentage of women living alone or with roommates rose 50 per cent. Among women of the traditional marrying ages of twenty to thirty-four the numbers more than doubled (Freeman 1975, 29). Furthermore, with the introduction of the birth control pill and the advent of the sexual revolution, the choice to remain single was no longer linked with remaining celibate. Instead of appearing as a radical and heroic alternative, the religious life was more likely to be regarded as an antiquated and oppressive sexual regime. Even the Sisters Survey suggested that the vow of chastity might be viewed as a hindrance rather than a way to liberate the individual for the realization of greater spiritual perfection. Sixty-five per cent of respondents agreed that 'the traditional way of presenting chastity in religious life has allowed for the development of isolation and false mysticism among sisters' (Wittberg

1994, 250). Since more women were remaining single without giving up the opportunity for intimate relationships and were enjoying greater access to education and careers, the benefits of the religious life seemed increasingly remote. With the introduction of such organizations as the Peace Corps, those interested in development and social justice work could now fulfil their ambitions without becoming missionaries. Sisters had to wonder what it was that they were offering in the convent that couldn't be gained elsewhere and with a lot more personal freedom.

By the end of the sixties, many sisters were out of the habit, out of church-run institutions, and out of patience with traditional Catholic attitudes towards feminine piety. Their increasingly strident position not only against church policies but also against American social trends was a far cry from the endearing portrait of new nuns at the height of the Second Vatican Council. Yet the campaigns for greater independence waged by sisters was neither recognized nor incorporated by the burgeoning feminist movement. The Conference of Major Superiors of Women was overhauled in 1971 to become the Leadership Conference of Women Religious, to the deep consternation of the Vatican, which refused to acknowledge this new group until the mid-seventies (Quiñonez and Turner 1992, 28). It became a much more politically activist and openly feminist organization, designed along the lines of the experimental structures of the women's liberation movement, including participatory democracy, consciousness raising, and collective decision making (92–4). Another grassroots movement emerged, the National Coalition of American Nuns, founded by Sister Margaret Ellen Traxler (formerly Mary Peter). She established a radical feminist mandate to work on issues such as welfare rights for women, the right for Catholic hospital workers to strike, racial integration within Catholic organizations, and greater independence for sisters from the clerical hierarchy. As Traxler argued in the pages of *Newsweek*, 'It's the nuns themselves who should determine whether they want to get out into the world ... not the men. They don't understand women – no man does' ('Battling for Nuns' Rights' 1969, 81). This was the only media report on this rather courageous initiative, and it appeared to have no backing from leaders in the radical feminist movement. Similarly, Read and Doherty's participation in NOW did not result in any public statement by that feminist organization concerning the freedom and equality of women religious in the Catholic Church. Nor is Schaldenbrand remembered as a birth-control activist.

Perhaps one of the reasons why sisters were shunted to the margins of the feminist movement was because their concerns did not always coincide with the priorities of other feminist groups. The divide separating sisters and secular feminists seemed to grow wider as the sixties progressed. When questions of sexual liberation and reproductive choice took precedence over employment and education, the celibate status of women religious made their participation incommensurate to some. Even though sisters were trying to forge alliances between feminism and the convent and were not afraid to challenge church doctrine in the process, the image of them as desexed or repressed kept reappearing. The celibacy of sisters became a kind of sore point with others who, in the early days of sexual liberation, saw vowed virginity as a sign of a repressed, prudish lifestyle. The decision from the Second Vatican Council to reduce the religious life to equal status with the laity further exacerbated the issue. One religious complained, 'Whereas formerly, religious assured the laity that, even though they were married, they could still attain true sanctity, now the laity have to assure religious that, even though they are celibate, they can still achieve true personhood and first-class citizenship as human beings' (Wittberg 1994, 250). Certainly, by the end of the sixties sisters were again grappling with the problem of being treated as human beings, just as they had when the reforms began twenty years before. Only this time, they were a lot more experienced in the workings of society and were not as eager to adopt the values of the dominant culture as they had been before.

With the advent of the Leadership Conference of Women Religious came a new kind of politics for the religious life in America that was far less about charming the public. Gone were the sweet pietic platitudes of before and the trusting embrace of new social movements. In some communities sisters began to rebuild the confidence of their badly depleted ranks through forays into feminist consciousness-raising and feminist liberation theology. Their work took on greater political urgency, and they even began openly criticizing the status of women in the Catholic Church. At the same time they formed sophisticated lobby groups to challenge government bodies to improve the health and education of the nation's poor. Yet even though sisters became more politically in tune with the goals of feminism during the seventies, their status as religious celibates posed a major barrier to their acceptance by the increasingly radical movement leaders. Furthermore, without the strength of an institutional hierarchy behind them they also lost prestige as the moral conscience of the Catholic Church. Where they were once the figureheads not only for a more liberated religiosity but also an appropriately liberated femininity, sisters no longer stood for either.

By the seventies women religious were in a no-win situation. They were either too radical for mainstream audiences to appreciate or too conservative to be embraced by radical movements. And yet their foray into postwar society speaks to so many issues within our current understanding of women's history and its relationship to popular culture and the mass media. Most obviously, the question of religion and its relation to gender has yet to be adequately addressed within cultural studies even though it has played a key role in representational strategies of independent, modern womanhood. Religion provided women with a kind of public authority at times when they were otherwise expected to remain quietly within the home. This historic role repeated itself in the 1950s when Catholic women religious began to organize themselves and encourage young women to see the benefits of a vocation that would allow women to lead active, fulfilling lives while adhering to strict doctrines of feminine obsequiousness. However, it was severely undermined by those same sisters once they increased their contact with the rest of the world and engaged with political and social debates about gender.

By examining the roles and representations of sisters before, during, and after the revival of the feminist movement, the primary focus on sexual and reproductive issues that continues in feminist cultural studies can be addressed from a very different perspective. Research can begin to include considerations of the convent as an alternative way of life for independently minded women, in which questions of labour, education, and social justice can and should be a significant area of feminist cultural analysis. In each of the five chapters that follow I trace the changing representation of the religious sister in different media across the twenty-year period under investigation. Beginning with film, then moving into sisters' own efforts with vocation books and popular music, and closing with a look at *The Flying Nun*, I examine how the nun operated as a kind of transitional figure that linked together two heretofore distinct moments of great social upheaval in both religious and gender identity. In so doing, more will be achieved than a simple retelling of an otherwise lost popular-culture phenomenon. I wish to present a challenge to feminist cultural studies to seek out other 'lost' groups of women who forged strategic alternatives to the dominant roles of marriage and motherhood but who, for whatever reasons, have been discarded by those invested in the creation of a cultural history of feminism.

2

Celluloid Sisters:
Nuns in Hollywood

The convent underwent enormous shifts in structure and values as sisters began adapting the religious life to conform to notions of modern independent womanhood. It is perhaps in film that these shifts are most easily identified, for a number of reasons. There were approximately fifteen films about nuns released in the fifties and sixties. The shifts in representation over this period provide a context for further examinations of the relationship between popular culture, the public role of sisters, and changing social values surrounding gender and religion. Film is especially relevant to this study because it was viewed as the most important medium of social communication by the Catholic Church and therefore subject to the most scrutiny. From the turn of the century until the era of Vatican II, 130 papal documents were published that directly pertained to film. Film bureaus, ratings offices, and advisory councils were run by local parishes and dioceses, most notably the notorious Legion of Decency, which staged boycotts of any film that did not meet its standards. However, by the postwar period the Catholic Church's influence on film production had steeply declined. Thus, the changes in the figure of the nun in films not only reflect shifts in gender relations and loosening values. They also speak to the waning authority of the Catholic hierarchy on its followers. It is nothing so simple as claiming that films about nuns mirrored the real-life struggles of sisters. Rather, they drew upon contemporary issues and reconfigured them in strategic ways that allow for alternative meanings and interpretative possibilities. The emotional journey of a nun in a film would inevitably lead to some kind of closure that usually resulted in one of three general resolutions. If she was the lead character, the nun would have to leave, or she would renew her commitment after exacting some minor concessions from a traditionalist hierarchy. And if she was a supporting character, she would be left behind in the story as an inspirational force for another's journey. Thus, the most interesting aspect to nun films is the dynamic between the nun and the other characters. The values mediated by her presence in the film often masked the exploration of social conflicts concerning questions of gender, religious, and national identity.

In 1966 there were nine films in production featuring nuns, leading the critic in *Cue* magazine to comment sardonically, 'Actors are known for their desire to play "Hamlet." Lately, it seems that actresses long to play nuns' (*The Trouble with Angels* [*TTWA*] MPAA File). The comparison of one classic heroic role for men to a generic character type for women is telling. It speaks directly to the problem of feminine identity during the postwar era as one not of individualism and self-awareness, but as a set of required attitudes and dispositions. The growing dissatisfaction among women with a society that relegated them to the home and curtailed their opportunities for education and careers found one particular outlet – albeit tightly controlled – in films depicting nuns as independent heroines engaged in meaningful labour and experiencing great adventures. Later on, as the sixties progressed, the nun retained an aura of sacrificial glamour, but her role as a serene exemplar of feminine heroics became increasingly troublesome. As women fought public battles for their social, sexual, and economic equality, the nun became less a figure of strategic independence than one of compromise or even capitulation. The relationship between femininity, piety, and American values was foregrounded in nun films to foster a new role model for zealous young women looking for alternatives to marriage and motherhood that would not radically depart from the expectations placed on women in society. As Brandon French has argued, the fact that these heroines were enrobed from head to foot in the religious habit and vigorously guarded their chastity served to limit the radical potential for women's liberation at which they broadly hinted (1978, 122).

While French's analysis is useful, it does not go far enough in determining why Catholic sisters were selected to fulfil this quasi-emancipatory role in films rather than, for example, Protestant missionaries like Katherine Hepburn in *The African Queen* (1950). The answer lies in the changing status of Catholicism and the reappraisal of religion in relation to everyday life. By shifting the focus of attention away from

America per se and onto American Catholicism, films featuring nuns could widen the scope of critique, while at the same time diverting it from any direct confrontation with American cultural hegemony. In this way nuns served as the repositories of displaced meanings about gender, religion, and culture (McCracken 1988, 106). To many in the postwar era, Catholicism represented traditionalism, submissiveness, and passivity. It was the antithesis of the American ideals of independence, freedom, and democracy. Not by coincidence were these traits assigned a gender so that the Catholic mentality could be associated easily with the feminine, and the American with the masculine. It is this process of feminization of religion in the postwar period, most specifically of Catholicism, that provides a deeper texture to nun films and can go to some lengths in realizing the extent of the relationship between gender and religion in postwar culture.

It would be going too far to suggest that nun films are a specific genre, but the trend in interest about the convent during the fifties and sixties was a particularly imaginative way to come to terms with seemingly unrelated issues of gender and religious identity in postwar America. Nuns had the potential to disrupt the discourses of femininity since they operated outside the confines of heterosexual domesticity. At the same time, the inherent traditionalism of the nun as invested in her habit, her cloister, and her pious virginity assured that the doctrines of femininity – a moral order of womanly submissiveness and sacrifice – would remain intact (Smith 1990, 171). Nuns offered women a unique alternative to the dominant ideals of marriage and motherhood at a time when higher education and professional careers were generally discouraged. To be sure, many social critics supported the idea of working women, recognizing that the number of women in the workforce rose steadily every year throughout the fifties and sixties (Freeman 1975, 30). However, the argument was that women should not work for reasons of self-fulfilment but as a sacrifice of their inherently passive nature for the enrichment of American socio-economic progress. As one article on women factory workers stated, '[Women] feel they are "doing a job for others" as well as for their families. They eschew noble phrases but there is no mistaking that meaning' (Samuels 1951, 13). 'Doing for others' was a major impetus of sisters that informed all their work. By making sacrificial labour crucial to their religious identity, they brought the feminine ideals for working women to a higher, spiritual level. They also countered the growing association of independent working women with their increasing consumer power, which often translated into sexual autonomy. A delicate balance between self-abnegation and heroic purposefulness directed towards others became central to the representation of nuns in film.

In choosing the films for analysis here, I looked for emphasis on some of these contemporary social issues with a nun as a central lead character. *Heaven Knows, Mr Allison* (1957) chronicles the transformation of an American Marine from an arrogant, selfish boor to a compassionate and sacrificing man because of his love for a beautiful nun, Sister Angela. *Lilies of the Field* (1963) is a gentle yet uncompromising examination of race relations in America through the friendship of an elderly East German nun with a young black drifter. These two films were released before the effects of the Second Vatican Council were to be widely felt and reflect that transitional sense of religion as nostalgia. In the mid-sixties, on the cusp of a sexual revolution that would lead to the women's liberation movement, nun films remained rooted in a conviction that feminine independence was still somehow containable. Two films that were released in the years immediately following the Second Vatican Council, *The Sound of Music* (1965) and *The Trouble with Angels* (1966), represent a kind of corollary relationship to the same nagging question of what to do with unruly, misfit girls who dared not to conform. By the late sixties, radical social movements were sweeping across the country, making it difficult to offer simple solutions of 'aut maritus aut murus.' *Where Angels Go, Trouble Follows* (1968) and *Change of Habit* (1970) focus on the challenges of religious sisters confronting sexual and social revolutions with their traditional spiritual devotion. These six films are not the only ones, or even the most acclaimed, to deal with nuns. That honour should go to *The Nun's Story*, whose production was mired in controversy and transatlantic negotiations. It will be dealt with separately in the next chapter.

Hollywood was not alone in discovering the dramatic potential of the convent. It was picking up on a trend in the media in which nuns were now news. One obvious reason for all the attention was that for the first time in their lives, sisters were encouraged to break down the barriers that kept them apart from the rest of society. As church officials relaxed the rules of cloister, habits, and daily routines, a long-suppressed curiosity bubbled to the surface. At first sisters were delighted, but they were unprepared for the media to take their way of life and use it in other ways to promote both a kind of idealized, industrious femininity as well as a benign, comforting religiosity. These characterizations persisted even as sisters became increasingly sophisticated about their public image. In the fifties sisters were almost giddy to cooperate with the media and, indeed, were often photographed laughing gleefully, whether they were in a classroom or on a roller coaster. By the sixties sisters were publicly expressing frustration with their frivolous depictions. As one put it, 'Sisters are not known as persons, "reserved," "sweet," "genteel," – all these adjectives are used to characterize sisters but they make the nun almost a minus sign as a person' (Schaldenbrand 1965, 161).

MaryAnn Janosik argues that Hollywood's ongoing fascination with nuns is fuelled in part by their historical association with the Madonna icon of nurturing, compassionate spirituality. She suggests that while representations of nuns in films tend to be reflective of the social conditions of women at any given time, the sense of eternal security generated by the image serves to mute the potential for social critique (1997, 81). Thus, the role of the nun is rarely fleshed out into a complex character, but instead acts as a kind of 'cultural afterthought, needing kitschy talents or quirky gimmicks to explore trite social problems' (76). Other film historians, including Les and Barbara Keyser, have echoed this opinion. They claim that nuns are idealized figures in Hollywood films rather than complex characters in and of themselves. The nun exists on screen to inspire other characters and the audience to strive for higher goals and become better people (1984, 141). It is their dual persona as idealized woman and idealized religiosity that propels this sentimentalized image of nuns.

Both Janosik and the Keysers appeal to a complete history of nuns in films to support these arguments. These range from wartime melodramas like *The Bells of St Mary's* (1945) and *The Song of Bernadette* (1943) to the more recent comedy *Sister Act* (1992) or the critically hailed *Dead Man Walking* (1995). It is unfortunate that they do not support these claims with historical evidence about changes in the status of women and, more specifically, of sisters in society. Instead, they bolster their arguments by creating different character types or genres. The Keysers rely mostly on aesthetic ideals to evaluate a film's portrayal of the convent. Thus, *The Nun's Story* is a good film about nuns because of its attention to detail and high-minded – not to mention big-budget –

artistry (151). They are critical of films that rely on melodramatic conventions wherein the nuns are 'designed to make audiences feel and feel
and feel' (141). It is telling that their complaints tend to be that nun
films are overly feminine ('pink-lampshade cosiness' is how they
describe them). Their concerns about the aesthetic value of the films
override any sociological analysis. Thus, they criticize films that incorporate feminine values and praise films that follow more masculinist
aesthetic principles. This reductionist association of art with masculine
values and kitsch with feminine has been a long-standing issue, especially as concerns material Christianity. Colleen McDannell points out
that debates about modern religious art and iconography have tended
to operate within this gender dichotomy, to the detriment of women
and femininity in general (1995a, 174). Thus, their claims of offering
any kind of gender analysis are undermined by their own unexamined
bias.

Janosik fares somewhat better by leaving questions of critical value to
the side and focusing on the character development of nuns. She con-
structs three categories of nun roles: the Earth Mother Madonna, the
Eccentric Aunt, and the Social Activist Sister (1997, 81–90). The first
type, the Earth Mother Madonna, refers to the image of the nun as a
stout-hearted defender of high morals and human dignity. Rosalind
Russell's Mother Superior in both *The Trouble with Angels* and *Where
Angels Go, Trouble Follows* is one example of this character type. The
second type, the Eccentric Aunt, is usually reserved for secondary characters as foils to the Earth Mother. Mary Wickes's character of Sister
Clarissa in the *Angel* movies or Kathy Najimy's role in the two *Sister Act*
films serve this function. They provide comic relief through an assort-
ment of wacky personality traits and eccentric behaviour. Finally, the
third type, the Activist Sister embodies a more adventurous heroism
than the Earth Mother and tends to be more susceptible to her own
human frailty as it conflicts with her spiritual ideals. The most obvious
examples of this type are Sister Luke in *The Nun's Story* and the Oscar-
winning performance by Susan Sarandon as Sister Helen Prejean in
Dead Man Walking.

It would be difficult to argue that these character types for nuns do
not exist. However, Janosik's method does not enable her to specify the
relationship of the role to the broader social context of the film. There
are almost forty years between *The Nun's Story* and *Dead Man Walking*,

yet by placing them in the same analytical category, Janosik is unable to support her argument that representations of nuns reflect the particular social conditions of women at any time (1997, 81). Shifts in the representation of nuns throughout the fifties and sixties were expressive not so much of types as of social issues regarding gender and religion in postwar society. My point here is not to look for those characteristics that diminished the effectiveness of the nun, as Janosik does. At stake are urgent moral and social concerns about gender and religion facing audiences that could be partially and temporarily resolved through a nun character. While the parameters of the cinematic nun's relationship to lay society expanded over time, there was ultimately little change to her persona. Thus, Sister Angela of *Heaven Knows, Mr Allison* emotes an incipient feminism with her youthful idealism and bravery against assaults to her vows from the outside world. Yet when Sister Michelle from *Change of Habit* faces similar conflicts over a decade later, she is less a hero than an example of muted independence through sexual repression and tradition-bound femininity.

In the era before the Second Vatican Council dramatically reconfigured the religious life, the traditional idea of a vocation dictated that nuns literally obliterate their own needs and desires in favour of others. As one priest expressed it in a book for young sisters, 'We make ourselves, for the love of God, holocausts, whole-burnt offerings. Just nothing is retained' (Moffatt 1960, 88). Even reform-minded sisters had great difficulty shaking off this attitude. In 1964 a member of the progressive Maryknoll religious community had this to say: 'I have a private theory that no woman is happy unless she is sacrificed on some altar. It may be her family and home; it may be the welfare of others: education, perhaps, or medicine or reclaiming alcoholics. Whatever it is, the woman who spends herself down to the last penny is the woman most satisfied with life' (Lexau 1964, xii). However, signs abounded that perhaps sisters did not subscribe wholesale to this theory of symbolic self-immolation. Sisters were just as likely to extol the virtues of the religious life because it liberated them from the yoke of domesticity under which so many other women chafed. This argument usually centred on the sexuality of sisters and their consecrated virginity. In an essay entitled 'The Meaning of Virginity in Religious Life,' one sister argued that the vow of chastity actually freed women to realize a greater capacity of love and fulfilment, not confined to a husband or children

(Malits 1965, 93). Another sister, who eventually became a missionary in Oceania, recalled how domestic bliss never held any charm for her as a child and she yearned to exceed everyone's expectations: 'From the time I was old enough to toddle, I had always strained for the horizon. In the days when baby-sitting was a cherished privilege and happy pastime for the little girls of my neighborhood, I had scornfully closeted myself with a book in my self-designated "studio" in the attic, to dream of the day when I would be, unquestionably, one of the world's greats' (Austine 1964, 32). Thus, a religious vocation was seen as one of the very few respectable – even honourable – alternatives to marriage and motherhood precisely because it preserved a sense of sexual containment. While it extolled the American virtues of ambition and idealism, it wrapped them in a thoroughly feminized cloak of pious virginity and selfless service to others. It is for this reason that when a nun appeared on film, she operated as a virtuous symbol of emancipated womanhood, one who hinted at, rather than openly challenging, the hegemony of domesticity (French 1978, 122). A nun film tended to be about nuns only at face value. Scratch the surface and the story opened up to a wide range of meanings relating to women's independence and the struggle for balance between traditional (i.e., feminine) and progressive (i.e., masculine) values. This balance was continually shifting throughout the fifties and sixties. Yet, in the beginning, the scales were definitely tipped in favour of notions of women's inspirational qualities rather than their own activism.

In *Heaven Knows, Mr Allison* and *Lilies of the Field* both nun characters operate as towering moral forces within narratives that do not lead to their own personal growth but to an awakening in their male companions. The former was a World War II epic about a stranded marine and missionary nun on a remote Pacific island. Sister Angela, played by Deborah Kerr, is searching for a missing priest when the rest of her band hears signs of a sea battle and sails away without her. The priest for whom she is searching dies soon after, leaving her completely deserted. Likewise, Corporal Allison, played by Robert Mitchum, is on sea patrol when his submarine submerges to head into the battle. He drifts in his raft until he lands on the same island as Sister Angela. Together, they retreat to a cave in the mountains and wait for a rescue team. Unfortunately, a Japanese corps arrives and establishes a base camp. They now need all their wits if they are to avoid capture. Their tense living situation inside the cramped cave is brought to a head after a drunken rage by Allison during which he sexually threatens the young nun. Frightened, she runs off into the jungle before collapsing from exhaustion and a high fever. His tender nursing awakens his own sense of remorse and a determination to control his animalistic tendencies. With Allison's moral regeneration complete, the movie ends rather falsely. Discovered by the Japanese while hiding in the cave, they are just about to be killed when the Allied troops arrive and rout the enemy – assisted in part by Allison's stealthy sabotage of the Japanese guns in the middle of the night. Allison is wounded but his sense of honour is restored as Sister Angela leads him off the island.

Lilies of the Field (1963) was different because rather than having a young, beautiful nun who would incite sexual tension, the lead character was the ancient and formidable Mother Maria, played by Lilia Skala. If Sister Angela fit the profile for the Activist Sister, then Mother Maria was most certainly an Earth Mother. As her character was described in the synopsis sent to the MPAA offices: 'Mother Maria has a single target: to serve God. A stubborn, Teutonic woman, she led her band of Nuns to a new world to escape a worship she could not believe [Communism]. In the strange and barren Southwest she will work for God, but first this resolute woman must wrest from the stubborn soil a living for her brood. She needs help – a man's help. To her the answer is simple: pray for it. Homer's arrival coincides with the prayer' (*Lilies of the Field* MPAA File). As the leader of a small band of East German refugee nuns now eking out a living on a barren farm in Arizona, Mother Maria is as harsh and uncompromising as the landscape. Yet she does not hesitate to place her most cherished dream of building a chapel in the hands of the young drifter Homer Smith, an Academy Award-winning performance by Sidney Poitier.

In the opening of the film, Homer drives up to the farmhouse as Mother Maria raises her eyes to the sky and pronounces, 'Gott is gut. He has sent me a big, strong man.' She and her nuns are lilies of the field, women who 'neither toil nor spin' but place their faith utterly in God. In this case God provides the nuns not with skills and abilities of their own but with Homer. He works two jobs, one at a highway construction company in town and the other at the farmhouse building the chapel, so that the sisters can enjoy a more comfortable standard of living. He even brings lollipops to the nuns every week – a band of four plain-looking women described accurately in the *New York Times* as 'a charmingly cheerful, chipper chorus' (Crowther 1963) – and grins appreciatively at their girlish squeals of pleasure over the small treat. The chapel gives Homer a sense of purpose and accomplishment, as the faith the nuns have placed in him is a new and thoroughly welcome sensation. The journey of self-discovery that first led him down the highways is finally realized by staying put and witnessing at first hand the power of faith and community. As he slips away from the makeshift convent after the job is done, there is no doubt that his wandering days will soon be over. In stumbling across the nuns, he has ultimately found himself.

Thus, in both films, the relationship between the nun and her new male friend plays out in terms that privilege the emotional development of the man. This situation speaks to the kind of double bind women found themselves in the period just before *The Feminine Mystique*, where they were to be passive in their femininity but also assertive and independent according to the new values of achievement-oriented Americanism. Women were encouraged to work hard on behalf of their families, even to leave home and join others on assembly lines. Yet the impetus was not their own self-improvement or independence but to assist men in their primary responsibilities as providers and protectors. Nuns were excellent examples for both elements of this double bind since they trained for hardy, demanding labour but were dedicated to obedience and humility in all their endeavours. However, even as muses, nuns were still more active and adventuresome than most other female heroines. Yet it was still ultimately for the betterment of a man, and not for their own sense of identity.

The underlying sexual tension between a beautiful nun and a rugged marine in *Heaven Knows, Mr Allison* results in scenes of domestic quietude as the brave nun who is prepared to fend for herself too easily slips into the role of compliant helpmate after the arrival of Allison. As she explains her situation to Allison, she demonstrates her own remarkable courage and loyalty by showing no resentment against the nuns who abandoned her or the priest who went missing at a crucial time. Unfortunately, once her character's fortitude is established, Sister Angela then abdicates all authority to him. While he makes plans for food and shelter, she retreats to one of the huts to find the priest's old pipe for her new protector. The easy transition from a dedicated missionary to a submissive woman finding a smoke for her man highlights the complexity of gender relations and the difficult question of women's self-reliance in the postwar era. At once the movie acknowledges that Sister Angela could take care of herself if necessary but that it is for the best that she has a man to do it just the same. Importantly, it is her status as consecrated virgin that confers upon her that added sense of competency and independence. As Allison puts it, 'What do you see besides a big dumb guy? I'll tell ya. A marine. That's what I am. All through me, a marine. Like you're a nun. You got your cross, I got my globe and anchor ... Other guys, they got homes and families. Me, I got the corps, like you got the church.' This link between the military life for men and the religious life for women illustrates how nuns were identified as the feminine equivalent of war heroes, embodying patriotism, adventurism, and moral courage while also exhibiting the innocence and placidity appropriate to their gender.

The most efficient way to ensure that Sister Angela could be portrayed as simultaneously heroic and meek was to make her character a foil for the salvation of Corporal Allison, rather than explore the boundaries of her own mettle. This was not a coincidence in the film but a deliberate strategy by the producer. In a memo sent to the MPAA offices, which sought to address concerns raised by the Legion of Decency, Sister Angela was described in this way: 'a motion picture based on this story would be a great tribute to nuns, in general, through the personalization of the story of one particular nun, who fights valiantly, both physically and emotionally, to persevere in her vows as a member of a religious order, and, by her fortitude and perseverance, she brings about the moral regeneration of a thoroughly evil young man' (*Heaven Knows, Mr Allison* [HKMA] MPAA File). Unfortunately, the need to appease Legion of Decency officials resulted in a rather pedantic portrait of an unquestioned vocation. Not even an attempted rape and a subsequent bout of malaria upsets Sister Angela's placid countenance as she thanks the marine for saving her life and apologizes for overreacting to his drunken advances before. Yet it appears that this was an image of nuns that resonated deeply with audiences. As one reviewer commented:

> Miss Kerr is pure delight in every scene, endowing her Sister Angela with natural and very human reactions – including a genuine if covert sense of

humor – but never for a moment allowing them to violate the purity of her vocation. Throughout she is the picture of spiritual grace, but even clad in her bulky white habit and her freckled face unadorned by make-up, she likewise is the picture of physical grace and beauty. (Proctor 1957, 4)

Sister Angela's supporting role is reinforced in the film by placing her under containment in a cave to hide from the enemy. Once the Japanese army sets up a base camp by the beach, the nun is barred from leaving the cave because her white habit can be seen from far away. While Allison is able to search the hillside for food, slip down to a cove and fish, or even sneak into the enemy camp to steal food and supplies, Sister Angela waits patiently in the cave and leaves it only when Allison gives her permission. Her only consolations are the few items she was able to rescue from the mission church before it was destroyed. The elaborate gold crucifix and long white tapers in the dingy cave give glamorous balance to her bleak cloister, reiterating a feminine need for beauty and adornment even in the most implausible circumstances. This is not to say that she was supposed to be portrayed as a helpless woman – few missionaries could afford to be – and her character was intended to show great courage and compassion. Yet the role of Sister Angela is ultimately relegated to a tiny space in the film, far from the centres of action. There she can offer comfort and support to Allison without actually engaging in any dangerous activity herself. This kind of characterization was deemed appropriately feminine:

But Sister Angela has no wish to get rid of her veil, comes from no love-less existence, has no frustrations to pitch into the river: no sooner have we caught a glimpse of her without [her habit] than she is cured and the veil back in its place again. The fact that everyone – director and actors – accept this as reasonable, likely, and not necessarily tragic gives the film a serene charm and, oddly enough, an air of being like real life, of having its feet firmly fixed on the ground, however outlandish the circumstances. (HKMA Clippings File)

The notion that it was 'reasonable' and 'like real life' for a woman to accept such severe restrictions to her mobility shows how Sister Angela was being presented as an ideal, if unattainable, woman. She delicately balances the demands of traditional femininity and progressive industri-

Sister Angela (Deborah Kerr) in *Heaven Knows, Mr Allison*.

ousness without complaint or any indication that she needs more to fulfil herself. The film never questions her motivations but remains
resolutely focused on Allison and his journey of self-discovery.

Similarly, Mother Maria brings about a moral regeneration, but hers
is thoroughly grounded in the contemporary social issues facing America in the early sixties. The relationship between Homer and Mother
Maria resonated because it spoke to a transitional point in postwar culture in which notions of humanity and the dignity of persons were
being strongly asserted. This transition was not marked by the nun, who
preserves old-fashioned values, but by the African American, who is
redeemed through her intervention. At the beginning of the sixties,

Herberg noted that the American way of life was overtaking denomina-
tional faith as a kind of civil religion that sought to reveal an authentic
sense of self through a results-oriented, achievement-minded, and
work-conscious sense of purpose. This was contrasted with the traditional way of life based on conformity and a need for belonging and
acceptance from the community (1960, 59–63). If *Lilies of the Field*
envisioned Homer as the sign of the new and Mother Maria as that of
the old, it needs to be asked what additional moral weight and sympathy was given to both positions by making Homer black and Mother
Maria a nun. Their relationship articulated certain tensions about race
and gender in an oblique and non-threatening way by mirroring images
coming out of the civil rights protests of young African Americans and
older white nuns joining hands together at the front of picket lines.

The feminization of the civil rights movement did not begin with
films featuring nuns but derived from an interesting conjunction of that
movement with re-emergent feminism and the new personalist movement. The women workers who volunteered to assist in voter registra-
tion drives and public rallies in the South were often linked to this
rather nebulous form of spiritual and social thought, which had its roots
in the highly feminized piety of postwar Catholicism. Influenced by the
writings of notable Catholics such as Dorothy Day and Thomas Mer-
ton, personalism did not directly challenge American idealism but suggested it be tempered with those values relegated to women and
religion (O'Brien 1972, 17). Thus, this alternative ideology shared
much in common with nineteenth-century feminization and its claims
to reintroduce 'women's values' to the political process (Farrell 1997, 8;
Evans 1980, 108). However, as both Sara Evans and Jo Freeman have
pointed out, while the values associated with women may have been
given greater credibility, women's participation in the civil rights movement was still limited to domestic and clerical work on behalf of male
leaders. Women often complained that they had two choices: either
work as typists and office girls to the male organizers or become the wife
(legal or otherwise) to a leader and earn prestige for your domestic and
sexual talents (Freeman 1975, 57).

In a movement that idealized feminine values while demeaning and
sexualizing feminine labour, it actually makes some sense, oddly
enough, that the nun should appear at the forefront in images of protest
marches and rallies. Their chaste, morally rigorous version of femininity

transcended the negative stereotypes assigned to women workers. Nuns served an almost completely symbolic role, linking civil rights to spiritual issues of human dignity and compassion. As one sister complained, it seemed at times that 'it is the habit, not the person, whose presence is sought' (Shea 1967, 61). Their sudden visibility in the most politically fraught issue facing America at that time challenged conventional thinking about the role of sisters in society. It was, perhaps, the first indication that the goals of the Conference of Major Superiors of Women to improve cultural understanding and community building between sisters and lay members of society were starting to take hold.

However, sisters soon discovered that they were fighting a battle not so much with the church hierarchy or concerned Catholics as with their own mass-mediated image. One sister recalled the early days of protest and the identity crisis it sparked from within the protective walls of the convent: 'The nuns had taken vows to be poor (like Him), unmarried (like Him), and (like Him) strictly obedient to the law of love. Why then was everybody surprised to find them standing in the streets with the poor and dispossessed? Was it, we began to ask ourselves, because in actuality we were perhaps closer to the movies than to the Gospel?' (Griffin 1975, 41). In contrast to that concern it could be argued that the movie persona of the nun as a sweet, naïve, and morally righteous woman informed the image of sisters arm-in-arm with young black men on the streets of Selma and helped to make the movement seem less threatening. By the early sixties America was at a crucial juncture where feminism, social protest, and even Vatican II had not yet really begun to make radical claims on the national psyche. Nuns seemed to be standing at these crossroads between the best of the past and the best of the future. Within the habit lay a richly textured symbol of the crisis of identity that was not just facing women but the nation as a whole.

The fact that *Lilies of the Field* won a host of awards from religious organizations, critics' polls, and audience surveys suggests that the relationship between nuns and civil rights activists resonated deeply in the American psyche. However, the film did not make the civil rights movement an explicit part of the story. There is only a fleeting scene of a confrontation between Homer and a racist contractor. Soon after this confrontation the contractor is quickly won over to the cause of building a chapel, partly through the moral urgency of Mother Maria and partly through his admiration for Homer's work ethic. In this the two main characters exemplified the best of their kind, in a rather trite way that was never fully fleshed out. Homer and Mother Maria never even acknowledge the racial tensions percolating at this time. The two unlikely friends are more likely to squabble over religious differences than racism. Homer is wary of Catholicism and refuses to attend mass with the sisters, claiming that as a Baptist it wouldn't be right. At one point, when they both appeal to biblical passages to support their position in an argument, he pulls out a pocketbook version that he always carries while Mother Maria has to lug a huge, ancient version from a side table. After listening to the sisters sing complicated Latin hymns, Homer teaches them a traditional gospel song with only one word, 'Amen.' His simpler, unfettered, and more forthright spirituality is subtly portrayed to be somewhat more authentic than the sisters' deeply ordered and ritualized community. Although both are on a search for deeper meaning and purpose in the world, Homer's faith is easy, transportable, and more democratic. In other words, more romantically American. *Lilies of the Field* sentimentalized the plight of black men by bringing it into contact with the unassailable morality of religious sisters. In so doing it turned Homer Smith into Everyman, making him the symbol of America's well-being and the nun the conduit for his redemption.

In the pre-feminist fifties and early sixties, the nun filled a badly needed role in postwar American film by deflecting some of the tensions mounting in society over enforced domesticity. Even in news reports of the time, the efforts of American sisters to organize through the Conference of Major Superiors of Women and the Sister Formation Conference were brushed under the carpet. Instead, the message seemed to be that their work was a natural outcome of their religious dedication. In this way, sisters were not given credit for their administrative, negotiating, or policy skills but were admired only as devoted, duty-bound virgins. This divinely inspired productivity stood in stark contrast to articles on working women who did not have a thousand-year tradition of religious obedience to mitigate any claims of independence. In a 1956 article in *Life* magazine, Robert Coughlan stated unequivocally that a woman who thwarted her natural proclivity for marriage and motherhood faced dire emotional and psychological consequences. Referring to the 'primary feminine qualities [of] receptivity, passivity and the desire to nurture,' Coughlan argued that any woman who put work ahead of family was necessarily 'an unhappy woman' (1956, 109, 116). It seems that nuns were able to circumvent such critiques because they never failed to reassert their naïveté and dependence even as they were embroiled in life-threatening challenges. The nun was used to substitute a different kind of cloister from the home and therefore to reiterate the doctrines of femininity regardless of the specific conditions of women's lives. Making a nun the main female lead expanded the possibilities not only of locale and time but also of character motivation and relationship to the male lead. It also reasserted the convention that women were better off kept in the background and should not be let loose on society unless they were somehow contained. It is interesting that rather than having this conciliatory aspect of the nun diminish as real-life sisters became more politically active in society, films featuring nuns reinforced that idea of the religious life as an acceptable compromise for women. The heroines of later nun films tended to start out as rebels, but the allure of the convent would eventually soften their harsh ways and bring them back in line with the doctrines of femininity.

Both Mother Maria and Sister Angela represented the traditional religious life and how, with a few modifications, it could be integrated into a complicated modern society as a kind of moral paragon. By the end of the Second Vatican Council, the double bind of nuns became more central to film plots but also more ambivalent. It is worth noting that by this time producers did not have to carefully construct their proposals to the MPAA in order to avoid any confrontation with Catholic officials. The Legion of Decency, which had tyrannized Hollywood in the pre-war era, had lost much of its clout with the American public by the fifties. In 1965 it was disbanded and the National Catholic Office for Motion Pictures took its place (Skinner 1993, 154). While apologias for films featuring nuns were standard practice prior to the Second Vatican Council, in the post-Legion of Decency era there was very little negotiation between Hollywood executives and the Catholic Church. Ideally, this should have left the field wide open for complex dramatic interpretations of the religious life. With the opening up of the convent, there was now much more dramatic potential in stories that focused on nuns and their own crises of self-discovery rather than as fodder for another's. It is surprising and more than a little disappointing that the films about nuns in the aftermath of Vatican II were far less ambitious and the image of nuns as independent heroines was muted and compromised. Two films from the mid-sixties best express the efforts to contain feminine independence through appeals to the convent. Both *The Trouble with Angels* and *The Sound of Music* featured a wild, untameable heroine who seemed to not fit in with society but who was eventually, gently guided into an appropriate form of femininity by the intercession of a motherly nun. In the first film, that path led directly to the convent. Interestingly enough, in the latter it went the other direction, towards a husband and children.

Based on a memoir by Jane Trahey, *The Trouble with Angels* appeared one year after the close of Vatican II, when the sister population rose dramatically before its long spiral downward. It thus serves as a kind of median point between the traditionalism of *Heaven Knows, Mr Allison* and *Lilies of the Field*, and the more sexually charged journeys of discovery depicted in *Where Angels Go, Trouble Follows* and *Change of Habit*. Producers sought out technical advisers and even shot on location at a sister-run school outside Philadelphia. The director, Ida Lupino, and the star, Rosalind Russell, were both well-known devout Catholics in Hollywood. Russell even arranged for the premiere to be held in St Louis, Missouri, as a benefit for her old Catholic high school, Marymount (*TTWA* MPAA File). The convent boarding school in which the film is set is a magnificent Gothic institution amidst a lush and expansive landscape. Within the walls are two kinds of women: brash and exuberant schoolgirls and kindly but emotionally remote nuns. The twist is that the cloistered walls of St Francis Academy entice the wildest young students, not the demure ones. The film portrays the antics of two rebellious teenagers. Mary Clancy, played by teen star Hayley Mills, has been kicked out of a number of boarding schools before arriving at St Francis. Her best friend, Rachel Deverey, is a refugee from the progressive school system. They are both quickly dismayed at their new surroundings. As Mary complains, 'The only difference between this place and a girls' reformatory is the tuition.' To which Rachel replies, 'And we got enrolled instead of committed.' Still, they do their best to upset the peace and quiet of the school by setting fire to the basement with contraband cigars, sneaking out from class excursions, and setting up practical jokes to disturb the solemnity of the sisters' cloister.

However, as the film progresses a change occurs in Mary. Although the ringleader and the one to come up with the 'scathingly brilliant ideas' that seemed only to land them in trouble, she is also the one to sneak a glimpse at the rich world of the cloister. Rather than the austere and cold prison she imagines, it is filled with beauty, dignity, and love. Late at night, she watches from a dormitory window as the Mother Superior gently places bits of bread for the birds on the statue of St Francis in front of the school. She hides behind a pillar in the chapel to see the Mother Superior say goodbye to a popular sister who has died suddenly in the night. Again she observes the sisters at Christmas time singing in the chapel, their faces made radiant by the candles they hold before the altar. Rachel is privy to none of this and never sees beyond what she thinks is cold-hearted reserve. It is telling, therefore, that the punishments for her bad behaviour are domestic drudgery. She is sent to wash dishes, scrub floors, and clean up dusty storage rooms. Mary, as the more difficult case, is threatened with expulsion but somehow manages to avoid the brunt of the chores assigned to her friend. With her natural ability to lead and her openly assertive behaviour, it is somehow apparent that she will not be able to fit the mould of appropriate femininity and follow her classmates into marriage and motherhood. Instead, the Mother Superior slowly awakens a religious vocation in her most rebellious student.

Advancing the religious life as a suitable alternative for unruly girls who could not fit into the restraints of domesticity was one way to manoeuvre around the other alternative being popularized by the likes of Helen Gurley Brown. This was at a time when there was still much anxiety over the threat to femininity by increased education and professional opportunities for women. On the campuses, strains of a new moral relativism challenged the doctrine of saving yourself for marriage and put a high value on sexual independence. Even for those women who did choose chastity, the emphasis was on personal choice, not social conformity or traditional values. In many ways, sex wasn't the problem but only the outward sign that women were not quite as docile as they were supposed to be. Cute was out, cool was in. As Gael Greene explained in her sensational study *Sex and the College Girl*,

> The name of the game is Cool ... The voice of the cool coed is speaking out at colleges and universities across the country, sounding the slogans, the boasts, and the doubts of a new sex freedom. Although definitely a minority voice, the cool coed, as champion of the new sex ethic, makes a

loud, impressive and persuasive noise. The more conservative college girl echoes the cool coed's slogans – often in the same hip language – although she would not dream of emulating her sexual behaviour. (1964, 34)

Faced with such attitudes, concern was high among the more conservative members of society that a woman who was not content with the traditional roles of wife and mother could put her femininity in jeopardy. A 1968 study of career-oriented women students tried to prove that their femininity was significantly lower than that of homemaker-oriented women. Although they demonstrated higher levels of feminine characteristics (to be useful and busy), their masculine characteristics were also considered higher than average, throwing their femininity into flux (Rand 1971, 163). The unproblematic assessment of feminine versus masculine characteristics in this study could easily be undermined, of course. What is more interesting is the way in which women looking to leave the confines of domesticity behind and take an active role in the world were considered either oversexualized or overmasculinized, or both. As Cynthia Fuchs Epstein argues, popular psychological profiles in the sixties continued to encourage women to stay 'in their place' in order to avoid any unnecessary disturbances to their mental and emotional stability (1970, 31).

Against such entrenched attitudes the convent stood out as a viable compromise for those women who could not be contained by domesticity but were unwilling to reject totally the doctrines of femininity. *The Trouble with Angels* depicts the religious life as a vibrant alternative that would foster but also subdue the wilfulness of even the most adventurous girls. As the Mother Superior explains Mary's vocation to a stunned and betrayed Rachel:

> It was her decision. You of all people should know how strong she is. She didn't yield, Rachel, she chose. And I'd rather have one like Mary who chooses than one hundred who yield. She has so much to give. All our sisters do but Mary will give with joy and laughter. And defiance I imagine. In fact I have a feeling that someday many people – even those in the highest places – will know that Mary Clancy came our way. She has some scathingly brilliant ideas.

The idea that the worst girls would make the best nuns may have seemed to upset the balance of femininity by rewarding unfeminine behaviour with a richer and more fascinating life. Yet it cannot be ignored that the reward was ultimately an interior one, existing within a protective cloister of habit, community, and strict religious discipline.

Still, for 'good Catholic girls' what options were there? Back on the college campus, some still felt their religion was enough to stop the tide of sexual confusion, although their resolve seemed shaky. Greene reported a conversation with young Catholic women: 'What keeps a girl from going to bed with a boy she loves?' I asked. 'I can answer in three words,' a Radcliffe freshman shot back, 'I'm a Catholic.' 'Come back when she's a junior,' an upperclassman whispered to me. 'See if she can still put it in three words' (Greene 1964, 110). Others equivocated with an 'everything but' approach or their own unique logic, such as deciding birth control for premarital sex wasn't a sin but would be once they were married (201). Even nuns were publicly expressing a struggle with the meaning of chastity, casting it as the most outward sign of their devotion to Christ. In their efforts to embrace sexuality as an integral aspect to their formation, they either reverted to themes of sublimated labour or spiritual marriage. Gone were the days of smug superiority. Love in any form – as long as it remained safely ensconced in either a home or a convent – was equally valid. Thus it was that another unruly girl was not drawn into the cloister but gathered strength from that spiritual world to become the quintessential pious wife and mother. Maria from The Sound of Music may not have been quite as delinquent as her counterpart, Mary Clancy, but she was as badly needing to be trained into femininity. While her path led in the opposite direction, the message remained all too much the same.

Often regarded as the best-loved musical and a classic in its own time, The Sound of Music appeared in the midst of a wave of nun-themed films. Not only The Trouble with Angels but also MGM's rival nun musical The Singing Nun were released closely following its block-buster opening. Unlike those two, however, this was not a nun film in the purest sense of the term. To be sure, Maria starts out as an eager but irrepressible postulant, literally coming down from the mountains to join the sisters in what she sees as an impossibly beautiful way of life. Yet the convent setting quickly melts away as she is sent out to become a governess to the Von Trapp family, a wealthy and influential house-hold headed by the formidable Captain, who has closed his heart to

love and to music following the death of his wife, leaving his seven
children starved for affection. The reason for her departure from the
abbey is so that she can better discern her vocation. However, in many
ways she is trading one type of cloister for another. The high walls and
bells are replaced by an expansive country estate with its own iron gates
and forbidding entrance. Maria's first impressions are of a house as austere and imposing as the convent – and about as inviting. As she stands
on the opposite side of the fence, staring forlornly at her new place of
employment and gathering up the courage to go forward, she is leaving
behind the open road and the beckoning countryside that have been
her only friends.

The coldness of the house is emphasized by the lack of music. It is the
singing of the nuns that had first drawn Maria from her mountain home
and into the abbey. Here, there isn't even that. Eventually, however,
her own spirited sense of self brings first music and then love back,
causing a crisis of faith that sends her running back to the convent. It is
telling that at no time is the convent seen as a place where love, joy,
and music have no place. It is the Reverend Mother herself who insists
that Maria return to the Captain and discover her true capacity for
love, the calling that God has laid out for her. In the bleak surroundings
of her dimly lit office, she sings 'Climb Every Mountain.' While the
choice to have that inspirational anthem sung in the close surroundings
of a convent with nary a mountain in sight was in part to diminish the
cloying sentimentality of the lyrics, it served a double purpose. The
convent was not a place to lose sight of dreams or abandon courage, but
a place where those dreams could be realized. The fact that Maria
returns once again to the abbey, only this time to be married to Captain
Von Trapp, reinforces such a message. The nuns dress her and send her
out into the world as they smile knowingly behind the grille. At this
point they all but disappear from the film, except at the end when it is
due to their own courage and compassion that the Von Trapps escape
the Nazis and climb that mountain to freedom.

The character of Maria is, despite her centrality to the narrative,
practically a cipher. She has no last name, no family, no origins at all
except some vague references to the mountains. She is a misfit in a very
real sense, belonging nowhere and desired by no one. With her close-
cropped hair and tomboy attitude, Maria appears almost childlike, less a
governess than a big older sister. Indeed, her eldest charge, Liesl, seems

more sexually aware than her, especially after she slips away from the house to have a tryst with Rolf, her boy suitor. Discovered by Maria, she is defiant even as she trembles with fear of being sent to her father. But Maria defies patriarchal authority – at least temporarily – by conspiring to keep it all a secret from the Captain and even lending Liesl a nightgown so she can change her wet clothes. The two seem more like dorm mates than anything else, with Maria definitely the more innocent one. In that sense, then, perhaps she is an alternative to Rachel Deverey more so than Mary Clancy: someone who can get into trouble if led by the wrong person. As the nuns sing at the crescendo of the song 'How Do You Solve a Problem Like Maria?':

> She'd out pester any pest; drive a hornet from its nest
> She could throw a whirling dervish out of whirl
> She is gentle; she is wild
> She's a riddle; she's a child
> She's a headache
> She's an angel
> She's a girl!

And being a girl means being a problem to be solved, one way or another.

It is only after marriage that a change comes over Maria. Her childish impetuousness seems smoothed over into a more matronly glow. She moves slower, talks softer, and even surrenders her lead singing duties to her new husband. As she glides across the abbey courtyard and down the steps into the chapel, with the nuns trailing behind her, it appears that a solution had been found. This point is driven home by the nuns singing now in triumph 'How do you solve a problem like Maria? / How do you hold a moonbeam in your hands?' Maria practically looks like a moonbeam in her voluminous wedding finery, but at last someone has taken hold of her, firmly and completely. The convent could not tame her, but it is within the convent walls that she is gently guided to her real vocation as pious wife and virgin mother. Liesl now defers sexual matters to her, asking advice over what to do about Rolf's cooling off. What had been a love song between the two youths is reprised as a gentle admonishment from mother to daughter to 'wait a year or two,' that love at 'sixteen going on seventeen' was too soon. That same advice

In *The Sound of Music*, the nuns solve the problem of Maria (Julie Andrews) by replacing one kind of veil with another.

was going out to idealistic Catholic girls across the country, although it seemed to be falling on deaf ears.

The character of Maria reflects a growing spiritual defence of consecrated celibacy as spiritual motherhood. As the literature on celibacy expanded in the 1960s, there was an increasingly urgent need for an interpretation of the vow that embraced positive, progressive, and personalist dimensions instead of the rather Jansenist, negative, anti-sex stance of the past. The justification seemed relatively simple, as one priest explained: 'First of all, by her vow of chastity, the Sister gives up the right to physical motherhood in order that she might become a spiritual mother and sister to the members of Christ's Mystical Body' (Dion

1965, 35). The unique lifestyle of the convent was a refuge of sorts for women who couldn't quite fit the mould but did not want to risk their emotional and spiritual health by spurning maternity. Some nuns admitted that 'a highly intellectual creative personality might be less willing to serve as a really good wife and mother' (Tate 1970, 63) and could, therefore, find an outlet in the convent but only if they found that capacity for sacrificial love elsewhere. Somewhat defiantly, some nuns insisted on the reality of 'spiritual maternity' (Valentine 1968, 91) and the positive value of a feminine mystique that emphasized women's other-directedness and need to find value through love of others instead of satisfaction in their own accomplishments (Malits 1965, 90).

This sort of argument drew on the existing pop psychology of motherhood, and the 'libidinal mother' who used her feminine instincts to love unconditionally and spontaneously and gently offered an alternative to the stark disciplinary tactics of the patriarch, who was now viewed as old-fashioned and out of step with the permissiveness of the times (McCleer 2002, 87). As Anne McCleer argues, *The Sound of Music* was a reactionary film in its attempts to build a shaky bridge between a nostalgic past of the pious, patriotic family and some of the less contentious elements of the contemporary progressive age, which valued the autonomy and authority of the person over the family. It therefore becomes crucial that Maria arrives direct from the convent, where her purity and chasteness would be unquestioned. Linking religion to the family in the magnificent wedding scene further insists that sexually mature womanhood doesn't come from experimentation or moral relativism. This point is doubly articulated through Maria's role as a virgin bride first to Christ and then to the Captain, followed by her assuming the duties of a virgin mother. Maria's simplicity, naïveté, and subordinated status in life are not overcome but properly sublimated into the rigorous confines of heterosexual domesticity, with her first husband's blessings (87).

For all its popularity, going on to break box-office records and to capture the Oscar for Best Picture, *The Sound of Music*'s message of pious, family-oriented joy was not greeted with open arms. Critics were almost uniformly negative. The *New Yorker* called it a 'tasteless blowup' (Gill 1965, 96), while others commented on the 'fatuousness of the plot' ('Ruritanian Reich' 1965, 100) that seemed always in 'peril of collapsing under its weight of romantic nonsense and sentiment' (Crowther 1965).

Pauline Kael was nearly apoplectic in her denunciation of the film (for which she was fired from *McCalls*), in particular the role of Maria: 'The perfect, perky schoolgirl, the adorable tomboy, the gawky colt. Sexless, inhumanly happy, the sparkling maid, a mind as clean and well brushed as her teeth. What is she? Merely the ideal heroine for the best of all possible worlds. And that's what *The Sound of Music* pretends we live in' (1970, 77). Not even the Catholic magazine *America* could find anything to love: 'The film's non-admirers, on the other hand, will be likely to call it vulgar, sentimental and phony, and suggest that it is a superficial and unbelievable treatment of serious subject matter with such extra flaws as the presence of silly, stereotyped nuns and the absence of any real religious feeling' (Review of *The Sound of Music* 1965, 375).

As the film continued its juggernaut, grossing over $60 million in its first year worldwide, some questioned how this could possibly be. *Esquire* attributed its success to many elements, but first and foremost to the presence of nuns. 'Only sea gulls can upstage nuns as camera material,' it claimed, especially if they were 'the gutsy, going-my-way kind, full of beans under those great costumes ... Saint Teresa crossed with the Wife of Bath' (1966, 20). The reviewers appeared aware of the trick this film was performing in claiming the possibility of pious, simplistic virginity as an ideal goal for women no matter what their circumstances. And yet that thorny issue of the sexual revolution refused to disappear but became even stronger and merged into a burgeoning women's liberation movement. Nostalgic affirmation would not be enough. The nun films of the late sixties could no longer avoid the real world but had to face it head-on, if only to then deflect it back. That was the underlying message of *Where Angels Go, Trouble Follows* and *Change of Habit*, two films caught up in the swirl of the counterculture before settling back to earth with their sights even more fixed on the power of celibate service.

Modern and traditional ideals of the religious life coexisted tenuously as the new nuns tackled the old-fashioned ways of the convent. In *Where Angels Go, Trouble Follows* (1968), the sequel to the Hayley Mills hit minus its star, the sounds of the counterculture rang throughout the convent in the guise of Sister George, a young activist nun with decided ideas on the renewal of the religious life. Her conflicts with the older nuns as they escort a group of students across the country to a free-speech rally echo the debates between traditionalists and reformists in the Catholic Church. Experiments with social justice and integrated

living were examined in detail in *Change of Habit* (1970), the story of
three young nuns who leave the protective confines of their uptown
convent to live in a Puerto Rican ghetto in New York City's Harlem
district. Their decision to remove their habits and conceal their religious identity leads to a great deal of confusion amongst their wary
neighbours. In these later films, the tension between traditional values
of religious obedience and humility clash with the newfound independence of young women who were no longer willing to remain in the
shadows and serve merely inspirational roles. Yet they both stop short of
outright support for the rebellious, activists nuns. Instead, they offer a
compromise to women as much as to sisters that reinforces the doctrines of femininity through the serenity of the religious life, even while
expanding the parameters of appropriate feminine behaviour.

Sister George, the swinging sister of St Francis who makes life miserable for the mother superior in *Where Angels Go, Trouble Follows*, was one
of the first attempts by Hollywood to come to terms with the changing
image of nuns. 'Vatican II has reached Hollywood as is evidenced by the
newest nun-fiction motion picture,' crowed one review (Review of
Where Angels Go 1968, 79). Although she still wore the full habit, this
particular nun was not the sort to wait patiently for a man to rescue her,
like Sister Angela and Mother Maria. Instead, the film opens with a
montage of her leading students in rallies and protests, being carried
away by police, and shoved into paddy wagons. Notably, her fervour for
social justice and political activism is not sympathetically depicted. She
is rude, abrasive, and insulting to the other sisters and complains frequently about their inability to adapt quickly enough to the times. She
even publicly berates another nun for her apparent incompetence in
driving the bus to a particularly important rally, implying that the political good of the rally supersedes any good that can come from keeping an
older nun active and involved in the affairs of the community. In an
angry retort to her mother superior during a discussion about the proper
role of nuns with respect to their students she says, 'You enjoy the whole
nun mystique, don't you, Mother, because it places you above the ordinary and makes you something special ... And you resent me because I
represent change and you don't want change!' However, by the end of
the film the mother superior is able to do what Sister George could not,
integrating the old and new and allowing all the nuns to retain a level of
dignity and sense of purpose.

Thus, traditional doctrines of femininity are ultimately reinforced rather than rejected through strategies of compromise and negotiation. Sister George is forced to recognize that the tranquillity and reserve of the religious life brings with it a unique kind of personal authority that spurs others to action far better than her shouting and placard waving. Meanwhile the rest of the community gladly introduce modified habits and an updated attitude more in keeping with the modern image of nuns. However, by the conclusion of the film the basic infrastructure of their lives is still circumscribed by institutions, order, and discipline. More importantly, Sister George no longer rails against it but acquiesces graciously. There was only one film in this era that delved into the dramatic possibilities of nuns outside the protective confines of the cloister. Although on many levels it is merely another B-list Elvis Presley vehicle, Change of Habit does not shirk away from the conflicted sense of identity that was facing young sisters. Instead, it deals directly with the challenges to their religious vocation in the wake of second-wave feminism. The central conflict in Change of Habit is not between nuns and male protectors, nor between traditional and progressive members of the convent. Rather, it is an internal conflict between the nuns' sense of themselves as women and as religious.

Inspired by the work of Sister Mary Olivia Gibson, a speech therapist and expert on juvenile delinquency, Change of Habit is an entirely fictional account of three nuns who doff their habits and move to Harlem to work with the black and Puerto Rican communities. In 1969 such a premise was considered very topical, as Box Office Magazine's 'Exploitips' recommended that the media 'set up radio-TV discussions on the role of nuns and priests in modern life' in tandem with the film's release (Change of Habit Clippings File). The magazine also suggested selling the idea of nuns out of the habit as the most dramatic way to express the radical changes happening in the religious life. In its opening credit sequence – which was also used for the film's promotional trailer – the problem of negotiating the role of woman and nun was made both sexy and humorous. As the sisters leave their convent and head into the city, they are treated with due respect and deference. A cop even stops traffic for them so they can cross the street safely without even looking up. Then the transformation takes place, filmed as a kind of chaste strip tease. Serge skirts drop to the floor while sheer stockings slide up shapely legs. Heavy veils are swept off and tousled heads languorously shaken. With a dash of mascara and lipstick the new nuns step back out onto the street to a very different reception. The courteous pedestrians are now leering men who prefer to stand directly in their way rather than respectfully step aside. The biggest shock is that traffic no longer stops for them. As they stride onto the street, again without looking, they are very nearly run down while the same cop from before yells angrily at them. Operating as both the opening sequence and as a promotional vehicle, this brief montage sets the stage for the conflicts facing the nuns as they struggle to discover their identity and, as Mary Tyler Moore's character Sister Michelle put it, 'be accepted first as women, then nuns.' What exactly that means to them is almost immediately put to the test when they report for work at the neighbourhood walk-in clinic.

Dr John Carpenter, played by Elvis Presley, is brusque and dismissive towards them, calling them uptown do-gooders who won't be able to handle the troubles of the ghetto. Sister Michelle testily retorts that she is a psychiatric social worker specializing in speech therapy, Sister Barbara is a lab technician, and Sister Irene is a registered public health nurse. However, their religious identity remains a closely guarded secret. This heated exchange was not far-fetched for many sisters preparing to leave the massive institutions run by their congregations in favour of small, grassroots urban ministries. Sisters had been protected from much of the frustrations felt by other women over educational and professional opportunities because their closed systems of education and administration gave them far greater opportunities. When they began to integrate into the social service networks outside their jurisdiction, they were often stunned to face the intransigence of male colleagues who treated women professionals as inferior (Wittberg 1989, 532). *Change of Habit* highlights this problem at a very early stage in sisters' feminist awakening. As nuns, their qualifications would have been unquestioned, but since they had to be women first, according to Sister Michelle, their professional commitment is suspect.

The doctor is not the only one who distrusts their motives. No one in the neighbourhood knows quite what to make of three attractive, obviously middle-class young women living on their own in a dangerous part of the city. Without the religious motivation, they are clearly out of place. Meanwhile, their local priest is thoroughly opposed to the whole experiment. 'I don't like underground nuns who wear bobbed hair and silk stockings,' Father Gibbons grumbles. With their mission in jeopardy, they are ordered to return to their habits and make their religious identity known. Although this regression is meant to convey the meddlesome interference of an out-of-touch, conservative church hierarchy, only as nuns do these women really begin to make a difference in the community. They begin to gain the trust of the wayward girls who previously viewed them as interlopers on their turf and competitors for the affections of the sexy doctor. After Sister Michelle offers her old lay clothes to the oversexed gang leader, an unexplained transformation takes place in which the girl begins to gain power from that transferred femininity. Her heavy eye make-up and tight jeans are replaced by demure dresses and pillbox hats, and she begins to attend church regularly again. Sister Barbara wages war on the local merchants who overcharge customers, including her when she was incognito, but who stop charging the nuns altogether once they appear in habit. Sister Irene takes the most dangerous chance when she borrows money from the local crime boss and then dares him to beat up a nun when she refuses to pay. Although he does punch her, she achieves her desired effect since the community's citizens who previously lived in fear of him rush to her defence. They are willing to risk their safety to protect a nun in a way they would never have done for a nurse. The sisters gain other small victories once they find ways to compromise their zeal for social justice with the traditions of feminine piety as shaped in the convent.

However, the rewards are not as desirable for everyone. Sister Barbara eventually cannot reconcile herself to a life of enclosure and leaves to pursue her new life as a political activist. Sister Michelle's struggle is more personal, as she finds herself falling in love with John. Like a woman torn between two lovers, she agonizes over whether to remain a nun or leave and marry. An attempted rape by one of the local boys, who sees her with the doctor, hastens her return to the convent. John, too, retreats to the church as the leader of an electric folk group. It is there that they have their final encounter as Michelle glances back and forth between the crucified Christ and the virile doctor to discern her options – both now safely encloistered and resolutely pious.

Perhaps the most dramatic transformation occurs in Sister Irene, a black nun who grew up in the ghetto and had looked to the convent as a means of escape. By returning to her roots, she is forced to confront her own conflicted sense of identity as both a nun and a black woman in an era of increasing racial hostility. Unlike Mother Maria in *Lilies of*

Sister Michelle (Mary Tyler Moore) tries to reconcile her love for Dr John Carpenter (Elvis Presley) with her vows as a nun in *Change of Habit*.

the Field, she is no mere catalyst for the moral awakening of a black man. Instead, the relationship between race and gender as it related to sisters was tackled directly. Ironically, in so doing, the film reinforced the idea that for women struggling with their identity, they were better off in a restricted environment where their inherent femininity would ultimately be protected.

Sister Irene is the least enthusiastic of the three nuns for the experimental living project and resents the loss of her protective habit. Arguing with Sister Michelle that 'there's a lot to be said for being different,' Irene reminds her middle-class white companions that 'I must have said

a million Hail Marys to get out of a neighbourhood just like this. I suddenly realize just how safe I felt in my habit.' It becomes increasingly
clear that Irene has sought out a religious vocation as an escape from
her own ghetto roots. However, the new religious spirit of community
involvement and social activism forces her back to confront her particular identity crisis as a black Catholic woman, a minority within a
minority within a minority. Her tense confrontation with two black
men in a dilapidated apartment building hallway highlights Irene's fear
and confusion about her identity as a black sister:

SISTER IRENE: Well, I'm a Negro. I think that's pretty obvious.
COLOM: Where you been, sister? We ain't Negroes, we're black.
HAWK: Not her. She's just been dipped in maple syrup.
SISTER IRENE: Don't you talk to me about being black. I've been black all
    my life, so I don't want to hear that.
HAWK: Everything but the soul. You copped out.
SISTER IRENE: I never have. I've done my part.
COLOM: For you, not for us. You see, you're locked in with those ol' beige
    chicks. Well, you can't have it both ways.

The problem of African-American sisters trying to reconcile the
demands of their faith and their race had recently been brought to light
at the First National Black Sisters' Conference, which was held in Pittsburgh in 1968. High on the agenda was the reawakening of a sense of
racial identity and outlining the special circumstances of black sisters in
an overwhelmingly white subculture. In an interview in *Ebony* magazine, the organizer of the conference claimed that 'the core of the racial
problem is basically spiritual.' She urged sisters to come to terms with
their dual responsibility to the African-American community and to
their religious congregations ('Awakening' 1968, 48). However, two
months later that same magazine published a feature by Saundra Willingham, a former sister, on why the religious life was incompatible with
black culture. She argued that the religious life demanded the oblitera-
tion of any kind of racial consciousness to allow for greater spiritual perfection. She stated, 'So instead of taking my ego and building it up,
religious life, like American life in general, in relation to the black
man, contributed to its disintegration' (Willingham 1968, 68). Her
comment is interesting because not only did it link the microcosmic

world of the convent with the larger problem of American society, but it also affiliated her with black men rather than with women. In this way religious, gender, and racial identity all collided into one larger problem of national identity and the continuing viability of the American way of life as the single tie that bound everyone together (O'Brien 1972, 209). The religious ideal from the early civil rights movement that all men are brothers, which put a black man and a white nun along the same moral continuum in *Lilies of the Field*, was an affront to Willingham and other black sisters because it whitewashed their own life experiences and left them struggling to harmonize their religious vocation with their growing racial identity (70).

The character of Sister Irene in *Change of Habit* epitomized this identity crisis but managed to keep the problem within the privatized sphere of religion, rather than be galvanized into a more overtly political life, as Willingham advocated. She explains her particular crisis to the clinic's doctor:

> We have to get involved. I've been running from reality ... I have to face it. I have used my vocation to get away from all the things I've ever known. Doctor, do you know what it is to be really poor, hungry, frightened? To be black? ... When little white girls were playing with dolls and wearing party dresses I was dodging drunks in dark hallways praying I could get away from the stench of the ghetto so that I could be somebody, not just another nigger in the streets.

Yet, despite her newfound urgency to be more involved, Sister Irene willingly returns to the convent and once again puts on the old habit. Her harsh demeanour softens and she tells Sister Michelle that she has finally found peace with herself. Coming to terms with her identity means not forging out into the world on her own, as Homer Smith did, but retreating back to a place of solace and contemplation. Her vocation stabilizes her crisis and curtails her politicization. Her role suggested once again that in the combination of piety with femininity, women could find peace amid the myriad crises of identity and belonging they faced and ultimately realize their authentic selves.

Thus, even in the depiction of nuns as crisis-riddled, adult women caught up in the midst of radical social reform, the ultimate solution continued to be a dependence on traditional feminine virtue. In that way, while nun films appeared on the surface to become incrementally more complex in keeping with the changes in the religious life, the underlying message was still entrenched in tradition-bound ideals of nuns as appropriately modified, sexually contained, independent women. The difference was that in *Heaven Knows, Mr Allison* or *Lilies of the Field*, there was no question of the boundaries of autonomy or self-fulfilment for nuns. In the films produced later in the sixties there was a hint of promise that was not merely snatched away but freely rejected by the nuns themselves. In other words, the later films demonstrated a creeping neo-conservatism in the representation of nuns, while the far more openly conservative films of the fifties and early sixties can be analysed as positive depictions of incipient feminism.

After *Change of Habit*, nun films ceased to be a prominent feature of the American film landscape. The next film to appear was a low-budget independent called *The Jesus Trip* (1971), about a fugitive biker and a runaway nun. The sexual tension between this unlikely duo was played to the hilt, as Sister Anna abandons her habit and her vow of celibacy for the charismatic rebel, Waco. The unbridled eroticism in the film was a far cry from a chaste Mary Tyler Moore, and the ease with which she trades her vows for sex was certainly a different take on the religious life. At the same time, exports from Europe, in particular Italy, flooded the market with soft-core nun porn, a whole new genre. The use of nuns in bawdy sex farces became commonplace, most obviously in *Nasty Habits* (1977), about a nun who wants to bring 'free love' into the convent. What is worth noting is that this film wasn't really about nuns but used the convent for an allegory about the Watergate scandal. What these examples from the seventies show is that once the feminist movement became more visible and more centred on notions of sexual independence, nuns were no longer viable representatives. By the time they reappeared on screen in screwball comedies like *Sister Act*, it was as if the reforms of the sixties had never happened. Cinematic nuns were back in full habits and living in vast institutions, hopelessly out of touch with the ways of modern society. The more radical real sisters became, the more conservative their image was in films. It is clear by this reverse relationship that the dramatic potential of nuns did not lie in the reforms of the religious life. Instead, nuns seemed to stand in for other issues facing society, not the least being women's independence and identity on sexual, political, and economic terms. In the postwar era, nuns were effective representatives of modified social changes in gender relations. No matter how far afield they went, how radical they behaved, their religious vocation to poverty, chastity, and obedience would eventually be reasserted and return them to the feminine fold.

Embodying elements of both radicalism and traditionalism, the representation of nuns in films made viable a contradictory ideology for women somewhere between the passive dictates of femininity and the active celebration of American initiative and independence. In film, nuns existed on the border between old notions of domesticity and the feminine private sphere and increased urgency among women to be more involved in the public realms of social justice. They were able to negotiate that position through their unique religiosity, which carefully guarded their sexuality and, therefore, kept in check their erotic power as individuals. This was an era when religion was hailed not for its strict organizational principles but for its ability to give its adherents a sense of commitment and moral authority in an otherwise harsh and anonymous world. The figure of the nun on film helped to reinsert feminine ideals of compassion, atonement, and sacrifice into the public arena and reconfigure political concerns into pietistic or moral concerns. Catholicism was crucial to this feminization of religion and social justice because of its subcultural role in American society. As a locus of ritual, tradition, and authority, Catholicism would appear as the conservative 'other' in the American Christian landscape even as it struggled to remake itself in the image of modern liberalism. Thus, the role of the nun was often placed in conflict not just with her surroundings but also with the vestiges of a grandiose religiosity, from the makeshift altar in Sister Angela's cave to the Upper East Side convent that didn't understand its new nuns in *Change of Habit*. Audiences were thus able to be both sympathetic to nuns and critical of the authorities who placed limits on their lives, while still appreciative of the haunting beauty of Catholicism as a locus for forgotten values in modern society.

3

Whose Story Is *The Nun's Story*?

The Nun's Story was one of the most celebrated motion pictures of 1959. It might have been remembered as the most important film of that year if another religious-themed film hadn't rode in on a chariot and stolen its thunder. *Ben Hur* ultimately went on to break the box-office records set by *The Nun's Story* and to sweep the Academy Awards. It is interesting to note that the battle for Hollywood supremacy was waged by two films dealing with religion. Clearly, interest in this area was gaining prominence. However, these two films could not have been more different. *Ben Hur* featured action-packed tension, breathtaking battle and race scenes, and rippling masculinity. By contrast, *The Nun's Story* was a ponderous film of one woman's self-discovery set against a background of Old World feminine tranquillity. At first glance, the ultimate success of *Ben Hur* over *The Nun's Story* would seem to run counter to my argument about the feminization of religion, were it not for one thing. *Ben Hur* was set in the distant past, a biblical epic about how people used to fight for their faith. *The Nun's Story* was ostensibly set in the years before and during the Second World War. However, in look, style, and language it seemed very much a story of the present. Thus, if anything, the two represent corollaries of the same anxiety over the appropriate gender of religion. As the flurry of media activity surrounding it suggests, audiences took *The Nun's Story* to be about contemporary convent life, not the past. It became a touchstone in the growing public debate about the struggles facing nuns in particular but, more importantly, about the limits of women's independence beyond the cloister.

Kathryn Hulme based her novel *The Nun's Story* on the real-life exploits of her partner, Louise Heberts, a former nun from Belgium. The two had met in Europe after the Second World War and became life partners soon after. Upon their return to the United States, Hulme set out to document Heberts's life before they met. She used specific events from Heberts's experiences as a sister and her knowledge of convent routine, but added dramatic flourishes and characters to help flesh out the story. This mixture of fantasy and reality would later prove to be a major stumbling block in gaining sisters' approval and would help those who resented the book to discredit Heberts. The book stirred up major controversy in Europe that soon reached across the Atlantic. Despite protests from religious sisters, Fred Zinnemann optioned the book and quickly set out to make an epic film that would be visually dazzling and artfully authentic. That meant gaining the support of sisters and clerical leaders in both Hollywood and Europe. The saga of the making of *The Nun's Story* is ultimately far more intriguing than either the book or film. In fact, both verge on the tedious and neither has survived the test of time. The lengthy process of research, negotiation, and compromise reveals heightened levels of mutual awareness between the Catholic Church and the entertainment industry. However, the final film, and the animated debate that circulated around it, suggests that claims to accurately and sympathetically document the convent may have been only a smokescreen. What became the primary theme of the movie was the tension between a strikingly independent and gifted young woman and the more conservative, traditional women who hold her back. That both sides drew equal levels of sympathy from audiences and critics speaks to the deep ambivalence over women's status in the years immediately preceding the rebirth of feminism.

While convent reforms had begun at the start of the decade, the organizational initiatives of sisters were not yet well publicized. The Call for Renewal had already sent word to convents to begin modifying habits, cloister rules, and daily regimens in ways that would make sisters appear more accessible. The Sister Formation Conference was taking matters into their own hands by 1954 with new educational and spiritual programs for young recruits. And the Conference of Major Superiors of Women had announced plans to incorporate community and cultural development into reforms on a national scale by 1956. Yet none of these projects received more than passing attention by the mass media. A few magazines carried pictures of the new habits, but more as a quirky fashion story, with no wider context. The Sister Formation

Conference was not mentioned by name until 1964, just before it was taken over by the Conference of Major Superiors of Women (CMSW). The CMSW had to wait one more year, 1965, before it was recognized by the news media in the *Harper's* cover story 'The American Nun: Poor, Chaste, and Restive' (Wakin and Scheuer 1965). Thus, in the fifties, although there was a sense that sisters were making changes to their way of life, it had yet to be well articulated or assessed by the mass media. Instead, there were human interest stories of active sisters and approving portraits of their hard work in service to others, such as the cover story of the Maryknollers in *Time* and the photo essay on the young nun-doctor in *Look*. These articles stood in uneasy tension with a lingering wariness of Catholicism in American society. The criticism that dogged John F. Kennedy right from the beginning of his political career was proof that the public was only so willing to accept Catholics into the mainstream of society.

Into this ambivalent situation for religious sisters the novel *The Nun's Story* appeared to almost unanimous critical acclaim and became an instant best-seller. The decision to turn the book into a film caused a major stir in Hollywood, and media speculation ran high throughout its production. At stake was the chance to merge traditional attitudes of the Catholic Church and its vowed members with more modern ideas about women's independence through the portrayal of the heroic efforts of sisters around the world. How this would happen and who would have the most say turned into a prolonged struggle between four different groups, all invested in shaping new meanings of the religious life. There were the entertainment executives and artists, who had just begun to realize the dramatic potential of the convent. Then there was the network of Catholic officials, including the Legion of Decency, the notorious censorship bureau that had been established in the thirties but by the fifties was trying to evolve into a more benign consulting agency. Assisting the legion in this cause were leading members of the Catholic press, a tightly knit network of Catholic-oriented newspapers and magazines spread across the country. Finally, and somewhat lost in the midst of the more powerful players, were sisters on both sides of the Atlantic, who generally despised the book and publicly rejected the idea of a movie.

The goal of each of these groups was strategically different. Both Hulme and Zinnemann argued that their desire was to provide a sympathetic yet dramatically compelling portrait of a fascinating way of life that had been concealed from the public for too long. Warner Brothers, the film studio that had optioned the rights to the book even before it was published, wanted a lush spectacle to highlight the talents of both Zinnemann and the star of the film, Audrey Hepburn. Neither the studio nor the artists were interested in producing a religiously righteous or even spiritually intense cinematic experience. On the other hand, Catholic officials saw an opportunity to depict the beauty and grandeur of the religious life and hopefully ignite public interest in the more romantic elements of Catholicism. By the 1950s Catholicism was in the grips of a profoundly emotive and sentimental movement that valorized suffering and sacrifice, especially when performed by a beautiful and graceful woman like Hepburn (Fisher 1989, 163). Such an image helped diffuse political tensions fuelled by Blanshard and others by feminizing Catholicism in ways that diminished its authority to a state of evocative influence. At the vanguard of this image shift were women religious. They became the public face of Catholicism in the mass media. Whether they were shown toiling in cramped hospitals or riding roller coasters, sisters were never implicated in any plots to undermine democracy, as anti-Catholic commentators feared might happen.

Perhaps it was because they had been thrust into the centre of attention so suddenly and unceremoniously that sisters felt rather sideswiped by *The Nun's Story*. They had been working diligently to improve the religious life and attract young recruits for more than half a decade. At a point where they were hoping to receive some recognition for their efforts, along came a novel that seemed to prove the public's greatest fears. It reinforced negative attitudes towards the convent as an imposing asylum where women were subjugated and demeaned in the name of religious obedience. This troubling depiction took a further turn for the worse when the book was used by the respected sociologist Erving Goffman for his 1961 essay on total institutions and treated as a factual account of the standard of living inside contemporary convents. It is little wonder, therefore, that many sisters were unhappy not only with Hollywood producers but also with leaders in the Catholic Church for allowing the movie to go forward. Those who took up the cause felt keenly the book's intrusion into their way of life and became obsessed with the details of its depiction. In the minds of some, they were owed a flawlessly accurate portrayal in the movie to compensate for the damage that they perceived the book had wrought.

When *The Nun's Story* was first published in 1956, the author was already well known as a new-style female adventurer. Kathryn Hulme had established a reputation for compelling non-fiction with her first book, *The Wild Place*, which had won the Atlantic Non-Fiction Award in 1953 (Chase 1956, 1). That book was based upon her experiences working at a displaced persons camp in Europe following the Second World War. It was there that she met Louise Heberts, a Belgian nurse who in the course of their relationship revealed that she had recently left the convent where she had been a sister for seventeen years. Heberts confessed that she could not return to her family because they were deeply ashamed of her for abandoning her religious vows. Hulme then sponsored her for immigration to the United States, and the two lived together until Hulme's death in 1981.

This kind of passionate friendship was not uncommon among former sisters or even secretly within the ranks of the sisterhood (Gramick 1989, 223). While some such relationships were explicitly sexual, others were expressed in the more sensual or erotic terms of deep, abiding love. Having sought out an intense homosocial community life, many sisters were unprepared for the shock of having those desires squelched in a repressive atmosphere that denied personal attachment and treated sexuality and erotic feelings as sinful. That is not to say that sexuality was a particularly strong or compelling reason for leaving the convent. Rather, sexual confusion often led to greater conflicts with the vow of obedience. This became more acute when elements of the sexual revolution merged into feminism and awoke a stronger sense of personal consciousness and autonomy (Schneiders 2001, 172). Certainly, in *The Nun's Story* there is no deliberate hint of lesbian desire on the part of Sister Luke, and neither Hulme nor Heberts publicly claimed that they were lovers, neither late in life nor even after Hulme's death. There is no indication that an element of criticism against Hulme was her sexuality. Even the clerics from the Legion of Decency, who took great pains to ensure no 'lesbian looks' in the film, seemed to have no problem collaborating with two women who were clearly in a relationship of some sorts.

The protagonist of *The Nun's Story* is Gabrielle Van Der Mal, the eldest daughter of a distinguished Belgian surgeon and widower. Following a pilgrimage to the shrine at Lourdes, she realizes her religious vocation and joins a missionary order. Renamed Sister Luke, the young novice is faced with the daunting task of reforming herself in the mould of a religious. Great attention is spent in the book on the petty details of religious training, which are described as 'the most exasperating and the most compelling challenge [Luke] had ever experienced. It demanded an all-or-nothing way of being, a conscious and complete submission of self' (Hulme 1956, 30). During her first two years in the convent Luke struggles desperately to control her wilful independence and pride in her work as a nurse, all the while harbouring a fervent desire to someday be selected for service in the Belgian Congo. She is sent to the School of Tropical Medicine, where her teachers single her out as an excellent nurse with a natural aptitude for diagnosis. In one of the most controversial episodes from the book, Sister Luke is asked by her superior to fail her medical exams to prove her humility, but she is unable to comply and as a result graduates fourth out of a class of eighty. Her superior congratulates her but remarks wistfully that 'your failure ... would have been a gift to God' (99)

Despite her academic achievement she is sent not to the Congo but to an insane asylum run by her congregation. She realizes that this is a test of her religious strength but is still determined to conquer her pride. Her goal is to become one of the Living Rules, those nuns so perfect in the religious life that if the rule were ever lost it could be regained simply by studying their behaviour. That desire is clouded by her encounter with a patient who turns out to be a former abbess driven mad by her obsession with the rule. She seeks friendship from another young nun but is traumatized when the sister is murdered by an inmate. It is, however, after she is brutally assaulted by the Archangel, a dangerous lunatic who is kept locked in a padded cell, that Luke begins to realize just how daunting a task she faces if she is to succeed as a nun. The shame of her experience with the Archangel, from whom she flees half-naked down the convent halls, leads to greater spiritual strength. She is rewarded with an appointment to the Congo, five years after her first entrance into the congregation.

Although initially disappointed that she has been placed at the European hospital in Stanleyville as chief surgical nurse, rather than at the bush station, Sister Luke still feels happy and fulfilled for the first time since joining her congregation. She is assigned to assist Dr Fortunati, a brilliant but arrogant surgeon who also happens to be an agnostic and is therefore a potential danger to any sister left alone with him for too long. Her skill as a nurse soon wins him over, however, and he becomes

On the threshold of two worlds: Sister Luke (Audrey Hepburn) in *The Nun's Story*.

a kind of confidant to her. It is he who first recognizes Sister Luke's problem with conforming to the religious ideal: 'You're not in the mold, Sister, and you never will be. You're what is called a worldly nun – ideal for the public, ideal for the patients. But you'll never be the kind of nun your convent expects you to be' (221).

No matter how hard she protests, it seems that Fortunati is right. She continues to face new obstacles, which remind her over and over again of her inability to reconcile herself to the constant demands of the rule. She earns praise from the colonial authorities for her training program in the hospital for young Congolese, but she is rebuked by her superior for failing to advise her of this innovation. She becomes increasingly alienated from the community as her nursing duties overtake the demands of attending communal prayers and mealtimes. The relaxed state of the Congo, coupled with the urgent demands of a new colony, temporarily relieve her of much of the burden of the religious life that she had found so taxing in Belgium. It is small wonder, then, that she is devastated when Fortunati decides to send her back home to accompany a colonial official who has had a nervous breakdown.

Back at the motherhouse, Luke is restless and longs to return to the Congo, but because war is threatening to break out she has to remain at home. She is encouraged by the mother superior to take time to renew her spiritual life, but she wants only to begin work again as soon as possible. With some reluctance her superior sends her to a hospital in Holland to resume surgical nursing duties. Not long after her arrival war is declared; Belgium is captured and Holland soon after. The convent is placed under Nazi surveillance, but the sisters are exhorted to ignore the war as much as possible and continue to work as if nothing has changed. This is too much for Luke, whose patriotism begins to take the place of religious idealism. A student nurse connected with the underground secretly informs her that her father has been killed while attending to refugees on the road from Belgium to Paris. She gives in at last to her hatred of the Nazis, and her lapses in religious discipline become more pronounced. Tormented by her desire for revenge and despairing at her inability to attend to even the most perfunctory tasks of the religious rule, Sister Luke realizes that she must leave the convent and return to the lay world. Despite pleading from her confessor and superior, she receives dispensation from her vows and exits the convent through a back door, armed only with the dowry her father had given the convent upon her entrance and a contact name in the underground, which she plans to join.

When the book was first released it was optioned immediately as the September Book of the Month Club selection as well as the Catholic Book Club and the Readers Digest Condensed Book Club selection.

That alone would have ensured it best-seller status, but the almost uniformly glowing reviews in major dailies across America singled it out as
an important book that deserved a wide audience, regardless of readers'
religious beliefs. It was called 'an enthralling narrative of a profound
experience' by Mary Ellen Chase in the *Herald Tribune.* She advocated
reading it twice, once for the story and once for its themes of unique
inner strength: 'For this novel, rooted though it is in the Roman Catholic faith, bursts all doctrinal bonds and transcends mere theology in its
fair, objective and merciful portrayal of the human conscience, of the
never-ending struggle of the awakened human spirit, intent on redeem-
ing, in whatever surroundings, its loan of threescore years and ten'
(Chase 1956, 1). The *New York Times* included a photo of Hulme and
Heberts and reiterated the same theme of humanity over theology by
describing the book as a story 'of spiritual defeats and of victories in the
cause of humanity' (Fremantle 1956, 1). The *New Yorker* reviewer
Albert Hubbell was more critical of the religious life than the other
reviewers but still found himself enthralled by the contradictions inherent in the characters. He focused particularly on the daily grind of the
rule and made special reference to the flagellation device used by sisters
in the book, despite the fact that it was mentioned only briefly in a
short passage. However, he also praised it as 'a book of great beauty' and
acknowledged that the convent sheltered 'women of first-rate minds,
ability, culture, and character' (1956, 138–44).

The *Nun's Story* received the most attention from the Catholic magazine *America*, a Jesuit-run periodical generally known for its liberal position on political and religious issues. The literary editor, Harold C.
Gardiner, SJ, became a champion of the book and later figured promi-
nently in the pre-production efforts of Warner Brothers to adapt it for
film. Unlike the reviewers in the lay media who tended to see a larger
story of humanity over religiosity, Gardiner praised the book first for its
spiritual, not secular, fortitude: 'Above all, the book is a most moving
incarnation ... to the spirit of devotion and utter dedication. Some critics of the novel have paid what is apparently their highest possible com-
pliment by saying that the dedication portrayed is reminiscent of the
spirit of Albert Schweitzer. Actually the dedication is more sublime, as
devotion to Christ and His work is more exalted than devotion to
humanitarianism' (Gardiner 1956a, 568). In an editorial published two
months after his review, Gardiner commented that other members of

the Catholic press did not share his glowing opinion of the book and he was concerned that their criticisms were not based on artistic merit but on prejudice and insularity.

Concerning those who criticized the book, Gardiner admonished them that it was 'the story of one woman meeting her peculiar difficulties. She was not a "normal" nun, whatever that may be' (1956b, 300). In an indirect allusion to the complaints of sisters that the book would harm vocations, he argued instead that any prospective postulant who felt the book represented 'the "average" American nun in an "average" American convent' would soon realize her error. In the meantime, readers might also admire those nuns who carried out their duties in the background and wish to emulate them so as not to endure Sister Luke's disappointments (301). He suggested that the beauty of the religious life was definitely present even if it wasn't centre stage. If anything, it was highlighted by the stark contrast between those who succeeded and the thwarted efforts of Sister Luke. He accused critics of 'clericalness,' a kind of reverse prejudice that protected sisters from examination by outsiders. He countered that the generally glowing and sympathetic reviews of *The Nun's Story* in the lay media mitigated accusations by sisters that the book painted a false, negative portrait of the religious life: 'I have not met one reaction of shock at the physical penances, of distaste for the discipline and rigidity (perhaps foreign even to American Catholic sensibilities) of the life, nor the conclusion that a group of women in religious life must be a creepy assembly of frustrated neurotics' (301).

To his credit, Gardiner did not give himself the last word but devoted the entire literary section of the 26 January 1957 edition to letters on the subject of *The Nun's Story*. The letters were organized into three categories: 'Laymen Have Their Say,' 'Clergy Pro and Con,' and 'Sisters Have At It,' which gives some indication of the stratification of the debate. Since each section included letters that approved and disapproved of the book, it is impossible to draw any conclusions about the differences between the three groups in terms of their general opinion. However, it is possible to note some of the issues that sisters seemed to emphasize more than other readers. Many of the letters by sisters expressed concern over the damage the book could do to vocations. This was, of course, at a time when vocations were deemed at a crisis level and congregations were taking tentative first steps in recruitment drives and quasi-marketing efforts to improve the public image of the convent. Sister M. Kathleen felt the book was a 'source of great harm' when it was considered in relation to the current vocation shortage. Mother M. Clotilde was even more alarmed at the book's negative potential. She chastised Gardiner: 'It is a source of special regret to have a review of this kind appear when we are in the midst of a great battle with parents over the right of their daughters to follow the call of Christ' (Gardiner 1957, 483).

There were of course letters from sisters who praised the book but not necessarily Sister Luke. They tended to be more impressed with the depiction of the religious life in general and a congregation that, so wrote Sister Mary, 'was 100-per-cent wonderful' (483). The clergy and laity, however, did not share these views. One priest suggested that it be required reading for congregation superiors as a kind of teaching tool for how not to treat novices. Meanwhile, the general reading audience seemed uninterested in these kinds of recruiting issues altogether. Their comments tended to remain focused on the drama of Sister Luke's personal spiritual journey, regardless of whether they enjoyed the book or not. It is interesting to note that Gardiner selected letters from sisters that supported his position – that *The Nun's Story* had some kind of obligation to promote and encourage vocations. This dual reading of the book, seen either through the eyes of its sole heroine or as a larger picture of a hitherto mysterious way of life, continued to resonate during the three years it took to make the movie.

Beyond the specificities of a pro-or-con argument over *The Nun's Story*, Gardiner's highly public and partisan position reflected some significant developments in the relationship between the Catholic hierarchy and the mass media. His role became even more crucial once preproduction began on the film version, which required Catholic assistance if it was to be successfully completed. Catholic officials had been deeply involved in the film industry since the 1930s when they formed the Legion of Decency. Since then they had enjoyed unprecedented privileges to monitor film content and had forced studios to adhere to their principles on threat of audience boycotts and public protests. By the fifties, however, relations were growing friendlier. The old guard who had once dictated the cultural habits of Catholics through the Legion of Decency began to lose ground to a younger generation of clerics who wanted more open and generous participation with artists and

entertainers from all walks of life. It was a transition that would perma-
nently alter the Catholic hierarchy's attitude towards the mass media,
which had been nothing less than adversarial since the early days of
Hollywood when the legion was first formed.

As a voluntary association, the Legion of Decency cemented its
power over Hollywood by demanding that all faithful Catholics recite
an annual pledge to boycott any film that received the dreaded 'C' for
condemned by its own hand-picked ratings board. Pope Pius XI was so
impressed by their coercive success that he drafted *Vigilante Cura* in
1936, an encyclical on the moral dangers of film. It was filled with
praise for the Legion of Decency and exhorted other countries to follow
their example. The extremely negative portrayal of the cinema and the
treatment of audiences as a passive, ignorant mass easily incited to violence and depravity remained the cornerstone of the Vatican's attitude
towards film until the fifties. The change in attitude coincided with the
midpoint of the papacy of Pius XII, in the 1950s.

It is important to make clear that Pius XII did not initiate the relaxation of the Legion of Decency's rigid moral standards. Rather, this was
more a reaction to the legion's diminishing credibility. It was facing
opposition not only from the studios but also from the courts and, crucially, its own Catholic followers. In the early 1950s it faced two major
setbacks from within its own ranks. The popular Catholic magazines
Ave Maria and *Commonweal* both criticized the prurient attitude that
the legion had fostered. In *Ave Maria*, Edward Fisher described a letter
that had been read aloud at the Catholic Press Association meeting in
1951. The author of the letter identified herself as a concerned mother
who frequently awoke at three o'clock in the morning fretting over 'the
smut' that was threatening her children. Ten years earlier, that letter
would have likely received thunderous applause. Now, the assembled
merely dismissed it as obviously 'the product of an unbalanced mind'
(Walsh 1996, 283). One year later, Walter Kerr, a well-respected drama
critic for the *New York Tribune* and a member of the Catholic University of America's drama department, disparaged the legion's obsession
with content to the exclusion of artistic and technical merit (287).
Also in 1952 the legion lost an important legal battle when the U.S.
Supreme Court ruled that no film could be banned for being sacrile-
gious. In 1953 the condemned film *The Moon Is Blue* played across the
country to packed houses. The legion even conceded that the contro-

versy they had ignited over an innocuous film probably helped fuel audience curiosity. It was only then that the legion had to acknowledge that its authority over individual Catholics was on the wane (Skinner 1993, 112–15).

It is not a coincidence that Catholics were becoming increasingly upwardly mobile at the same time that the Legion of Decency was slowly loosening its grip on their cultural practices. Sociologists such as Andrew Greeley and Will Herberg noted that Catholics no longer made up the marginal, immigrant underclass as they had in the first half of the century. Catholics were entering into the suburban middle class and taking pride in the liberal-democratic values of independence, individualism, and success to the exclusion of traditional Catholic values of authority, sacrifice, and suffering (Greeley 1971, 166; Herberg 1964, 596). However, as Riesman commented, their access to Americanism was by no means socially secure even if economic barriers had been broken (1951, 272). Foreswearing the old-guard hierarchy over such things as popular film was one way to make a very public claim that the parochial system was no longer in control. By the late fifties, 32 per cent of Catholics had completed high school, compared to 27 per cent of Protestants. Nineteen per cent of Catholics held managerial positions, almost on a par with the 21 per cent of Protestants. A significantly higher percentage of Catholics had an average income greater than five thousand dollars, 52 per cent as opposed to 45 per cent for Protestants (Wakin and Scheuer 1966, 206). With these kinds of gains, the new generation of middle-class Catholics chose to integrate rather than isolate themselves from mainstream, middlebrow culture. Such a transition was a blow to the heart of the legion's separatist philosophy.

With the Legion of Decency defanged, Hollywood was free to explore the potential of turning a book like *The Nun's Story* into a movie without having to whittle away at the dramatic conflict and whitewash the representation of convent life. However, it could not simply ignore the still-powerful, if somewhat chastened, Catholic hierarchy. Zinnemann had seen fit to declare publicly that he would not be involved in any adaptation that did not have the full endorsement of the Catholic Church. He claimed that 'If we didn't have that cooperation it'd be like making "From Here to Eternity" without help of the Army' (*The Nun's Story* [*TNS*] Clippings File). Yet seeking the involvement of Catholic officials for what amounted to technical support was a far cry from the days when the Legion of Decency could exert control over content and thematic material. In the same interview Zinnemann was careful to state clearly his artistic intentions:

> Zinnemann said he is determined to capture the spirit of the Kathryn Hulme story as written, with ending (the nun leaving her order) to be left intact. 'I am against showing nuns on the screen as just a habit,' he noted. 'They are human beings and we must give them dimension. I've talked to a lot of nuns since drawing this assignment and I found they react as individuals ... But I have no intention in any way of presenting [Sister Luke's] dilemma with any comment. The film will be done with respect, and with no overtone of sensationalism.' (*TNS* Clippings File)

To accomplish his artistic goals, Zinnemann and his producer, Henry Blanke, put together a team of advisors and negotiators from the studio, the Hollywood Production Code, American Catholic representatives, and their European counterparts. It was only after this all-male network had been developed that any sisters were approached to give their opinion.

One of the first men to come on board was Jack Vizzard of the Production Code Office, himself a former Catholic seminarian. Vizzard had worked with Warner Brothers in the past to help them negotiate with the Legion of Decency over such films as *A Streetcar Named Desire* (Walsh 1996, 244). In August 1957 he joined Blanke and Zinnemann at a meeting with Monseigneur Jack Devlin, the head of the Los Angeles chapter of the Legion of Decency. The group discussed the filming of *The Nun's Story* and agreed upon those elements from the book that needed to be either toned down or removed altogether. Among the concessions was the removal of scenes that emphasized some of the more neurotic characterizations of nuns in the book. These included nuns fainting in chapel or the disciplines and refectory penances. Sexuality was still a taboo to the Legion of Decency, at least as it concerned women religious. There was a request to avoid any homoeroticism between Sister Luke and the Archangel during their fight. Heterosexual tension was equally off the table, especially any hint of romance between Sister Luke and Dr Fortunati. Perhaps the most important agreement to come from that meeting was that above all the story was to be 'that of a girl who enters religious life with a false concept, and struggles valiantly but hopelessly to adapt herself to this impossible and destructive idea. She has to step aside lest the false ideal destroy her' (*TNS* MPAA File). Thus, very soon in the development of the film the religiosity of the story was relegated to a kind of romantic prelude. What was really at stake was one woman's quest for authenticity and the damaging consequences of a narcissistic false consciousness. This fell neatly in place with the social discourses of personal discovery and an authentic way of life based on American ideals of heroic independence. Armed with letters of introduction from Devlin, the three Hollywood executives were able to move forward as a team and solicit support from the legion's European counterparts in the Office Central Catholique du Cinéma.

The problem in Europe was that the book had been regarded as a harsh indictment of the religious life. Thus, no sisters were willing to assist in the film's production for fear that it would lend credence to Hulme's version of the convent. It turned out that despite the author's efforts to disguise the congregation and maintain its anonymity, it was nonetheless well known to be the Sisters of Charity, who had their motherhouse in Ghent, Belgium. There had been a disclaimer that the book was only true 'in its essentials,' and it was obvious that the book was set thirty years in the past. Apparently, that was not enough to prevent readers from believing that it was an entirely accurate account of the contemporary religious life. Cardinal Suenens, who would later write *The Nun in the World* but who was in 1957 the assistant to the Archbishop of Malines in Brussels, advised Blanke that the book 'has caused a general painful impression in Belgium and that it can easily be harmful to religious vocations, since the story describes the religious life as somewhat inhuman' (*TNS* MPAA File). Not even the intervention of Harold Gardiner helped secure the assistance of the Belgian hierarchy. He pleaded with one priest:

> I do not believe that the book gives a false picture of the 'religious life.' There is peace, joy and happiness in the nuns who surround Sister Luke, though she herself missed these elements. That is what can, I feel, be very well and convincingly brought out in the film version, if the film is handled well – and it probably will not be handled in the best fashion unless the writer and the director get some guidance from the order which is concerned, or from some other authority, such as yourself. (*TNS* MPAA File)

In one last attempt to break through the intransigence of the clergy, Devlin wrote to Father Leo Lunders, a Belgian priest and executive with the Office Central Catholique du Cinéma. He assured him that Vizzard, Blanke, and Zinnemann were entirely trustworthy. He said that 'they have manifested, very definitely, a sincere application of my concern about this story and have complied with all my suggestions, corrections and omissions without any question or argument' (*TNS* MPAA File).

Devlin's intervention finally won them the cooperation they needed. However, there still remained delicate negotiations with the sisters in Ghent. Although Lunders took pains to assure Vizzard that he 'adores the book, just as it is,' he was quick to point out that sisters were highly unlikely to cooperate (*TNS* MPAA File). He suggested offering no formal approval but arranging to have an 'ecclesiastical assistant' to help with technical details. In the old days when the Legion of Decency seemed to have final say on any picture, such a compromise would have seemed very generous. However, Zinnemann wasn't looking for moral support. He wanted to ensure the highest levels of authenticity, and for that he needed direct assistance from a convent. It is significant, then, that the Hollywood players refused to back down and sent a letter back to Lunders making clear that the film could not be in any way controlled or diminished:

> You say that you suspect there would be considerable dragging of feet on the part of the nuns. Would it be persuasive to them to point out that the picture is going to be made anyway? If they fear that the film will terminate in giving greater currency to the book, may I argue that this is going to happen, no matter what? Is it not better to cooperate in the making of the film, so that the image of the book which they find distasteful, will be corrected? (*TNS* MPAA File)

Such subtle threats seemed to be enough to make the sisters relent. They agreed to meet with Vizzard in Belgium to discuss their concerns. What Vizzard did not realize immediately was how far they were to take his offer to correct the image of sisters from the book.

The assistant to the mother general in Ghent, Soeur Godelieve, agreed to meet with Vizzard to discuss their complaints. Lunders had warned Vizzard that if the meeting did not go well, the sisters might be

inclined to speak to their bishop, who could arrange to have every convent in Europe closed to the production. Vizzard was therefore very
concerned to appease the sisters. Soeur Godelieve presented him with a
thirty-page mimeograph that elucidated in point-by-point fashion all
the factual inconsistencies in the book. As he reported in a letter to
Blanke, 'she traces item and item, and shows how they were woven into
a cloth with a semblance of authenticity, but which are, in truth, not
factual as far as Sister Luke is concerned. So much for that, but it will
make clear why they did not want to cooperate in the making of the
film, lest it seem that they admit that their order was as inhuman as
depicted in the book' (*TNS* MPAA File). Three days later, Vizzard was
able to claim victory based on, he felt, his conciliatory attitude, the letter from Devlin, and the revised script, which had incorporated many of
the changes suggested during that August meeting in St Victor's Rec-
tory. The sisters still refused to give any kind of public endorsement, but
they promised to assist in technical matters. They also cleared the path
for any future involvement of other congregations who would be willing
to take in actresses and train them in convent practices (*TNS* MPAA
File). However, one paragraph in that letter was a portent for much
more involvement than anyone in Hollywood or in the Catholic hierarchy expected. Vizzard wrote:

> [Soeur Godelieve] proposes that in the scene in which Sister Luke
> receives a telegram, telling her that she is going to the governmental hos-
> pital, and not into the bush, she shows an open rebellion. She is trying to
> write out some dialogue for this, to give the idea. I admitted that this
> sounded good, since it was basically dramatic, and would likely meet no
> resistance from Fred. On this, I simply took the chance. (*TNS* MPAA
> File)

Soeur Godelieve did not come back with just one scene rewritten but
with about a third of the script revised and annotated, with new dialogue and stage directions included. One can only hazard to guess how
annoyed Zinnemann and Robert Anderson, the scriptwriter, must have
been with such an unexpected level of interference.

While it is not surprising that Anderson chose to use very little of
Soeur Godelieve's exact wordings and whole scene rewrites, it is nonetheless interesting to examine what changes he did incorporate. It

appears that it was in the small details, rather than the big picture, that the sisters felt their lives were being misrepresented. Godelieve's version of the script, which has been preserved in the MPAA file, focused primarily on the first part of the movie, when Sister Luke is in her postulancy at the motherhouse and taking daily lessons in the religious rule. Frequent requests were made for less stern representations of the sisters in charge of convent affairs. In the estimating script that was given to Soeur Godelieve for approval, the sisters rarely smiled and meted out reprobation to the younger sisters with rigid efficiency. For example, it described the mistress of postulants, Sister Margherita, as 'a bit vinegary, a disciplinarian.' After Godelieve's plea that she not be 'too disciplinarian just now at the first moment,' the character description was removed altogether from the script and a more friendly, smiling sister was substituted. Another sister gives a surreptitious wave and a smile to the young postulant and her father, after it is noted that she has worked with both of them at the local hospital. Although such a subtle difference may seem trivial at first sight, this change went to the heart of the debate over the representation of women religious in the book as emotionally repressed, bitter individuals, and what the sisters wanted rectified in the movie. As Gardiner had explained to Zinnemann in preliminary discussions on how to gain the support of the Catholic hierarchy both in Hollywood and the European film industry:

> I do think that one thing that could help to put the story in proper perspective would be to highlight somewhat the peace and contentment that surrounds Sister Luke. Many readers concentrated their attention on her so much that they missed – as she herself missed – much of the joy that was evident in her sister nuns. But there *is* joy in the book and I think much can be done to make the film less myopic than Sister Luke's view was – this, as you know, was one of the major criticisms of her story – 'there's no joy in it.' (Zinnemann Collection)

In this way, the film was seen as a corrective to the book. Background images of contented nuns were difficult to convey in the novel. Film was a better medium to present this balance between a conflicted protagonist and her contented counterparts. There were hopes that the film would succeed where the book had failed to express the beauty of the religious life without limiting the psychological drama of Sister

Luke's struggles. Something so simple as relaxing the facial expressions of the nuns who surrounded Sister Luke would go a long way to appeasing the real sisters, who identified far more with the characters in the background than with the heroine.

Perhaps the most influence Godelieve exerted was over the haircutting scene as part of the noviciate ceremony, when Sister Luke and the other postulants are given their first habit. In the early draft the scene is played for full melodramatic impact. The novices are sent to the laundry room, where a paper bag is placed over their heads and their hair is cut in such a way that none falls on the floor. This so appalled Soeur Godelieve that she typed boldly across the page 'THIS WILL MAKE THE SCENE RIDICULOUS!' She also insisted that the location be changed. As for the nuns in the scene, one has hysterics as her hair is cut while the one looking after Sister Luke speaks conspiratorially of disappointment and repression:

> NUN (whispering): It's cold at first until you get used to it (she adjusts the sac on Gabrielle's head). Our Sisters in the Congo say it's fine for the heat down there ... I wouldn't know ... I wanted the Congo, but ... (she starts to fashion the serre-tête). The tighter you draw these strings, the better you will restrain your imagination. I draw mine very tight. I suggest you do the same. We do not waste God's time with daydreaming selfish hopes. (Best Collection)

Needless to say, Soeur Godelieve requested that the dialogue be removed, and in this instance Zinnemann and Anderson were prepared to accommodate her. In the end the scene was shot in silence with only Sister Luke and the haircutter in a side chapel. There were no tears and no confessions of disappointment in the religious life.

Other scenes struck Soeur Godelieve as too intrusive into the private lives of sisters. In the estimating script, Sister Luke's cell has no mattress, only a bare board, with loose straw on the floor as in a stable; the straw was supposed to crunch audibly in the cold stillness of the dormitory. Godelieve requested that at the very least the straw be removed, and in the film it was clearly shown that Luke had a proper, albeit narrow, bed with a real mattress and a clean floor. Long scenes of communal dining in the refectory were deleted, including one scene particularly disliked by Godelieve in which Sister Luke is revolted by the eating habits of a rough country girl in her postulant class. The metal crickets used to signal to postulants whether to rise or kneel during religious ceremonies were removed from most scenes at Godelieve's request, although a new scene was added to the film that shows the postulants training for a ceremony in the classroom by rising and bowing according to Sister Margherita's click of the crickets. Scenes of group recreation were initially written to show the restrictions made on personal attachments and projected a kind of hollowness to community relationships. Twice Soeur Godelieve tried to inject a more light-hearted mood in order to acknowledge that sisters also enjoyed fun and relaxing recreation. Although her suggestions were not taken in the final script, it is interesting to note that both scenes of postulant instruction on friendship and on recreation times were ultimately deleted from the film. This spared sisters from any in-depth speculation on their emotional ties to one another and a public discussion over 'particular friendships.' Thus, both sisters and the general public received a brief reprieve from any overt scrutiny of the sexual psychology of the convent. That Hollywood was so willing to cede this point is indicative of its own anxiety over female sexuality, which was threatening to erupt and become a key element in women's claims for autonomy and authority over their lives.

After one year of negotiations, filming began in early 1958 and the movie was ready to show executives and religious advisors by April of 1959, before its official release one month later. The involvement of the European hierarchy came to a close and attention returned stateside to find a mass audience for a film about Old World European nuns. With its release, the film sparked even greater debate than the book had on its publication in 1956. In the pages of *America*, Gardiner brought together his friends Hulme and Zinnemann, movie critic Moira Walsh, and three anonymous sisters identified only by their congregation for a special symposium on the film and its differences from the book. While both the author and the director tried to emphasize the necessity of dramatic conflict in order to make the story of Sister Luke interesting to those uninformed of the religious life, they also tried to positively represent the underlying heroism of the convent. They both expressed sensitivity to complaints from sisters that they had ignored the joy of the religious life. Hulme took a sneaky shot against a popular nun memoir called *A Right to Be Merry* when she wrote, 'If my nun protagonist did not seem to some critics as "merry" as nuns they knew, this was simply because my principal character saw nothing playful or merry about trying to please God' (Gardiner 1959, 468). Zinnemann was even more precise in dispelling criticism that Sister Luke was not happy enough to ever succeed as a nun: 'Kathryn Hulme's book wiped out, once and for all, the thousand cloying, sentimental notions about nuns – particularly the notion that nuns are just like anyone else, except that they are especially jolly and "good joes." ... Above all, it pointed out the difficulties that arise and the heroic demands that are made on those who follow their vocation.' (469)

The sisters on the panel were, by contrast, unanimous in their dislike of the film. All three expressed concern that it would somehow harm vocations, either by scaring off the kind of girls convents wanted to attract or encouraging neurotic and confused women who might think erroneously that the convent would shelter them from the troubles of the world. The Ursuline sister suggested that any girl seeking to enter would have to be questioned about her opinion of *The Nun's Story* and have those misconceptions corrected before being able to proceed. The Sister of Charity saw the problem slightly differently and suggested that maybe the film would 'contribute left-handedly to the spiritual health of sisterhoods by dampening the ardour of unstable, confused or slightly neurotic girls. Every community has experienced its Sister Lukes, but certainly the fewer the better.' Perhaps the Sister of Notre Dame made the most succinct argument over the value of *The Nun's Story* as a recruitment film. She stated plainly that the religious life had been reduced to 'a series of lectures and processions and exhortations. Frankly it all seemed boring to me' (470).

The participants in the *America* symposium were not the only ones to raise the issue of vocations and recruitment. At the Catholic Press Association meeting in 1959 Sister Mary Augustine had this to say:

THE DISASTROUS THREAT to vocations with especial reference to the Catholic hospital apostolate is the lingering impression, as one leaves the showing, that Sister Luke, an intelligent, progressive, zealous religious, was somehow 'ahead' of her rather backward community and that if she was a beautiful, bewildered misfit unable to adapt herself to the constricted thinking (or lack of it) of her noble heroic companions, it was somewhat a shame that the Rule was so rigid. That even the essentials of

religious life are so little recognized was evident in the remark of one
woman to another, sitting in back of me at the preview, sympathizing
audibly with poor Sister Luke at the very height of her endeavours undertaken outside the framework of obedience: '... but what did she do wrong?'
(Augustine 1959)

Augustine was in a unique position to voice such concerns in a highly
dramatic way. As the first woman president of the Catholic Press Association, she was a rarity in the church. While many sisters were professionals, most were in education or health care; very few were
journalists. This was still early in the Call for Renewal, when the media
were practically off-limits to sisters. Now she was at the vanguard of a
new era of publicity and recruitment. As one of the few women with
training and access to the media, it fell to her to make clear the frustrations of sisters in trying to dispel such misconceptions about the convent that seemed to be central to *The Nun's Story*. Thus, while her
comments may seem hyperbolic, she was standing up for all sisters
against a near-impregnable wall of masculine clergy and Hollywood
executives who gave them only a supporting, ad hoc role in the negotiations for a film that was about their way of life.

In June 1958 Augustine had written a pamphlet produced by her
congregation, the Marist Missionary Sisters, which exposed many of the
factual errors and incongruities in the book in an effort to undermine
the real Sister Luke and any vestiges of truth surrounding her story.
That pamphlet was updated and put into circulation again once the
film was released. She had decided to rekindle her campaign against
The Nun's Story after a man approached her on a train. He told her that
he had just seen the movie and wanted her help in having his own
daughter released from a convent before her personality was shattered
and her sense of identity stripped as had happened to Sister Luke
(Marist Archives). Her pamphlet caused much dismay for Gardiner,
Hulme, and Heberts. Gardiner requested a rebuttal from Heberts to
publish in *America*, but Hulme insisted on protecting her partner from
the harsh glare of the limelight. She wrote back, 'it truly *is* best, Fr. Gardiner, that she not be called into this little fray. There were many things
in that little pamphlet that not only cut her to the core but which also
raised her righteous wrath. Were she to "set the record straight" it
would not be with velvet gloves' (Zinnemann Collection). Augustine

did deal harshly with Heberts, accusing her of trying to unburden herself of guilt over a failed vocation and of conceit and betrayal against her former congregation, who had treated her well. She asked rhetorically, 'can time and life obliterate every trace of all one has seen and heard and learned for seventeen years, leaving only the memory of a few material facts, emptied of any real significance, and presented from a misleading angle?' (Augustine 1958, 26).

It can be argued that sisters were so unaccustomed to dealing with the media and having their lives open to public scrutiny that they could not accept the idea that nuns may hold meanings beyond their specified role in the Catholic Church. Yet the representation of nuns could not be held strictly to the very narrow concerns that sisters had about their vocations and the mental health of new recruits. *The Nun's Story* was a major Hollywood feature, expected to garner much critical praise for Zinnemann and Warner Brothers. Neither wanted to be seen as producing a 'Catholic propaganda picture.' In an interview with the *Los Angeles Times* just before the release of the film, Zinnemann tried to downplay the religiosity of the movie and emphasize the personal struggle of a strong-willed woman. 'The story is a conflict of conscience, the interior conflict of the woman; it just happens to be set against a religious background ... SHE is the battleground. In the end she leaves the convent' (*TNS* Clippings File). For whatever reason Zinnemann saw fit to give away the ending, it is clear that he did not want *The Nun's Story* to be seen as a religious movie. If the background of the movie was, in his opinion, mere happenstance from which to explore the conflicts of a woman who cannot reconcile obedience to others with her own wilful independence, then it suggests that the meaning of nuns at work here had more to do with gender relations than they ever did with religion.

Brandon French claims that the use of nuns as the lead characters in American films of the 1950s asserted women's professional and intellectual equality with men, while still safely enrobing that position in a chaste religious habit to undermine any possible threat to male dominance (1978, 122). She argues that the sublimated representations of sexuality through Sister Luke's relationship to both Fortunati and her father provide the strongest thread binding her decision to both join and subsequently leave the convent. While there is some merit to this argument, it does not appear to have been reflected in the responses by critics and audience at the time of the film's release. It is certainly difficult to surmise what was going on in the minds of those who saw the movie. However, it is possible to draw some conclusions through the existing material available and to try to reconstruct a partial picture of audience response to *The Nun's Story*. The film was a touchstone in which negotiations over the figure of the nun reached unprecedented levels of urgency. The final composite image of nuns from this film helped to establish a set of rules about their representation, their meanings, and their value outside the religious milieu that resonated across all popular culture media long after the film ceased its theatrical run.

Reviews of the movie were as glowing as had been those of the book. They continued to find the central drama in the struggle of a gifted and independent woman against an overbearingly depersonalized institution. In this way, the film offered an image of an 'organization man' for women in postwar culture, despite its obvious setting in pre-war Europe and Africa. Jack Moffit of the *Hollywood Reporter* made this connection explicit in his review: 'In a larger sense, the problem of Sister Luke is the problem of our times – of whether the individual, particularly the richly talented individual, can function best in or out of an organization' (*TNS* Clippings File). Other reviews also commented on this conflict. *Variety* noted that one of the greatest faults of Sister Luke was her tendency to single herself out, but remarked that 'the lay world would characterize [this] as "expressing oneself." So it is ... a life against nature.' The *New Yorker* described Sister Luke as a 'self-reliant heroine' struggling to cope with the regimen of a convent in which 'any tendency toward individualism is suppressed summarily.' The *Film Daily* called Sister Luke 'a heroine torn between the conflict of the spirit and the human condition.' Bosley Crowther in the *New York Times* singled out the film's 'feminine appeal' in dealing with that same theme identified by both *Variety* and the *Hollywood Reporter*, 'the lasting conflict of a strong individual with a depersonalizing philosophy.' Even the Protestant Motion Picture Council praised the film, not for its religious value but for its valorization of the individual: 'While this masterful production may be taken by many as a consideration of Roman Catholic religious orders and convent life, it is essentially the development of a girl's personality from repressed confinement to the finding of herself by free choice' (Zinnemann Collection).

Many assessments of the meaning of the film referred to ongoing debates among social critics such as David Riesman, William Whyte,

William Herberg, and others. Among the concerns of the late fifties was that the individual was under attack by institutional bureaucracies that privileged conformity. What is interesting is that these debates rarely, if ever, included women. In fact, the manifestations of institutionalized behaviour were often criticized for their effeminate characteristics. This implied that women were not generally expected to suffer the plight of the 'organization man,' who was spiritually and physically drained by systems that put the perfectibility of society ahead of the assertion of individuality (Whyte 1957, 24). If anything, women were supposed to provide the locus for the positive benefits of increased belonging and togetherness that were otherwise disparaged by the critics. Their inherent 'other-directedness,' as Riesman defined it, led them to be more conformist and concerned with gaining popular approval from those around them and not to be as absorbed in the 'inner-directed' needs of personal integrity and authenticity (Riesman 1969, 15). What is interesting is that in *The Nun's Story* critics saw a woman in the predicament of the inner-directed organization man, struggling to free herself from a stultifying society. However, the cast of blithely happy-go-lucky nuns behind her undermined the potential of the film to make a direct intervention on the gender politics of this social debate.

The failure of the film to incite a gender critique was exacerbated by the socially accepted restrictions placed on women at that time regarding access to meaningful education and employment opportunities. According to a 1959 study, the rate of women in higher education was dropping precipitously, from 47 per cent in 1920 to slightly more than 35 per cent in 1958, and only 37 per cent of those who enrolled in university actually completed their degrees. Meanwhile, the average marrying age was dropping to below twenty years. And while women were increasingly part of the workforce, they tended to be clustered around low-paying, low-skilled jobs in factories or offices (Friedan 1963, 368; Freeman 1975, 20–3; Oakley 1986, 291–5). At the time that *The Nun's Story* was released in the late fifties, marriage and motherhood were viewed as the most desirable roles for women, not merely on a personal level but in terms of women's contribution to a national state of well-being. Even the church had begun to shift its own value system for pious femininity, privileging maternal nurturing and devotion over celibate obedience and humility (McDannell 1995b, 311). Work and education were treated as supplementary activities to help improve the household's overall spending ability, thus boosting the nation's economy and ensuring prosperity for everyone (Blackwelder 1997, 149–52; Haralovich 1992, 137).

Yet if all this was true, it brings to light just how compelling a film about a strong-willed and independent nun must have been at this time. To focus on the trials and tribulations of a woman clearly outside the suburban domestic milieu seems to have been in direct conflict with the lifestyle women were urged to adopt everywhere else in the mass media. What's more, her crises were not about herself in relation to men or to personal love relationships, but about her need to contribute something heroic for the betterment of humanity, which would ultimately improve her own sense of identity and self-worth. That her sexual identity was, for the most part, bracketed was all the better since it kept the film from being too radical. Instead, it offered women a containable level of independence that still reinforced notions of selfless service and near-slavish devotion to others as central to the feminine character. Removing erotic or libidinal desire from Luke's motivations curtailed her own autonomy and resisted any notion that her rebellion would lead to an undermining of social structures that denied women their sexual independence and only offered outlets that conformed to the feminine mystique.

In 1959 there had yet to be widely articulated any sense of dissatisfaction or general malaise by women. Yet the tendency of critics to focus on Sister Luke's struggles for independence against an overbearing institution does seem to suggest that the woman question – that centuries-old debate about women's place in a society that was both hostile and idealizing towards them – was slowly re-emerging. Perhaps the nun provided a dual kind of release for the examination of women's particular struggles against those social systems that curtailed their involvement in public affairs. By removing the heroine from a home with husband and children, the film protected the inviolability of the family from critical introspection. Furthermore, it liberated the female lead to explore her identity without having to abandon her family and thus risk losing the sympathy of the audience. However, it was still apparently inconceivable to have the heroine on a quest without any kind of limits placed on it. Unlike Homer in *Lilies of the Field*, Gabrielle Van Der Mal could not head down the highways of personal self-discovery. She had to become someone else altogether, Sister Luke, and submit to a different version of patriarchal authority. In this way it can be understood how Zinnemann was on the right track when he suggested that the convent was merely a dramatic backdrop for a much bigger story. Criticizing the Catholic Church for its oppressive institutions was a much safer option than turning the camera on the oppressiveness of the suburbs.

At the same time, despite such a prevalent characterization of the convent as 'depersonalizing' or 'against nature,' many of the reviews nonetheless also spoke respectfully of the religious life and the heroic stamina of sisters. *Variety* called the religious life 'super-human' (*TNS* Clippings File). The *Hollywood Reporter* commented on the public's 'compulsive curiosity for many years concerning what goes on in a convent' and assured that 'the picture leaves no doubt that the life of the dedicated nun is courageous and filled with self-sacrificing service.' The *Motion Picture Herald*, which was owned and operated by Legion of Decency founder Martin Quigley, commented that as 'a most remarkable and compelling film' it was also 'instructive about a way of life that is completely unknown to most of [the audience].' In the *Beverly Hills Citizen* the reviewer argued that 'if there are any who, through ignorance, prejudice or scepticism, are lacking in admiration for Catholic nuns this film should certainly change their minds.' Even the real-life Sister Luke, Louise Heberts, gave her opinion of the inspirational quality of the film. 'I'm never going to see it again,' she said. 'Because if I do I'm going to run right back to the convent. When you see the chapel, all those nuns ... I could just sit there and cry my eyes out, not with regret or anything, but because of the beauty of it' (Zeitlin 1959, 144).

Between commentary on one nun, Sister Luke, versus whole communities of nuns, it appears that critics held two vastly divergent opinions. They had only praise for the woman who had rejected the impersonal autocracy of the convent, but they also spoke highly of those who embraced religious rule and turned it into a life of heroism and beauty. This remarkable contradiction speaks to the crux of the double bind that women faced in the years before the re-emergence of the feminist movement. According to critics, the power of *The Nun's Story* came from what should have been two mutually incompatible forces. There was the woman-against-society theme, which turned Sister Luke into a heroine for her refusal to capitulate to an overbearing system. At the same time there was a sacrificial-virgin theme, which revelled in those sisters who humbly submitted to the same system rejected by Sister

Luke. To elaborate upon Hulme's and Zinnemann's call for dramatic conflict, it can be argued that the success of *The Nun's Story* did not lie in the conflicts of Sister Luke but in those audience members who read, and then watched her struggle and felt torn by their own divided feelings. In that, perhaps there is more reason to sympathize with the puzzled woman who asked Sister Mary Augustine, 'What did she do wrong?' She certainly was not the only woman on the cusp of second-wave feminism who felt confused over where her sympathies should lie.

The Nun's Story was a huge box-office and critical success, taking first place for two months after its release and continuing to break revenue records once it went into general release in October (Zinnemann Collection). It was nominated for eight Academy Awards, eventually losing in every category. However, it did win the New York Film Critic's Award for best movie and actress, the Ciné Revue Grand Prix in Europe, and was a regular feature in American critics' top-ten lists for 1959 film releases. The men who had first envisioned turning the book into a major motion picture had every reason to be proud of themselves. Not only had they collaborated on a critical and popular hit, but they were all able to claim victory in their stated intentions. The film was recognized primarily for its eloquent rendition of a unique and sympathetic heroine. Meanwhile, the lavish reproduction of convent life satisfied Catholic representatives and their desire to promote some of the beauty and romance of their religion. Yet as far as rendering an effective portrait of a convent that would be recognizable to sisters, *The Nun's Story* continued to disappoint. As late as 1964 one sister recalled how many 'heartily objected' to both the book and the movie and detailed the many complaints she still held (Dorcy 1964, 69). At the heart of this criticism was the difficulty sisters had reconciling the widespread interest in their lives with their own desires to shape their image in order to increase vocations and secure the future of the religious life.

It was partially out of this frustration that sisters looked to themselves to produce less-conflicted portrayals of the religious life. Beginning in the early fifties, congregations began to publish vocation books, illustrated stories for girls about the positive benefits of entering the convent. They provide an interesting counterbalance to the image of Sister Luke in their approving portraits of independently minded and fun-loving women who also happened to be nuns. These stories made heroines out of the ones who stayed, not those who, in their eyes, lacked the spiritual stamina to withstand the challenges of the convent. However, their exuberance in many ways masked some hard truths about the religious life. The minor changes to convent routine begun by the Call for Renewal were in no way adequate to address pressing concerns of an overburdened, understaffed convent network of schools, hospitals, and social agencies. While the Sister Formation Conference and the Conference of Major Superiors of Women were trying to combat the difficult problems of sisters' educational, professional, and spiritual development, they were still in their infancy. Thus, underlying the carefree attitude in vocation books was a lurking desperation for more and younger recruits. Sisters redoubled their efforts to insert themselves into debates over gender and religion by winning the hearts and minds of young girls who, like Sister Luke, wanted a more heroic and adventurous life than that which marriage and motherhood could provide.

4

Adventurous Souls:
Vocation Books and Postwar Girl
Culture

The growing interest in the religious life for women could not have gained such a foothold in popular culture without some effort on the part of sisters themselves. Opening their doors to the media for interviews and profiles, and assisting on films as technical advisers were good options. However, sisters also sought ways to directly connect with young audiences and encourage them to consider a religious vocation. Thus, beginning in the fifties and continuing until just after the Second Vatican Council, vocation books were widely published and circulated within the Catholic school system. These were books targeted at teenage girls, often including photos or illustrations, which extolled the virtues of the religious life. Although varying widely in production quality and content, they all had one purpose in mind: to make the convent appear as an attractive alternative to the limited career options offered young women in the postwar, pre-feminist era. Some were elaborate photo essays. Others were more like brochures than books. Even the clerical hierarchy wanted in on the trend, publishing the *McCarthy Guides to the American Sisterhood*. These reference books had a one-page description of the community accompanied by a picture of a nun in the habit, causing some to dub them 'bird books' for their similarity to nature guides. All told, there was a wide range of sources for girls to explore the possibility of a vocation.

These were volatile times with massive shifts in the image of modern sisters, not to mention feminine independence more generally. Yet the general tone of the books differed very little from the earliest text to the latest. Despite the dramatic changes that swept across convent life, the image of happy-go-lucky girls skipping up convent steps trying not to

trip on their new habits did not waver. As Sister Elizabeth Kolmer comments, 'At times realistic, at times romantic, these books were frequently used as apologia for convent life. They showed the ups and
downs of the young woman in process of becoming a nun, attempted to
depict religious as real people, and convent life as not so rigid and dull
after all. None of them raised the question of changing the traditional
practices of the religious life' (1984, 27). The conservatism of these
texts locked them into a unique discursive space where time seemed to
stand still. Indeed, specific references to dates or public events tended
to be kept at a minimum. Descriptions of school, clothes, and parties
before entering gave little indication whether they were referring to
events thirty years in the past or thirty days. There were no names of
popular singers, magazines, or movies that would anchor the authors'
girlhoods in time. What these books offered instead was an unbroken
chain of sexually contained spiritual ambition across generations, tempered by such down-to-earth and singularly feminine concerns as
appearance, family, and a suitably womanly career.

By far the most ambitious of the books was *Bernie Becomes a Nun* for
the Maryknoll community, which featured photos by George Barris,
better known for his portraits of Marilyn Monroe. The other book to
meet such high standards was *Those Whom God Chooses*, with photos by
celebrated *Life* photographer Grey Villet. Based primarily on these two
books, certain themes emerge and become more prominent as other
sources are woven in. Probably the most compelling thread is the bridal
motif apparent in the early stages of a vocation. References to showers,
wedding dresses, betrothal, and the like were juxtaposed with appeals to
a different kind of Mary that emphasized her courage and sacrifice more
than her status as the Virgin Mother. Reinforcing the call to become
Brides of Christ were promises that women who forewent the messy,
unpleasant duties of a wife and mother would reap greater rewards as
spiritual mothers and lovers whose virginal status came with unprecedented opportunities for travel, education, and meaningful work.

A major drawback to the liberating potential of vocation books was
their overarching sense of middle-class conformity. In a religion of
working-class immigrants, congregations were clearly seeking out those
who had assimilated just enough to assist Catholicism in its efforts to
appear more modern, more liberal; in short, more like bourgeois Americans. Highlighting shopping, dating, parties and the like implied that

the girls they were seeking were already part of the consumerist generation, with extra spending money that could only come from rising
socio-economic status. With the increase in Catholic incomes, however, there was a concomitant intellectual flowering. The shifts in the
Legion of Decency spearheaded by Fr Patrick J. Sullivan were reflective
of these changes in the Catholic mentality. Doubleday Books responded
in 1954 with a new series called Image Books, for the 'intellectual
Catholic public.' Their best-selling title, A Popular History of the Catholic Church, was second in quality paperback sales only to Riesman's The
Lonely Crowd. Riesman himself hailed Catholics as the future of the
'good American' in an article published in 1951, one year after that
seminal text (Hudnut-Beumler 1994, 69). By 1960, Catholics had
positive role models in the two Johns – their pope and their president –
to provide the moral authority to continue on a path of spiritual and
civic zealousness. In that sense, then, vocation books achieved a certain
level of symbiosis between the allure of the individual in public life and
the conventions of middle-class domesticity, fired up by new forms of
liberal religiosity that became the organizing principle of postwar
Catholicism.

   Vocation books were not hard-hitting accounts of convent life but
officially sanctioned texts designed for the express purpose of encouraging girls and their families to consider the rewards of a religious vocation. As such, they have much to say about the social organization of
Catholic girlhood in the postwar era. They speak to the role of religion
in their everyday lives as they came to terms with their status as women
and as Catholics. By the 1950s, sisters were sounding alarms that there
were not enough new recruits to maintain their vast health and teaching institutions. At the same time, educational and employment policies for women streamlined many high-school girls into the dead-end
paths of vocational schools and part-time or temporary jobs while privileging marriage and motherhood. Vocation books were a way to bring
these two seemingly disparate problems together, without upsetting the
doctrines of femininity that sought to curtail women's erotic power as
autonomous individuals. Although the intention of the Call for
Renewal was to build a more supportive environment for sisters, its
lengthy list of reform initiatives actually helped increase their workload. Underlying it all was a fervent desire on the part of the hierarchy
to keep the sisterhood growing. If sisters were to keep up their heavy

load of responsibilities in the schools and hospitals, they needed more recruits than ever before. Thus, even though the number of women taking vows rose steadily until the late sixties, Catholic officials still spoke urgently of a vocation crisis. Without a huge influx of new recruits, the entire parochial network would be in jeopardy.

Why, if the number of sisters was rising steadily, was there such a foreboding sense of crisis in the convent? For one thing, the total number of Catholics was increasing at a faster pace, thanks to the baby boom. Because of the work they did, there needed to be a lot more sisters in the system than, say, priests. Although men also staffed their own schools and other social institutions, for sisters this was their primary function, barred as they were from the clerical hierarchy. That led in turn to a twisted logic in which the economic demands for women were justified as a spiritual calling. In 1961 *America* asked rhetorically 'What's with the Girls?' Including seminarians in its report on vocations, the article showed that from 1944 to 1961 the total number of men with vocations had increased by 42,754 while the numbers for women had risen by only 36,453. According to the Official Catholic Directory, which only included priests and monastic brothers (not seminarians), in 1961 there were just over 170,000 sisters to approximately 66,000 male religious. This was a decline in ratio from a high of 3.1 in 1953 to 2.6. However, in total numbers, the sister population grew steadily every year until 1967. It appears, then, that anything less than a clear three-to-one margin between female and male religious life was unacceptable behaviour on the part of the 'pious sex' ('What's with the Girls?' 1961, 359). Although the significance of the decline was mostly symbolic, it cannot be denied that women were deemed more valuable recruits to the religious life. While this might be explained away as simple economics, there was a certain assumption about women's role in the church that made this appeal to crisis somewhat disconcerting. As the *America* article hinted, according to Catholic tradition, girls were expected to be more pious and devotional than boys. Maintaining a wide margin between the two sexes in terms of vocations helped bolster this particularly Catholic aspect of postwar gender ideology.

The vocation crisis was most deeply felt in Catholic schools, likely triggered by the baby boom following the Second World War. By the early fifties the first wave of children was starting school, and the demand for teachers rose beyond a level that could be accommodated.

Even though 58 per cent of all nuns were teachers, they were constantly playing catch-up to meet the staffing needs of their schools. Even in 1950 the ratio between teaching sisters and students under Catholic instruction was unmanageable at one sister for every fifty-eight students. By the end of the Second Vatican Council the number of students per teacher had risen to more than one hundred. Lay teachers were hired to offset the load, but that was not the ideal solution. For one thing, lay teachers demanded market-level salaries, while sisters received little more than a stipend (Beane 1993, 17 and 23). Aside from economic concerns, parents tended to have a stubborn emotional attachment to the image of the teaching nun. As one article on the crisis in the Catholic schools noted, 'Many parents who nostalgically recall their own favourite Sister-teacher are troubled by this situation. The nun, they feel, has given Catholic education a very special flavour, one that they would prefer to keep' (Star 1963, 40). The sentimental appeal of the teaching sister spoke to a widespread ideology that idealized a form of sacred femininity and liked to see it materialized in the form of pious virgins patiently instructing children on how to be good Catholics.

This sentimental attachment to convent schools can be linked to a Marian revival in the postwar years. Nineteen-fifty was declared a Marian year by Pius XII, who formally recognized the Assumption of the Virgin as Catholic doctrine. An increased emotional attachment to Mary by Catholics of all levels of class and education became linked to a broad-based feminine ideology that women were innately predisposed to suffering and submission. They were, therefore, better equipped to take on a sacrificial role in society (Fisher 1989, 163). This is evident in much of the writing targeted at girls considering a vocation or having just entered a community. In a 1963 book sponsored by the Sister Formation Conference, women were esteemed for their role as helpmate and lover in God's divine plan. It stated that 'It is only love, love of God or human love of another, that makes a woman content. Love of self, no matter how exalted one may disguise it, is bereft of the altruism that becomes a woman's love, and, therefore must unmake a woman. Her very nature cries out for love' (McGoldrick 1963, 27). To be sure, this connection between devotional love and sacrifice was not exclusive to Catholicism. Yet the Catholic Church's tradition of Mariology bolstered women's idealized submissiveness. In its special issue on the

American woman, *Life* made the connection between women, love, and religion explicit. More importantly, it used only Catholic examples to support its claim:

> Women have excelled in every high Christian calling, from the pure mysticism of St. Teresa to the militant patriotism of St. Joan. Early saints were mostly men, those since the Reformation are mostly women; but in every age woman proves the diversity of her genius: the Seventh Century abbess of Whitby, St. Hilda, who, by encouraging the peculiar gift of an old man named Caedmon, became the mother of English poetry; the widowed Queen St. Elizabeth of Hungary, who fought the famine of 1225 by feeding 900 daily at her gate; tough and purposeful Mother Cabrini who left schools and hospitals all over this hemisphere in our own time. And thousands more. ('Woman, Love and God' 1956, 36)

Thus it appears that women religious were singled out over and over again to play a special role as the stalwarts of faith and femininity in society. When their numbers seemed to be in decline, at stake was not only the institutional and economic life of Catholicism but also its unique image of quixotic devotionalism. Maintaining the feminized face of piety on all fronts was therefore a crucial concern for clerical leaders.

When Pius XII sent out the Call for Renewal in 1950 his main focus was to replenish and hopefully even increase the population of sisters. When he first proposed sisters undertake efforts to modernize the religious life, he made it clear that the reason was not to make the lives of sisters easier for their own sake. Rather, it was to make the convent more attractive to Catholic girls. These new recruits were most likely to come from sister-run high schools, and recruiting efforts were organized to reflect that. According to the Sisters Survey from 1966, most congregations expected entrants to have completed high school, but additional education or work experience was not essential (Neal 1984, 37). Of course, high school was the preferred location to foster a vocation because girls would be exposed almost daily to the virtues of the religious life as represented by their teachers, mentors, and friends. As a former nun recalled, her school days were 'islands of femaleness where (save for the janitor, the retreat master, and the band director) the Second Sex was first' (Griffin 1975, 11). Congregations had both minimum and maximum age limits for new entrants, usually ranging somewhere between sixteen and thirty. Any older, cautioned Joan Lexau in *Convent Life*, and the candidate could be 'too set in her ways to adjust to religious life' (1964, 11). She also argued that it was better for the candidate to enter before beginning college. In that way, her superior could decide on an educational program that would best suit the needs of the entire community, as well as the temperament of the new sister (11). Thus, when sisters or the pope talked about potential recruits, they did not discuss women but were explicit in their preference for girls.

The bias towards youth was obvious in a 1956 vocation survey published in the *Sister Formation Bulletin* (Judith 1956, 1–7). Questionnaires were sent to high-school and college students, student nurses and parents across the country. The organizers received fifteen thousand responses. A major point the survey made was that sisters were often seen as irrelevant to the modern world and ill informed about the issues facing young women. It was stressed that sisters had to first make contact on girls' turf, and from there awaken a vocation: 'I know of apostolic-minded priests who subscribe to *Vogue*, to *Junior Miss*, and read them from cover to cover. Their motive is love for souls. To work with these young people one must know their world. The world of the student, however, is not only the teen-age world of dance, song and sports. These may be the entering wedge, but students expect us to follow through with solid stuff' (3). This two-pronged approach was to include a greater openness among sisters to share aspects of their lives with students and show by example the great happiness they experienced in the religious life. As one respondent complained, 'If only one Sister had ever been more informal, understanding, and informative to the girls in this room, at least 20 per cent of us would have a desire to become Sisters (4). Another concurred: 'I believe the Sisters' life is one of the happiest, but I wish that some Sisters could smile even once a week. This is the only difficult thing to understand. Being as happy as they are, why do they have a perpetual frown? (5). Yet, as the author of the report noted, asking sisters to keep up with all the latest fads and fashions, oversee vast social institutions, maintain rigid adherence to the religious rule, and be perpetually chipper about it all was pretty much impossible. They therefore set about to reform the religious life in keeping with the edicts of the Call for Renewal to simplify their rituals, streamline their daily routines, and modify their cumbersome habits. The initiatives of the Sister Formation Conference and the Conference of Major Superiors of Women in the fifties and sixties were instrumental in creating a nationwide revolution in the convent. However, their efforts still needed to be communicated to young women, who were not looking to the church for moral guidance as much as they used to but were increasingly caught up in a wave of new ideas that were based as much on socio-economic shifts as they were on new psychology about individual autonomy, sexual maturity, and explorations of the self. As young women's consumer power grew, it merged into a culture of liberated sexual expression. This did not fit in well with a religious culture that stressed humility, poverty, and virginity. Therefore, creative ways had to be found that implicated the convent into a girl culture of dating, parties, and shopping, while suggesting it would ultimately not be enough to satisfy the truly heroic idealists. Playing upon the cultural double bind that exhorted girls to be both independent and docile, and to place service of others at the heart of their personal ambition, vocation books were able to offer the convent as a provocative, if not exactly radical, alternative to a seemingly untenable social conundrum.

When dealing with subjects such as nuns and the convent, it can be all too easy to avoid another side of postwar girl culture, which can be grouped under the catch-all term the 'sexual revolution.' After all, as some may suggest, these girls abandoned their sexuality before they had even begun to explore it. However, without reducing the idea of sexuality to a kind of prurient speculation on illicit activities behind the cloister, it cannot be ignored that sex was an underlying, if not explicitly articulated, concern for young women no matter what their spiritual calling. In the 1950s the church was still almost incapable of anything other than a hysterical reaction to any suggestion that sex might have a significant role to play in people's lives. Children were reared to believe their bodies were so sacred that to touch or even look at them was to commit a sin (Mission Helpers 1954, 16). In a pamphlet designed to lay out a sex-education curriculum appropriate to a Catholic upbringing, the nuns of the Mission Helpers of the Sacred Heart linked this sort of rigorously maintained chastity directly to the Cold War and how children could do their part by treating the body as they would uranium:

> God put that treasure [uranium] there thousands of years ago. It is a great
> treasure for good or for evil. During WWII, it was used to destroy lives and
> entire cities. Scientists are now experimenting with atomic energy in the

fields of medical science, physical science, and industrial science for a beneficial use of atomic energy. That is the way God intended that it be used. Some day, we may see our ships and planes propelled across the ocean, our homes heated and disease arrested through the right use of atomic energy. (78)

In what can only be deemed one of the most unfortunate Freudian slips ever, the pamphlet encouraged Catholic youth to continue this milita-ristic approach to their sexuality by joining 'the Fighting 6 9.' Based on the values of the Sixth and Ninth Commandments (Thou shall not commit adultery and Thou shall not covet thy neighbour's wife), this was a youth league whose members pledged to uphold their virginity until marriage or, even better, until a religious vocation that would secure the pledge forever:

A nation's goodness or badness depends upon the youth and that means YOU. A nation, even our wonderful nation, is no stronger than the young men and women who are to be the future fathers and mothers. Sons and daughters of Mary Immaculate, 'Be pure!' Be faithful members of the Fighting 6 9. That is God's will for you today. Say your 'Yes' as Mary did, then you will be worth far more to God and to your country than all the uranium and all the atomic energy in the universe. (84)

Needless to say, not all Catholic girls heeded the call or saw virginity as a particularly patriotic duty. As Susan Douglas recalls, priests ranting against the evils of sexuality and birth control seemed badly out of step with her youthful understanding of what it meant to be good.

Being raised Catholic, as I was, meant going to church and hearing the priest all of a sudden start screaming about birth control, which I quickly learned was a really, really big sin. (We're talking a beeline to hell unless you said 500 rosaries and put a big contribution in next Sunday's collection.) ... This pill idea sounded pretty good to me, so I started getting confused some more. Didn't this represent progress and wasn't progress, especially medical progress, what made America America? (Douglas 1994, 62)

Even sisters felt pangs of confusion over what constituted a properly moral response in this battle between corporate and personal responsibility. For many who joined congregations right after high school in the fifties, questions of sexual identity were left in some nebulous void that suddenly emerged about a decade later as a crisis of faith that helped spark the personalist movement in the convent.

The timing of this crisis peaked during the mid- to late sixties, and while it would be too simple to suggest that the rule of celibacy was primarily responsible for the departure of many sisters from the convent, it was nonetheless a catalyst (Schneiders 2001, 135). As some argue, the twin eruptions of the sexual revolution and second-wave feminism altered feminine consciousness within the walls of the cloister (160). Even those vowed to virginity were faced with the urgent need to discover their sexual identities and integrate them into a way of life that had for centuries deemed such matters dangerous to vocations. Their earliest initiatives were tentative and occasionally defensive, tending to refer back to some kind of mysticalized femininity couched in marital and maternal language. Although one sister admitted that these kinds of invocations to spiritual marriage were 'intolerable to the New Breed's philosophy of fierce personalism and commitment,' she insisted that such spousal imagery was 'rooted in the authentic tradition of the Church' and vitally linked to the realities of the feminine mindset (Malits 1965, 91–3). It didn't hurt that appeals to marriage also counteracted any homoerotic intrigue that would naturally stem from public interest in a cloistered, all-female world. Vocation books were resolutely, imperiously heterosexual in their orientation; not only through the bridal motifs but also in the infantilization of women religious as sisters and daughters of the church instead of independent, adult women. Great pains were taken to assure that 'normal, healthy' girls were attracted to the convent for all the right reasons, not the neurotic or the sexually confused.

When *Cosmopolitan* ran a feature on Bernadette Lynch, the heroine of *Bernie Becomes a Nun*, it stressed two things: Bernie was a normal, everyday girl, in the psychological lingo of the times; and church leaders encouraged her to lead an active, sociable life before making any final decisions. The article stated that

> Bernie had no emotional problems. She had no desire to give up the world, no negative impulse ... On the advice of her confessor, Bernie agreed to wait a few years before taking a definite step. Though impatient,

she went to work as a stenographer in an insurance-brokerage house in downtown Manhattan. For a year and a half, she worked dutifully, dated, danced, went to parties – then surprised her friends by entering the Mary-knoll convent. ('Bernie' 1954, 119)

Almost ten years later *Life* magazine ran a similar feature based on *Those Whom God Chooses* ('Girl Sets Out' 1963, 68). *Seventeen* also featured an article on a girl who was considering a vocation. Like the vocation books produced by sisters, this short article insisted that aspiring girls were neither especially holy nor contemplative before entering but were merely seeking an elusive sense of 'something more' in their lives ('Face to Face' 1966, 117).

Growing into womanhood in the fifties and mid-sixties meant being subject to a barrage of conflicting messages about your duty to become a model American and to improve upon your femininity. The nationalist ideal encouraged higher education and technical training for girls so that they could be assets in the fight against Communism. This link between women, education, and national security was made explicit as early as 1951 when the American Council on Education sponsored the 'Conference on Women in the Defence Decade' (Blackwelder 1997, 171). There were two schools of thought about how this new curriculum should be shaped. Liberal reformers wanted to see more girls in college preparatory courses and increased science and math requirements. The National Manpower Council argued that schools were not training girls to think about a lifetime of employment but only a few years of work until marriage and children kicked in. Conservatives insisted that the family was the backbone of American democracy and the greatest weapon in the national arsenal. They supported rigorous home economics programs to provide girls with the necessary skills to juggle marriage, children, and work. Further, they insisted that work outside the home must always take a back seat to the demands of family, something liberal reformers did not argue against too vociferously (171–2). Both sides ultimately seemed to agree that women's responsibility lay in a combination of service industry, part-time, and volunteer labour. However, neither side could come up with a way to reconcile women's work with their ultimate responsibilities in marriage and motherhood, and no one wanted to even consider the idea of the sexually liberated single career woman.

The emphasis on training girls to be wives and mothers first and professionals second was not limited to the education system. Scouting programs for girls, in effect across the country since the First World War, also began to privilege domestic training and started to move away from the earlier tradition of adventure stories and survival skills. Since the 1920s, the Girl Scout movement had emphasized character building, resourcefulness, and independence alongside efforts to cultivate domestic and mothering skills. These were a tonic for girls who had only confining roles available to them, providing an outlet for them to at least imagine alternatives and build the necessary skills to realize them (Inness 1997, 233). Prior to the fifties, Girl Scout programs had as much to do with building a strong sense of civic responsibility and national pride as they did with shaping girls into good wives and mothers. By the end of the Second World War the emphasis had shifted from a robust adventurism to a more feminized message of social adjustment and domestication (Blackwelder 1997, 174). This shift reflected a larger transition in society, which critics like William Whyte and others challenged. Whyte complained that the Protestant ethic based on hard work, autonomy, and self-reliance was being usurped by a vision of a docile society dedicated to such concepts as togetherness and belonging (1957, 24–6). However, there seemed to have been no outcry by social critics over how the changes affected girls. Instead, the narrow opening for girls to experience adventures beyond the home, based on a nationalist discourse of individualism and preparedness, suddenly closed in the fifties in favour of a feminized nationalism of compromise and conformity. Instead of stories on aviation or wilderness survival, Girl Scout publications began to emphasize the development of good dating habits, personal hygiene, and deportment (Blackwelder 1997, 175).

Not surprisingly, the debate over the education of girls and their future adult role resulted in a state of confusion. While many girls were zealous about making a noteworthy contribution to national welfare, they could not help but feel intense pressure on many fronts to abandon higher education or a career in favour of an early marriage. A picture of an ideal woman who managed to juggle intellectual, professional, emotional, and civic responsibilities and still have time to do her hair began to emerge as the model aspiration for girls. In a special issue on the American woman, *Look* magazine painted an enticing but near-impossible picture:

No longer a psychological immigrant to man's world, she works rather casually, as a third of the U.S. Labor force, and less toward a 'big career' than as a way of filling a hope chest or buying a new home freezer. She gracefully concedes the top job rungs to men.

This wondrous creature also marries younger than ever, bears more babies and looks and acts far more feminine than the 'emancipated' girl of the 1920's or even '30's. Steelworker's wife and Junior Leaguer alike do their own housework ... Still, despite whacks from the critics, she is groping her way toward a new true center, neither Victorian nor rampantly feminist. ('New Look' 1956, 35)

While such an image could have resulted in a kind of cultural paralysis, it also gave girls a chance to experiment. Many cultural historians of postwar femininity argue that the resulting confusion helped to establish the conditions for women's sense of dissatisfaction. Even in the 1950s it was not all poodle skirts and promise rings. Wini Breines examines the liberating possibilities available in an otherwise 'culture of containment' (1992, 10), and she notes the underground movements of civil rights and pacifism, which had not quite entered into the mainstream. Culturally, the advent of rock and roll and, even more sublimated, the beat movement of poetry and jazz provided some outlets for rebels-in-waiting. Once *The Feminine Mystique* and the sexual revolution exploded into the mainstream, other opportunities for young women to turn their backs on societal conventions appeared on the horizon.

The American postwar economy of ever-accelerating consumerism elevated girldom, with its emphasis on beauty and shopping, to new heights of cultural importance. Granted, that status was really only accorded to women who conformed to an ideal American image: attractive without being overtly sexual, suitably educated but not brainy, and, above all else, white and middle class. With this new bourgeois appeal came a sense of sexual independence focused on individual fulfilment: a sexual economy of erotic power, pleasure, and identity (Radner 1999, 3). By the mid-sixties such sexy, independent women were visible in popular culture, trumpeted by Helen Gurley Brown in her revamped magazine, *Cosmopolitan*.

As much as the media seemed to be obsessed with nuns, there was equal if not more time given to the idea of college girls having sex.

What's more, it seemed that even good girls were doing it, and their reasons had to do with righteous values such as independence, personal responsibility, and authenticity. Still, one could not deny that it also had to do with the privileges of class. As *Newsweek* noted, 'Knowledge and sophistication alone do not make a social revolution. It also takes money and freedom of action, and, unlike most of their predecessors, the offspring of the affluent and permissive society seem to have enough of both' ('Morals Revolution' 1964, 52). The smug tone reflected in such popular sociological exposés as Gael Greene's *Sex and the College Girl* solidified this 'cool' attitude while implicitly maintaining its middlebrow appeal. Religious-based morality was for 'the nonthinking masses,' sniffed one Catholic girl who was sexually active with her Jewish boyfriend (Greene 1964, 110). However, that sexual sophistication was still deeply enmeshed in a heterosexist and domestic ideal. Full-scale promiscuity and homosexuality remained clearly out of bounds. Greene pointed out that not one of her college subjects referred to lesbianism as part of this culture of sexual experimentation (26). The vast majority insisted that 'sex with love is the new morality.' Without it, it was just 'a waste' (154). In her own report from campus, 'The Moral Disarmament of Betty Coed,' Gloria Steinem noted that 'What is shocking now is only real promiscuity or homosexuality or sex in which more than two people participate, and even then no one would dream of interfering unless one of the participants is being forced' (1962, 155). She went on to point out that in a culture that had adopted a style of cool rebellion but was fundamentally conservative under the surface, some women were feeling coerced into a quasi-liberated lifestyle that was framed by bourgeois, heterosexual, domestic values (156).

By making consumerism and sexuality the keystones of political and economic independence from domestic drudgery, new barriers were placed around women who did not want to be defined through their heterosexual desirability. Ilana Nash argues that the introduction of the Lolita figure into 1950s popular culture reflects an era of fetishization and exploitation of girlhood that was reflected in consumer strategies to target girls where they were most vulnerable – alone in the bedroom with their bodies (2002, 341). As she concludes, girls subsumed into this apparently liberating subculture had, as Humbert Humbert said, 'absolutely nowhere else to go.' (355) Sexually, intellectually, professionally, and romantically, there were many conflicting options available to girls, all of which came with their own level of compromise, sacrifice, and potential disapproval. It therefore comes as no surprise that this growing sense of dissatisfaction and frustration manifested itself in second-wave feminism and became increasingly more radical as the fifties wore on into the sixties.

For the most part, women's magazines responded to this 'moral disarmament' by promising women the chance for meaningful experiences in the world, but only if they capitulated to the tenets of domestic bourgeois heterosexuality. They cast the conflict in terms of a national duty to be both a model American and a good girl. The insurgent feminist consciousness of the fifties derived from this confusion of roles for women and the media's promotion of both working independence and domestic submission. Gertrude Robinson points out in her content analysis on women and work in magazine articles from 1950 to 1977 that the media often took a leadership role in promoting women's work in the postwar era. Public opinion, reinforced by public policy, may have preferred women to focus on child rearing and homemaking. Nonetheless, many magazines promoted career planning and profiled exceptional career women alongside articles on the virtues of marriage and motherhood (Robinson 1983, 95, 102). While her findings may seem at first to conflict with those of Radner, Nash, and others, they really just highlight the level of confusion and conflict for girls. The media exhorted them to work – but not too hard; to be attractive – but not too sexy; to be independent – but not promiscuous; and to give to their country – but put their families first. Susan Douglas recalls her own confusion: 'Was I supposed to be an American – individualistic, competitive, aggressive, achievement-oriented, tough, and independent? This was the kind of person who would help us triumph over *Sputnik*. Or was I supposed to be a girl – nurturing, self-abnegating, passive, dependent, primarily concerned with the well-being of others, and completely indifferent to personal success?' (1994, 25).

Thus, while education and careers were encouraged to a degree for girls, they still were considered temporary or part-time efforts and had to be shrouded in a veil of demure desirability. A girl's major ambition was expected to be finding a husband and having children; to accomplish this she had to put her looks ahead of her intelligence. Two studies of girls during the fifties discovered that being popular and attractive to boys was an abiding concern for girls as young as twelve years old. Furthermore, as girls grew up they became less and less sure about the future. Since they believed their future was inextricably linked to that of an as-yet-to-be-discovered husband, girls approaching the end of high school were less likely to have plans for education or work until the more pressing concern of marriage was resolved (Breines 1992, 106–11). Despite such disconcerting trends there were still girls with dreams of meaningful work, creative outlets or intellectual discovery. While some would choose a more radical route into the submerged counterculture of beatniks and swingers, others sought a way to achieve those dreams without having to reject the doctrines of femininity, which not only gave some structure to their sense of identity but were also a source of pleasure and self-satisfaction. For girls like this, the convent as envisioned by vocation books offered a rich opportunity.

Vocation books had a very specific audience and tended to address their readers directly, pulling them in and out of the narrative with passages of motherly advice alternating with first-person accounts of missionary life or postulant celebrations. It is interesting to note that these books did not seem to speak only to girls considering a vocation, but also to their friends and families. This intended readership was made explicit on the book jacket of ... *And Spare Me Not in the Making*: 'This understanding [of the religious life] is important not only for young women who are thinking of entering the convent, but also for parents who fail to comprehend the goals of religious life' (Frederic 1954). Thus, the books beseeched girls and their families to consider the thrill of the religious life despite – or perhaps because of – its underlying entrenchment of traditional femininity. They suggested a strategic alternative for girls who may not have wanted to follow the customary path of feminine fulfilment into marriage and motherhood, yet who were not so disenchanted that they wanted to reject those doctrines altogether in favour of an all-out immersion in the highly sexualized counterculture. In many ways a religious vocation must have appeared as a viable way for girls to extricate themselves from a culture that urged them towards higher education and work while it simultaneously pushed them into early marriage and motherhood. The vocation must have also seemed a way out of the confusing swirl of sexual experimentation extolled on campuses as part of personal self-discovery. Vocation books organized a particular discourse about the religious life expressly for girls that combined elements from the depiction of sisters in the mass media, generalized references to popular pastimes for girls like shopping or dating, and steady reminders that nuns were once normal teenage girls too.

Vocation books emphasized being the right kind of girl for the convent. By this they meant a fun-loving, popular, and attractive girl who was looking for more in her life than could be found through the usual routes open to women. Simultaneously, they maintained the doctrines of femininity while putting a decidedly religious spin on American idealism and the desire to do something grand in the world. In this way a religious vocation acted as an effective mediator between two conflicting postwar discourses and gave some girls a chance to overcome the double bind in a particularly romantic and heroic fashion. Pains were taken to dispel any image of overwrought, melodramatic young women grimly set on a life of sacrifice and dour piety. In *The Springs of Silence*, Sister Mary Gilbert recalled two such girls who had entered in the same class as her. Their severe haircuts, unsmiling disposition, and tendency to respond glibly to any questions pertaining to convent routine conveyed the stereotypical attitudes that many people associated with postulants. That stereotype was neatly upset by the fact that neither girl lasted a year (1954, 25).

The criticisms levelled at girls who sublimated their femininity by neglecting their appearance included the claim that they misunderstood God's plan for women. In the age-old battle between Mary and Martha, it appeared that in the postwar era Martha clearly held the upper hand. Girls were cautioned, 'You like to be alone? Slip quietly into church and spend hours there? You hate to be disturbed at your prayers in order to do some work around the house? I beg of you, – stay far from the convent!' (del Ray 1956, 4). And another complained about girls who confused a careless appearance with piety: 'These individuals seemed to see a symbol of unworldliness in looking frumpy or dowdy. A more chic (while not expensive) uniform or a better choice of clothes and hair-do, plus a touch of make-up for the more pallid ones, would have forestalled this unnecessary disaffection. Perhaps a better understanding of the place of material things in God's plan might help all concerned' (Faherty 1964, 172). It seems, therefore, that just because a girl planned to enter the convent there was no reason for her to not put on some lipstick and invest in a home permanent. These sorts of pleas to a consumer culture of beauty and budding female sexuality served multiple ends. They reinstated an ideal of bourgeois domestic femininity, as promoted in the 1956 special issues of *Life* and *Look* on the American woman. They 'normalized,' in the sense of het-erosexualizing, the convent, despite its obvious homosocial culture. And they made a direct appeal to the pleasures of being a girl, suggest-ing that they wouldn't be lost even after the lipstick was put away for good.

Girls who were reasonably pretty, enjoyed parties and dances, had plenty of friends, and did well – but not too well – at school were gener-ally the preferred candidates for the convent. Some defined it poeti-cally, as Sister Catherine Frederic did in ... *And Spare Me Not in the Making*. She suggested that all sisters required three special bones: a backbone, so that they could withstand any setbacks or negative reac-tions from friends and family; a chest bone, to represent loyalty, valour, and the courage to strive for the highest ideals; and a funny bone, so that they could always see the humour of the religious life (Frederic 1954, 57). Others were more prosaic in their recollections of their plea-sure in everyday life and their love for family and friends. As the con-templative sister from the Poor Clares recalled, she had been afraid that her priest would not recommend her because she was not heavily into mysticism or other exuberant forms of religiosity. She admitted as much to him: 'I am a very ordinary person. I want to enter the cloister because I think God is asking me. I like to dance and I like to sing. I love people and I love this university. I like books and I'd like to teach. And I would not give up any one of these things for anything less than God' (Francis 1957, 36). The girl in *Could I Measure Up?* was also candidly self-critical about her lack of overt religiosity. She took great pleasure in her comfortable home life, where her mother always made sure her party dresses were clean and ready and her father praised her budding culi-nary talents. 'Besides,' she continued, 'there were good times with school friends, too. There were barbecues on the lake shore, proms and parties, with the fragrance of lavender and corsages.' However, despite such a model middle-class lifestyle, she recognized that she wanted to do and to give more. In that moment she realized her vocation (*Could I Measure Up?* 1957, 5).

Even after the vocation had been acknowledged there was no reason to miss out on any fun. Girls were encouraged to continue their round of shopping sprees and parties and even to keep on dating. One book recommended that girls 'play the field' and remarked dismissively that 'going steady is for those who need social security ... It must be so boring to go with the same boy all the time, and the way it ties you down, you might as well be married' (Maureen 1967, 43). On the surface, this kind of advice sounds strangely liberal and freewheeling. However, it was part of a strategy to keep girls from getting too close and falling into that dangerous moral trap of 'sex with love.' Having a steady boyfriend could be a temptation, according to the Mission Helpers:

> Another danger to chastity is 'going steady.' Keep with the crowd. In numbers there is safety. Junior high is too soon to begin going steady! There is lots of time ahead, besides, you are losing out in the fun. Two people soon become tired of each other. Then there is the danger of kissing and petting. Why are they wrong? Because they can cause immodest and impure thoughts and desires. (1954, 72)

A steady boyfriend could also lead to an awkward moment when he would have to be told that the relationship had no future. There were pictures of Bernie's former fiancé hovering in the background at her farewell party, although he was not identified as such. In *Springs of Silence* Sister Mary Gilbert remembered that she waited until after her prom to tell her steady escort. He did not take the news well but nonetheless escorted her to her last party. He was never referred to again, as if the boy's feelings in this matter were not a great concern (Gilbert 1954, 14). In fact, Sister Mary Maureen argued that the experience of dating a girl who was planning to enter the convent all along might actually prove beneficial to the young man by helping to awaken his vocation to the priesthood (Maureen 1967, 43).

The final entering-day outfit became a part of the total ritual of a girl laying aside the first part of her life in order to join a religious community. Much attention was paid to selecting the perfect suit to wear to the convent before it was exchanged forever for the habit. Bernie's outfit, once discarded and hung neatly on a clothes rack, became a symbol of that liminal transition. A full-page photograph of it with the simple caption 'I had entered!' captured both the excitement and the sacrifice of her vocation (del Ray 1956, 41). Another sister fondly recalled the lavish attention she spared on her final outfit, much to her mother's confusion:

First, I got a crisp new permanent. Then I bought a new pair of silk hose (nylons were as yet to be invented) which item was definitely not on the Sister's list. I applied brilliant lipstick, with matching polish on my fingernails, and put on my favourite red high heels. I wore my newest silk dress, and completed the ensemble with rhinestone earrings, white gloves and hat. (Now, only on very special dates did I wear gloves or hat.) What Mom didn't realize was that this time I was keeping the biggest date of my life. Everything, even the tiniest detail, was significant to me – and to Him. (X 1958, 101)

Again, there was the implication that girls should not confuse piety with disdain for feminine appearances. Yet this particular recollection suggests another key theme that permeated vocation books. The idea that entering a convent was the same as 'keeping a date' with an important and demanding suitor was a common trope. It went further than just dating. In the postwar era sisters were still regarded as 'Brides of Christ,' the lovers and mothers of all humanity. This appellation was to prove embarrassing to those reform-minded sisters of the post–Vatican II era. They remarked on its 'incredibly bad theology,' since the term 'Bride of Christ,' from the Old Testament's *Song of Songs*, was meant to refer to the Catholic Church, not to Catholic women nor even to a particularly holy set of women within the church (Novak 1966, 25). However it did prove useful in vocation books since it provided an opportunity to inspire girls with tales of love and romance and fostered a convent culture in which bridal motifs were deeply woven into almost all rituals.

In an era in which marriage seemed inevitable to girls, it is not hard to understand why vocation books incorporated so many bridal motifs into their stories. Various studies in the fifties placed the average marrying age for women between twenty and twenty-two, depending on the survey. They also reported that 70 per cent of women in America were married by the age of twenty-four and only 9 per cent remained single throughout their lives. During the peak years of the baby boom, more than four million children were born annually (Breines 1992, 50; Oakley 1986, 291; 'Women Have It' 1957, 94). The overwhelming inclination towards marriage and motherhood greatly affected the kinds of educational opportunities available to girls and circumscribed their extra-curricular activities. Vocation books obviously were not interested in promoting the benefits of matrimony. Yet they could not avoid the pervasive pressure on girls to eventually marry and settle down in the suburbs. Rather than directly challenge this domestic ideology, they managed to find ways to highlight how the religious life incorporated the most fun aspects of marriage – the showers, parties, wedding dresses, and elaborate ceremonies – but with even greater rewards awaiting those who willingly wed themselves to the Catholic Church. This is not to suggest that congregations adopted bridal–like ceremonies in order to appeal to potential new recruits. The ceremonies and traditions had been in place for a long time, but like everything else about the religious life, they were not well known to the public. In the fifties, marriage-like rituals were expanded to incorporate the time spent preparing to enter a convent so that, overall, the Bride of Christ image was heightened in vocation books to conform to the attitudes and dispositions of postwar society.

Sometimes vocation books opened with teasing references to wedding customs. Sister Mary Gilbert remarked, 'My trousseau was reasonably complete by mid-July' (1954, 1). Sister Maryanna started with, 'Like many another bride, I wore white. My wedding gown was no Dior original; in fact, the model was about seven hundred and fifty years old, but I loved it' (1964, 7). By invoking images of traditional wedding rituals right at the start, both books made an immediate connection to domestic ideology. They also hinted at an aura of romance that pervaded vocation books. Indeed, there were very few customs associated with marriage – from the purchase of a special trousseau to elaborate wedding gowns and gold rings – which did not have a corresponding tradition in the convent.

The trousseau was so named because every girl entering a convent was expected to bring with her a very precise wardrobe, much of which had to be specially purchased. Many of the books relate with humour young women roaming department stores in search of old-fashioned rubbers, heavy black cotton hosiery, or pens with silver – not gold – trim. The lengthy lists of clothes, writing and sewing supplies, and religious accessories could often be overwhelming. That is why some vocation books recommended that friends throw a special convent shower in honour of the new entrant. *Bernie Becomes a Nun* included pictures from one such shower along with a helpful list of gift suggestions. It included ornamental ideas such as crucifixes and small statues of religious figures alongside more practical selections of boy-sized handkerchiefs, black gloves, and unscented soap (del Ray 1956, 17–20). Of course, just as it was for all brides-to-be, the pleasures of trousseaus and showers were mere stepping stones to the big event itself. For girls entering the convent, the excitement of a wedding ceremony was not to be denied them even if they had rejected marriage for what was supposed to be a higher spiritual calling.

When they first entered, girls were called postulants and were not required to wear a habit or conform strictly to the religious rule. After this period, which lasted anywhere from six months to a year depending on the congregation, they would then move on to the second phase of the religious life as novices. In a special reception ceremony (also known as the investiture ceremony or the clothing ceremony) they wore lay clothes for the last time in their lives before receiving the habit. After a year or more of service and instruction, they were invited to make their first vows. These would be temporary, requiring renewal every one to three years until final, formal vows were taken. There was no ambiguity about the vows being the equivalent of a marriage. Even the more progressive communities, such as the Marists in *Those Whom God Chooses*, stated unequivocally that 'With these vows, she promises to live at God's side, belonging only to Him and serving Him through love. She looks upon profession as the equivalent of marriage. Her vows mean that she has 'forsaken all others,' that she will never look back in regret to another life, that she will stifle the lovely songs of memory and the call of her desires for the world' (Villet and Villet 1966, 62). At least she still got cake, as one of the accompanying pictures featured a young professed nun standing before an elaborate wedding cake with a statue of Mary replacing the more usual bride and groom on top.

For the momentous occasion of investiture it is no surprise that the postulants' final lay dress should be a spectacular one. Not all congregations included wedding dresses as part of the ceremony, but a good many of them did. ... *And Spare Me Not in the Making* included a drawing of postulants dressed in flowing gowns with short bridal veils covering their faces and carrying bouquets of lilies as they marched down the church aisle. Sister Catherine Frederic recalled the thrill of the moment: 'What emotion filled my heart as I donned the bridal satin, and reflected that it was no earthly groom who was to take me for his spouse, but the heavenly Bridegroom Himself!' (1954, 48). Sister Mary

A newly professed nun celebrates her marriage to Christ by cutting the wedding cake. In *Those Whom God Chooses*.

Francis described one woman as a 'princess' and painted a picture of a blushing bride as romantic as any story in *True Love* magazine:

> Kathy wore palest ivory satin and lace. She looked like a debutante, and was one in the very truest sense of the word. Her long satin train was looped up over her arm, waiting to trail its full glory in the chapel. The dark curls were not flattened back today, but fell loose and shining about her face under the cloud of veil with its creaming lace panels. Kathy had a corsage of white roses against her shoulder and a string of pearls about her neck. The Irish eyes were not pools of blue laughter this morning; they were dark and dreaming. We all caught our breath, as we always do – all a little shy of this lovely young bride and most of us seeing her through a faint mist of the tears a great tenderness always evokes. (1957, 82)

With imagery such as this, she concluded, 'it would require a heart totally devoid of poetry and quite dead to romance not to be touched and quickened' (83).

The connection to marriage did not end once first vows were taken. Becoming a sister continued to be defined in terms of traditional heterosexual relationships, not as a heroic act of one individual woman defying convention. This tendency to define women's identity in terms of their relationships was not unique to vocation books. Janice Radway has commented on the tendency in romance fiction to define heroines in terms of their roles as lovers, wives, and mothers. By making feminine identity always a question of 'relational destiny,' the romance reasserts the inability of women to be accepted as self-reliant, autonomous individuals (1984, 207). Radway's definition of romance has much in common with the vocation books of the postwar era. Aside from such narrative conventions as a doting attention to clothes and other incidental features of the heroine's environment, there seemed to be the same kind of ideological pull towards a lasting relationship with the hero. As *Her Prince Charming* concluded, 'Finally, when she has reached that point in her life when the PRINCE sees that she has completely given herself to this transforming work – when she has fulfilled the pattern and is fully the princess she is meant to be – she will find herself already in eternity, living with her PRINCE happily ever after.' Sister Mary Gilbert also resorted to the conventional 'happily ever after' conclusion. She wrote, 'He had taken her at her word while she was still young and strong in faith; before the judgement of shortsighted men could err. She was all His – irretrievably His – and forever!' (1954, 208). The twist to each of these romantic endings was that the sister-heroine in both cases had died, thus adding an extra dimension to the romance with an evocative deathbed scene.

If the romance did not end in an early death, then it followed a predictable path into motherhood. It seemed that not even consecrated celibacy could let a woman escape the demands of maternalism. The attention to childcare in vocation books was not simply ideological, however. The reality of the religious life was that sisters would likely be in steady contact with children either in schools or orphanages or hospitals. Perhaps it was felt that by creating a fiction of family life and mothering within the convent, the enormous workload of sisters would appear to be no less than those of other women. Certainly, there was an attitude in the vocation books that, despite their celibate, communal lifestyle, sisters still needed their maternal, nurturing instincts fulfilled. Sister Mary Gilbert made this overarching sense of maternal duty explicit: 'God made women to be mothers ... And unless you utilize that capacity for motherhood, you can never attain to the fulfilment of your powers. You renounce motherhood in the natural order only to become mothers in a higher and spiritual order. You have no other choice. Either you must cultivate that God-given instinct, or you must be sour old maids' (1954, 114). Sister Maryanna concurred with this explanation of how the vow of chastity in fact awakened an even deeper sense of maternalism in sisters: 'By her vow of virginity a Sister renounces marriage and children of her own, but she does not renounce her maternal instincts or her other natural qualities as a woman. Chastity is not a negative restraint which represses her God-given gifts as a woman and a mother, but rather it is a positive force effecting their spiritual fulfilment through union with Christ' (1964, 45).

This imposition of a traditional but sexless family structure onto the stories of the convent began first by relating a girl's earliest sense of a vocation to the rituals of romance, wooing, and marriage. It was deepened by associating her religious duties and responsibilities with a naturalized ideology of maternalism. Finally, it was made the foundation of the religious life by taking the titles Sisters and Mother Superior literally and turning a congregation of adult women into a kind of all-female foster family. The loss of close family ties was studiously downplayed in vocation books. Sister Maryanna recalled her lack of sorrow that her father – her only living relative – had not come to her reception ceremony. Instead, she informed her superior that her family had indeed come. 'I had a Mother and a couple of hundred sisters,' she insisted (27). The blitheness with which a young woman could turn away from her first family and embrace a community of near-strangers as her new family was considered a sign of vocational strength. In *Those Whom God Chooses* the fact that one postulant was overcome with fear the night before her entrance and sought out her father to console her was a kind of foreshadowing that her vocation would not last (Villet and Villet 1966, 12–7). After her departure, the mistress of postulants reminded the rest of the class that they needed to transform their sense of family in order to thrive in the religious life: 'Turn your thoughts only to Him and you can gain for your families a supernatural grace that could never otherwise be theirs. Let your sisters be your family ... You are entering a new family – one that includes your own but one which is much greater' (35).

Taken as a whole, the family structure of the congregation coupled with the idea of a spiritual marriage and a supernatural sense of motherhood were strategies for cultivating a traditional sense of bourgeois heterosexual femininity as integral to the formation of a religious. However, the hidden subtext of all this was a fear of homosexuality in particular and a dread of female sexuality in general. Infantilizing new recruits as spiritual daughters to the religious hierarchy went hand in hand with a culture that policed personal or particular friendships. While the idea of 'PFs' was rarely addressed directly in vocation books, it nonetheless made its presence felt in the overall absence of anything to do with close, personal relationships and in the emphasis on childish group activities, such as a snowball fight depicted in a two-page spread in *Those Whom God Chooses*. PFs were dissuaded as signs of 'delayed adolescence,' and cautions were raised that 'a nun with strong homosexual tendencies would encounter grave and permanent difficulties' (Rousset 1955, 202).

By the mid-sixties more progressive sisters were seeking to temper this homophobic attitude, without actually going so far as to suggest that homosexuality was not a sin. Sister Judith Tate argued that, spiritually, all nuns were bisexual and friendships could be an outlet for sexual frustration that would otherwise manifest itself in homosexuality (1966,

80). Interestingly, in the name of personalism and spiritual authenticity, the ban on PFs was lifted in the sixties, and it became prestigious for a nun to have a personal or passionate friend above all others, to prove that she was with the times (Raphaela 1989, 82). Perhaps this was a compensatory attitude towards a society that was increasingly sceptical of celibacy. As Margaret Mead told one sister, 'American society no longer appreciates choices which are perceived as contrary to the prevalent notion of sex as physically and psychologically necessary to the well-adjusted "whole" person' (Oberg 1967, 68). Nonetheless, even with these relaxed rules, the message of the vocation books remained rife with traditional values of spiritual marriage and motherhood, perhaps to offset the possibility of enticing women for whom the convent seemed a respectable escape from what they saw as the drudgery of domestic heterosexuality.

Vocation books certainly must have offered some attraction for those women who were looking for a way out of the suburbs, with their promises of heroic, exciting, and exotic adventures in far-flung places. On the back cover of *With Love and Laughter*, there is the promise of 'an unusual Mother, several hundred Sisters, over a thousand children, and the joy of travel and literary creation' (1964). Sister Mary Maureen also referred to the benefits awaiting those who left their families behind to answer the call: 'Most of us have been given the opportunity of a better than average education; many of us have done extensive travelling' (Maureen 1967, 40). Unlike the usual 'happily ever after' endings of romances, the heroines in vocation books did not retreat into the sunset to bear children and clean house. Instead, they travelled the world doing important work or studied diligently to attain graduate degrees and professional accreditation. The allure of exciting adventures was not contrapuntal to the matrimonial theme but was offered as the logical outcome of embracing the natural feminine instinct for love and raising it to a supernatural level. Only by a deep and abiding sense of love could a woman be elevated in her aspirations and realize the total fulfilment of a vocation.

It was very important that girls not confuse a vocation with ambition. The single most important difference between the two was defined as love. Love was treated as an inalienable virtue in women that could not be overcome, but had to be intensified and broadened to a higher spiritual calling. As Sister Mary Gilbert explained, 'it is love that gives motive and meaning to her every action. Love is the vital current which charges all her activities – even the apparently inconsequential – with a mysterious power' (1954, 115). This overwhelming sense of love that was cultivated in all young sisters was trumpeted as an act of supreme selflessness that would, deceptively, lead to opportunities for enhanced self-awareness and personal enrichment. The model of this double-pronged love in the vocation books was the Virgin Mary. However, unlike in domestic Mariology, it was neither her self-effacing demeanour nor her sacrificial sense of submission to the will of God that was promoted. Rather, Mary was presented as a model of energy, passion, and commitment. Sister Catherine Frederic recommended her as a thoroughly up-to-date woman who could guide girls through their most difficult times: 'Is she then not the most modern of women, understanding as she does the problems of each particular country and period? Mary, the Mother, the Co-Redemptrix, the Healer, the Advocate, is truly the model for all career women to follow' (1954, 5).

Sister Mary Maureen echoed that image of Mary as an independent, confident woman who could act more as a role model and less as a maternal figure for young aspirants. She claimed that Mary was 'far from being the sweet, plaster-faced, innocent little thing whose image we see above side altars. She is smart; she is infinitely deep; she is hard-hitting and she means business' (1967, 60). Transforming the identity of the ultimate mother and virgin into a sophisticated career woman was rather innovative, to say the least. It expanded the potential of pious femininity while still containing its radicalness. The lesson of Mary was that a career was simply not good enough for women. They needed to strive for something greater in the big picture of their lives. In that way, vocation books could promote exciting opportunities in the fields of education, medicine, and the arts without actually deviating from the conventional societal attitude that women lacked ambition and only worked to make life better for others around them.

Even as late as 1968 a study on personality characteristics among college women confirmed traditional gender stereotypes in concluding that women who sought only a career and not marriage tended to behave in a more masculine manner. This conclusion was based upon a continuum that defined conservatism and conventionalism as feminine traits while deeming leadership and intellectualism to be masculine. Those women who did not rank 'making sacrifices' or 'being well liked' as important life goals were considered more likely to seek out a career exclusively and place their femininity in jeopardy (Rand 1971, 160–2). The study concluded that career-oriented college women had therefore 'deviated from the traditional feminine role' (164).

Sisters steered clear of any such criticisms by their doctrine of supernatural love manifested in a network of pseudo-family relationships including a divine spouse, foster children, a spiritual mother, and a host of sisters. Yet that didn't prevent some women from looking to the convent not as a greater spiritual calling to the bonds of love, defined on strictly heterosexual terms, but as an escape hatch. In the landmark book *Lesbian Nuns: Breaking Silence*, more than a few admitted that their vocation was not exactly God-given. As one of the editors admitted, the purpose behind the book was 'to find my Lesbian sisters who had entered the convent, not only as a response to a call from God, but as a refuge from heterosexuality, Catholic marriage, and exhausting motherhood' (Curb and Manahan 1985, xx). That is not to suggest that all lesbians who entered did so without faith. Sister Vickie, for example, was able to admit much later in life that her desire to join a convent had to do with the fact that she 'wanted desperately to do something different with my life, to be special and unique' (1989, 102). Despite her sexual crisis, exacerbated by a repressive structure that tried to prevent her from exploring her homosexuality, she eventually found reconciliation within herself, based on a personalist theology of passionate love for humanity.

Aware of the allure the convent would have on girls not interested in snaring a husband, vocation books were able to encourage girls to experiment with their intellectual and professional potential and cross gender boundaries without upsetting sexual mores. This was due to an unrelenting association of women's service with love couched in heterosexist language but fluid enough for some to transform it into a personalist quest for an authentic, passionate self. Safely embedded within this culture of supernatural love were all kinds of opportunities available to girls who wanted to join a convent. In the course of *Bernie Becomes a Nun*, the heroine became a teacher in New York's Chinatown and later sailed to Bolivia to begin her missionary career. She also learned plumbing and other useful skills that few women would have had in this era (del Ray 1956). *Those Whom God Chooses* was neatly divided into two parts, the first dealing with the girlish pleasures and anxieties of joining the convent. By the second half, the giddiness of cake and girlish capers were replaced by the harsh reality of missionary life. Sister doctors and nurses ventured into the slums of Peru to offer care and comfort to the world's most dispossessed. One image of a sister hovering over a dying child was especially provocative. Evoking a sense of the nativity, the sister is nonetheless an active, forceful presence, not a passive Madonna. It is clear that she comes with a near-supernatural authority to the peasants who so desperately need women like her, willing to give up her world for theirs.

Yet the books took pains to insist that girls not use the pretence of a vocation in order to fulfil other dreams. Sister Mary Francis put it dryly: 'the cloister is not a placement bureau. A girl who enters the Order to write or to paint or to develop any other real or supposed talent is making a gross and pathetic error' (1957, 69). This warning did not necessarily mean that girls could not develop their talents, but that they had to be willing to sacrifice those talents at first in order to ultimately realize them on a deeper level. Sister Mary Gilbert described a young sister who loved to paint but did not really enjoy teaching. Why she ever decided to join a teaching congregation was not questioned. Instead, the sister decided that she had to live with her decision and make teaching her passion. She went to the mother superior to hand in her art supplies but was surprised when her act of sacrifice was rejected. Her superior, well aware of the young sister's dilemma, was only waiting for a gesture of heartfelt sacrifice so that she could be assured of her vocation. Once that was given the sister was freed from her sense of failure and sent to an art college. As the story concluded, 'today that nun is a college art teacher, one of the best in her field, and a well-adjusted individual' (1954, 123). That final comment speaks to the importance sisters placed on being considered normal, average, and healthy women – in other words, embracing middle-class and heterosexual values – even while they argued theirs was a supernatural way of life. The religious calling was thus a way to meet two otherwise incompatible goals, to keep girls contained by the doctrines of femininity while they strike out on adventures all their own. Put another way, unlike the college students of the 1968 study, vocation books promised girls that they could simultaneously assert their independence and intellect and keep their claim to feminine beguilement securely intact through the demure chastity of the habit.

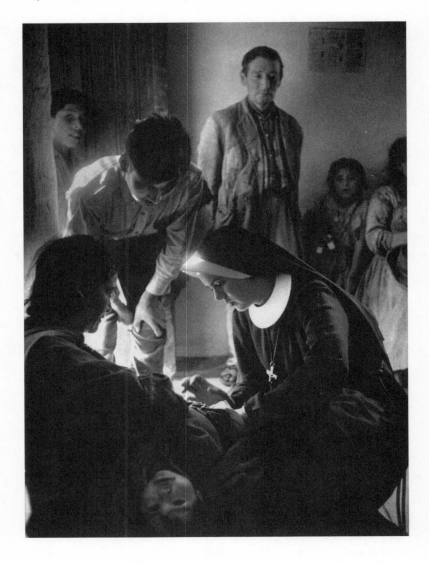

Sister Mary Thomas More, a doctor, tries to ease the suffering of a dying child. In *Those Whom God Chooses*.

The religious life was represented in vocation books as a richly rewarding experience filled with love, romance, adventure, and all kinds of girlish frivolity. Over and over again, vocation books emphasized a sense of vivacity and joy permeating the convent but most apparent in the communities' youngest and most sincere recruits. As one book put it, 'Postulants have a reputation for being giggly creatures. You see them all around the convent, flitting here and there in shortish black dresses, usually ducking around corners with other postulants and just bursting with some new adventure' (del Ray 1956, 27). Others spoke candidly of the great adventure of religious life. Sister Catherine Frederic concluded her book with the straightforward statement, 'That is what I would like to emphasize – the adventure and romance of the religious life' (1954, 93). At the heart of every vocation book was the promise that sisters would have a bigger, bolder, and more exciting life than their schoolmates who had gone the usual route of marriage and motherhood. At a time when schools were fixated on promoting domesticity as the primary goal for their female students, vocation books promised girls unprecedented opportunities to travel to exotic lands, learn new skills, and encounter different cultures. However, these promises were tightly wrapped in sexually repressive discourses that did not criticize or question domesticity but rather elevated it to a supernatural level. In effect, the religious life was remodelled to fit the expectations society had already placed on middle-class girls.

It was not until late in the sixties that sisters really began to assert a public position of radicalness and challenge the attitudes that they themselves had previously fostered. It was neither an easy nor a quick transition. As the remarkable similarity in the vocation books show, whether they were published in the early fifties or late sixties, critical introspection on the religious life was reserved for those books directed at vowed sisters and adults who were interested in the religious debates of the day. In the critically themed book *The Changing Sister*, Sister Marie Augusta Neal complained that the idea of treating the community as one big family fostered a kind of infantilism among religious sisters, who could not think or act without first seeking approval (1965, 35). It is perhaps telling that when the Immaculate Hearts of Mary congregation first began to splinter into traditionalists and reformists as early as 1967, one of the first acts of the reform-minded mother superior was to reject her religious name and title of Mother General Humiliata.

She insisted that she be called Sister Anita Caspary and her title be changed to president ('Priests and Nuns' 1970, 55). Yet even the later vocation books published after Vatican II still retained a sense of congregational familialism. As Sister Mary Maureen explained, 'Most religious are reluctant to tell young people about this. Perhaps they feel that it might make us too human. But we are human. We live a family life, with all the give and take, the ups and downs, the heartaches and headaches that this implies' (1967, 38). Other issues such as habits, rules, and authority systems were identified by M. Charles Borromeo in *The New Nuns* as some of the most pressing issues facing women religious in the aftermath of the Second Vatican Council (1967, 208). Yet in vocation books sisters were rarely shown in modified habits, even though the edict to modernize came in the early fifties. Additionally, a great deal of emphasis was placed on adherence to the rules and submission to the authority of the mother superior through the invocation of a family structure.

It is important to point out that not all the conventions of the vocation books were being swept away by the sister reformists. In *The Changing Sister*, Sister M. Elena Malits praised the unique workings of the feminine mind with its focus on love and personal, rather than professional, fulfilment and reiterated the idea that the religious life was a supernatural state (1965, 90). Even as late as 1969 a book on the religious life for women, written by a man, reiterated the traditional doctrines of femininity and asserted that a woman 'has the need to be of service to others and the need to surrender' (McAllister 1969, 106). Although this book received only a qualified endorsement from the sister who wrote the preface, she still supported the argument that love and personal fulfilment spurred women to action more than any kind of professional, intellectual, or creative ambition. This is not necessarily a criticism either of vocation books or of the myriad books on the religious life that sought a more adult audience. Clearly, entering the religious life did – and still does – require an enormous capacity for love, compassion, and sacrifice. However, it took sisters some time before they could come to terms with how these ideals could be best expressed and communicated during the two-decade period of reform. What began as sentimentality over the religious life slowly transmuted into personalism, a more politically astute response to changing times, but one steeped in romanticism and the middle-American values of belonging and togetherness.

5

Sing Out, Sister!
Sacred Music and the Feminized Folk
Scene

By the beginning of the Second Vatican Council the role of the nun in
the world was just beginning to be formulated. Films and books had yet
to find a way to make the revolutionary changes in the convent dramatically interesting. Thus, the religious life was, in the early sixties, still in
a fixed state of enlightened feminine industriousness as far as the mass
media were concerned. Vocation books did little to help this image, especially with their girlish, near-frivolous approach to the religious life. As
a result, the most accessible medium through which sisters could really
begin to make their personal, spiritual, and political struggles known was
popular music. Throughout the sixties sisters began to explore the potential of song to communicate the renewed sense of popular piety initiated
by Vatican II. They also sought to establish themselves within a matrix
of social progressivism that had more in common with beat poets and
folksingers than it did with old-fashioned religious values of obedience
and discipline. However, the reforms to Catholic music at this time
spoke little to the immediate circumstances of women's lives but rather
to that other, more nebulous side of the analysis presented here. I am
referring to the troubled sense of religiosity in relationship to postwar
American values and the rise of a feminized form of spiritual and civic
responsibility that came to be known as personalism. The image of singing nuns became a signifier of new forms of piety and forged a link early
in the sixties between the burgeoning counterculture and the renewal of
the religious life. Unfortunately, this image quickly froze into the idealized stereotype of the new nuns, a feminized image of radicalized spirituality, social consciousness, and demure sincerity.

Music was one of the most strictly regulated practices in the Catholic

Church and the only form of artistic training for all vowed religious. It did not fall under the same rubric as film, television, or radio broadcasting insofar as they were considered media of social communication. Musical practice was a cornerstone of the Catholic liturgy and a form of prayer. The liturgy – the system of public worship in church – was, until the sixties, firmly in the hands of the clerical hierarchy. The contribution of sisters to sacred music production was in their monastic regime of regular prayer and chant according to ancient rules and customs. Thus, for sisters to record albums in the early sixties was an unprecedented leap into the culture of their times. That some choirs chose to record popular songs from Broadway or Tin Pan Alley must have seemed incredible to those who had only ever seen sisters sing medieval chants and hymns behind a grille during mass. It would be easy to dismiss such efforts as innocuous or even as kitsch, but such a dismissal would neglect to acknowledge the purpose of such efforts to reach out to audiences outside the confines of the parochial network. It also would not take into account the recording industry's interest in exploiting the spiritual enthusiasm taking over the country.

The Singing Sisters of Mount St Mary and the Jesus and Mary Choral Group recorded in the early sixties with the support of Columbia Records, which encouraged them to use popular standards in addition to, or even instead of, hymns or other sacred music. Their goal in recording was not so much spiritual as it was financial; namely, fundraising for their respective congregations. Nonetheless, they strove to incorporate inspirational messages of joy, hope, and faith by virtue of their presence in the religious habit and their sweetly harmonic performance. Later, when sisters began to write their own material using the idioms of popular music, they were again on the cusp of revolutionary changes to Catholicism – a fact that did not endear them to the hierarchy any more than did their shortened skirts and missing veils.

Sister Miriam Therese Winter was at the vanguard of these reappraisals of sacred music. She was one of the first nuns to write and perform original songs based on scriptural passages using popular and folk arrangements, and relying more on guitars and bongos than the traditional church instrument of the organ. Her venture may not have been so readily received had it not been for the phenomenal success of a young Belgian sister, Soeur Luc-Gabrielle, aka Soeur Sourire or The Singing Nun. Her song 'Dominique' rose to the top of the pop charts in

1963 and turned her into a cultural icon. In America the craze for The Singing Nun brought to mass attention the enormous importance of the Second Vatican Council and helped spark initial interest in the new nuns. The troubadour stylings of these sisters were considered part of their experiments with urban ministries and community outreach in keeping with the convent reform movement. Thus, these shifts in sacred music were not incidental to *aggiornamento*. Rather, they were the culmination of reform efforts that had begun over fifty years earlier and were reflective of larger shifts in the social and political conscience of vowed religious.

During the first half of the century, sacred music was defined strictly as art music and was the privileged domain of men charged with overseeing the liturgy. Over the years both lay and clerical reformers sought to incorporate 'worldly music' that would resonate more with the faithful than esoteric chant. By the time that Pius XII had loosened the restraints on sacred music in 1955 with his encyclical *Musicae Sacrae*, there had already been significant shifts in the make-up of American Catholic society that placed triumphalism in jeopardy. This separatist policy was established early in the century to preserve traditional Catholic values against encroaching modernism and liberalism. As Catholics joined the middle class and moved out of their close-knit urban neighbourhoods into the suburbs, the cultural boundaries that had previously divided them from Protestants began to blur, leaving church rituals as the most clear-cut distinction between the two. Since religious affiliation was the most obvious marker of cultural difference, it also became the most contentious.

Catholics were eager to participate in the American dream but had lurking fears that their religion, which had been treated with disdain and distrust in the past, could block their access to middle-class complacency. However, postwar debates over Catholicism were based only on the thorny issue of Catholics in positions of authority and decision making. Critiques of the material culture of the religion, its practices, and its rituals were kept to a bare minimum (Welter 1987, 52–3). As Paul Blanshard, the rabid anti-Catholic critic, wrote:

> It is for this reason that I am addressing Catholics fully as much as non-Catholics in this book. American freedom is your freedom, and any curtailment of that freedom by clerical power is an even more serious matter

for you than it is for non-Catholics. I know that many Catholics are as
deeply disturbed as I am about the social policies of their church's rulers,
and they are finding it increasingly difficult to reconcile their convictions
as American democrats with the philosophy of their priests, their hierarchy, and their Pope. (Blanshard 1958, 4)

As long as Catholicism remained disconnected from public life it could
be viewed as a romantic and evocative tradition, giving people a link to
a past they had never lived. Assigning Catholicism these secondary values feminized the religion in a way that defused tensions between Catholics and Protestants and did not interfere with Catholics' aspirations to
become fully Americanized in all other aspects of their daily life.

The feminization of Catholicism was so thoroughly accepted that
Walter Ong, the popular social critic and Jesuit priest, complained that
Catholic authority had a weak hold on men and that women had been
misguidedly left in charge of matters of faith (1961, 26). Obviously, he
was not suggesting that women were taking on clerical duties, but that
they were the primary exemplars of Catholicism to the rest of society.
Furthermore, since they were not in any position to act as authoritative
voices of the Catholic Church, their efforts could only be evocative or
suggestive of the benefits of Catholic piety rather than instructional or
dogmatic. Perhaps, in this era of civil religion, the quixotic representation of women religious helped belie the suspicions of those who agreed
with Blanshard and his ilk. Yet there were still many obstacles prevent-
ing sisters from reaching out to the public. Contact with secular society
remained strictly limited until closer to the end of the Second Vatican
Council, so that interviews or public discussions about the religious life
would still have to wait. The Conference of Major Superiors of Women
and the Sister Formation Conference were working hard to modernize
the religious life, but their focus was on first building networks between
congregations and the hierarchy and then branching out into the world.
The vocation books were helpful insofar as recruitment to the convent
was booming with over twenty thousand more sisters at the end of the
fifties than at the beginning. Still, sisters were looking for ways to
improve their public profile as well as earn some badly needed funds to
accommodate all the new entrants. With the more relaxed attitude
towards music, many congregations formed non-liturgical choirs for
concerts and recordings geared mainly to a lay audience.

It is easy to understand why so many congregations turned to music. Musical training was mandatory for sisters and part of any postulant program. The Sister Formation Conference actively supported musical training as a fundamental element in the development of a religious, regardless of the specific apostolate of her congregation. Despite such a commitment, there were still many limitations on sisters' musical training. For one thing, liturgical singing was only to happen within the confines of the convent chapel and only when no men were present to sing in their place. Pius X forbade outright the presence of any women in the choir since it could imply that they were playing a quasi-clerical role (1903 V:13). Fifty years later Pius XII modified that edict to allow for the discretion of the parish priest, but he insisted that women be placed outside the sanctuary of the altar and be properly separated from the men (Carlen 1981, 288). With such restrictions in force, it seems that sisters were in a better position to take advantage of the recently relaxed rules on extraliturgical singing rather than try to improve their role in the liturgy proper. They thus became the initial promoters of a spiritually inflected popular music tradition within Catholicism.

One of the first congregations to experiment with popular music was the Religious of Jesus and Mary in Hyattsville, Maryland. Looking for a fund-raising venture to build a badly needed noviciate dormitory, the sisters decided to forego the traditional money-making activities of specialty foods or fancy needlework. Instead they formed a seventeen-member choir from the postulant and noviciate ranks and recorded an album. Their first attempt in 1960 was a modest effort that sold only through the convent and its school. However, it caught the attention of George P. Morse, the father of one of the postulants in the choir, who pushed the sisters to try again with a more professional product. With his help they formed a production and marketing committee and recorded *Patterns in Song*, which was released by Empire Records late in 1960. What makes this particular record interesting is that the sisters divided their repertory into religious and non-religious music. On side one there were Gregorian chants and traditional hymns, in keeping with the direction for sacred music sanctioned by the pope. Side two, however, was filled with folk songs and Tin Pan Alley standards such as 'The Woman in the Shoe,' selected to highlight the congregation's space crisis. The success of this album was more than any of them had anticipated. In less than three weeks they sold more than ten thousand copies, and orders continued to pour in. Promotional packages were sent to radio stations across the country with a promise from Mother Mary Immaculata that they would place any DJ who played their record on their own special 'prayola' list, a knowing reference to recent payola scandals (Religious of Jesus and Mary [RJM] Archives). The sisters even produced their own half-hour special for the local NBC affiliate television station. Entitled *The Sisters in the Shoe*, the show featured songs from the album and gave audiences a chance to see the choir members up close.

Not long after the release of *Patterns of Song*, the congregation was contacted by Ernie Altschuler, an A&R producer at Columbia Records. They soon changed record labels and began production on their follow-up album, a Christmas collection called *Gesu Bambino*. By this point the recording project had become a full-fledged cottage industry for the sisters, with production, publicity, and distribution all run from the convent. As Columbia quickly learned, the rules of cloister made it difficult for the novices and postulants to leave the convent. By way of a compromise during the recording of the first album, choir members temporarily donned the full habit and veil of the professed sisters, so that their cloister was maintained at a symbolic level. However, once it appeared likely that recording would continue to be a major part of the new entrants' everyday life, the sisters insisted that the studio come to them. Columbia complied and would arrive annually with an army of equipment and personnel.

The choral group recorded four albums for Columbia, until 1963. Each was a mix of folk songs, popular standards, and traditional hymns. The only exclusively religious album was *Life of Love*, which was released in 1963, right before their second Christmas recording, *Joyfully Yours*, the more successful album of the two. The group's association with Columbia also brought them into contact with other professional music artists. Mother Mary of Joy's solo rendition of 'O Holy Night' was included on Columbia's all-star Christmas album in 1962, alongside such performers as Frankie Laine, Doris Day, and Aretha Franklin. The choir appeared on the *Perry Como Show*'s Christmas special in 1961. The jazz guitarist Charlie Byrd was the guest accompanist on *Joyfully Yours*, flying right in the face of Catholic tradition, which abhorred both jazz and the guitar equally. The albums were favourably reviewed across the country, causing Mother Mary Immaculata to maintain subscriptions to *Variety*, *Bill-*

board, and *Cash Box* so she could track sales and promotion. Once the sisters had raised more than enough money for their capital improvements, they decided to stop recording professionally. By that time the Second Vatican Council had just begun and new directions in the religious life were beginning to be suggested. The Jesus and Mary Choral Group had achieved its goals, and in so doing awakened the potential for music as a vehicle for the promotion of the religious life. Their success encouraged other congregations to experiment with popular music for their own fund-raising needs. One of the more successful of these was the Singing Sisters of Mount St Mary, in upstate New York.

The Sisters of St Dominic were facing the same problem as the Religious of Jesus and Mary when they, too, decided to venture into the music industry. Vocations were booming and the college they ran, Mount St Mary, had a ready store of eager new entrants every year. By 1961 it was clear that new housing would have to be built, and so out of necessity the Singing Sisters were formed. Unlike the Religious of Jesus and Mary, there was no choir already in place at Mount St Mary, but one of the sisters had studied music before she joined and agreed to put together a choral group for the project. As luck would have it, another member had a brother who was a priest in Rochester, New York, and was acquainted with Mitch Miller. By this time Miller was a well-known record producer and showman. As an A&R producer with Columbia Records, he had nurtured the career of teen heart-throb Frankie Laine. By the sixties he had become disillusioned with the direction of popular music and decided to create a venue for the Tin Pan Alley standards he loved. First there was the *Sing Along with Mitch* record series – eleven in total – followed by a television variety show of the same name. The mother superior, along with the choir director, Sister Jeanne d'Arc, and the priest's sister, Sister Rose Anita, arranged a meeting with Miller. Perhaps because Columbia was already enjoying success with the Jesus and Mary Choral Group, Miller was eager to provide every assistance to this new group of singing sisters. As Mother Leo Vincent said in a memo to her congregation, 'His magnanimity left the Sisters rather breathless but most grateful' (Dominican Sisters of Hope [DSH] Archives).

On Miller's recommendation the sisters selected a repertory of popular standards, Broadway show tunes, and folk hymns. Traditional Catholic religious music was discouraged since it would likely not appeal to a broad audience. They sent him their list and he made the final selection based on a theme he had chosen for them, joy, which became the title of the album. In the meantime a sixty-five-member choir was assembled from the motherhouse and the smaller mission houses across the country. With Miller's help they were able to receive professional training from arrangers and vocal teachers. A management and publicity team was also formed with eight sisters handling distribution, tour bookings, and media relations, among other duties. The album was cut late in 1962 at Columbia's state-of-the-art recording studios free of charge. The record company did not take ownership of the album but suggested that the sisters handle sales themselves so that they could receive one hundred per cent of the profit. Within a year they had raised over one hundred thousand dollars and received special permission from the bishop to appear on *Sing Along with Mitch*, where they sang 'Maria' from *The Sound of Music* and 'Seventy-six Trombones' from *The Music Man*. A follow-up album, *More Joy*, was issued in 1964, but by that time the necessary funds had been raised for the capital project and the mother superior put an end to their singing careers. 'We're a teaching order, not entertainers,' she told an interviewer (DSH Archives).

The success of sister choral groups was not unnoticed by the major media outlets. In addition to their television appearances, both the *New York Times* and the *Saturday Evening Post* gave prominent space to stories on the new phenomenon of singing nuns. In many ways their efforts signalled the beginning of the image of the new nuns. As Father John Cannon, the priest who had hooked the Singing Sisters up with Mitch Miller, explained, 'It was a step that marked a departure in many ways ... This whole tendency that is developing is very much along the lines advocated in a book by Belgium's Leo Cardinal Suenens, *The Nun in the World*' (Aronowitz 1964, 66). Certainly, their presence charmed audiences and critics who were not put off by the habits, as some had feared. If anything, the religiosity of these choirs lent a particularly spiritual sheen to otherwise innocuous fare like 'Seventy-six Trombones.' However, whatever spirituality was imparted through the music was neither necessarily Catholic nor even particularly religious but was more a sense of inspiration and an invocation to an emotive piety based on joy, hope, serenity, and love beyond the confines of institutional religion. Mother Mary Immaculata suggested that this inspirationalism was more an after-effect than an intended goal of the music:

Mitch Miller leads the Singing Sisters of Mount St Mary through a rehearsal for his television variety show, *Sing Along with Mitch*.

After reading letters of praise and gratitude for [*Gesu Bambino*], I became convinced that our happiness could be shared by our singing, that we could let people catch our contagious spirit of joyful living through these recordings. Because we can love purely, unselfishly, freely, we find a joy unequalled, a peace unparalleled. Though as we grow older, our bubbling enthusiasm may sometimes diminish and even disappear, the joy only grows deeper, an overture of the profound happiness of an eternal day, the reward of a sustained sacrifice to bring Love Himself into a world which, too often, has time only for its own selfish whims and caprices. This is the secret we share with you as best we can in our happy, carefree, singing. (RJM Archives)

Thus it seemed that through the singing of the sisters, the edifice of the Catholic Church was giving way to something less tangible and more inner-directed, as went the popular psychology of the day. This was evident in the album covers, which eschewed pictures of convents or churches in favour of sisters against open landscapes, grottos, or hillsides.

This transition from an institutional foundation to emphasis on more natural and personal settings was the beginning of the breakdown of traditional Catholicism (Greeley 1971, 111). By 1962 the Vatican had caught up to the innovations swirling around them and had convened the first major council of the century. The intention was to re-evaluate every facet of Catholic life and bring it in line with the emerging cultural climate of personal autonomy and social responsibility. In America the timing was almost uncanny since the whole nation was undergoing a subtle transformation in which unwavering belief in progressivism was being challenged. The first generation of youthful baby boomers was clamouring for new models of living that ran counter to the traditions of civic responsibility and national pride. These changes in both religious and national values collided in the early sixties and found their expression in a new musical idiom of folk revivalism that, as the name suggests, had its roots in a romantic sense of the past and an embedded sense of feminized values. The emphasis on emotional expressiveness in the music of convent choral groups was indicative of a growing trend in which authenticity was less a question of tradition, canon, or history and more about personal integrity. These ideals extended well past religion, however, as individualism and democracy became increasingly more central to postwar values. Of course, exactly how these foundational values were to be understood was not universally accepted, and there were many different interpretations of this nationalistic creed. As Herberg pointed out at the time, they referred simultaneously to civil rights, free enterprise, and social equality without foregoing concepts such as competition and upward mobility (1960, 78). Yet the exact combination of these values was always a source of great debate.

The new style of popular sacred music preferred by sisters was intrinsically connected to the social movement of personalism, that quasi–ideological perspective which had at its base a moral belief in the dignity of persons. This differed from dominant conceptions of the rights of the individual because it emphasized the obligation of individuals to care for others around them, regardless of whether they were personally affected (Farrell 1997, 6). Personalists were wary of social systems or structures because they did not uphold the dignity of persons first and foremost. Those who adhered to personalism sought grassroots alternatives to institutions and bureaucracies. They called this a 'revolution of the heart,' an enacting of personal moral conscience to awaken nation-wide social consciousness over poverty and inequality. Through this harmonization of personal and public life, social change would begin with people first, organizations later. To accomplish this, social activists needed to find ways to bridge ethnic, racial, and class divides so that people could stand together and work for change. Folk music became the soundtrack of personalism in the postwar era because it was deemed the authentic voice of dispossessed persons. As Robert Cantwell points out, folk music suggested a kind of nostalgic pastoralism based on a belief in a simpler way of life and a more forthright communication of affirmative values (1996, 55). At the same time, by reviving a myth of an enlightened folk, the music evoked both a critical historical perspective and an alternative model for cultural organization, as befitting the goals of personalism.

Differing significantly from the populist politicism of the thirties folk-music scene, the manifesto of the revival was published in a 1959 issue of *Sing Out!* magazine: 'The emphasis is no longer on social reform or on world-wide reform ... The effort is focussed more on a search for real and human values' (Cantwell 1996, 22). The new artists were not much interested in reconstructing the music of the past or going out into the rural backwoods to track down and preserve the music of Appalachians, ex-slave communities, or migrant workers. To them, authenticity was not a question of class, ethno-racial background, or social marginalization. Rather, as members of the folk revival argued, 'folk music becomes a singing protest against the glossy complexities of our civilized affluence, which is so greatly responsible for modern man's alienation, absurdity and insanity. The way of life it represents is an alternative to suburbia insofar as it offers a simple and authentic human way' (DeTurk and Poulin 1967, 22). If the music was heartfelt and incorporated certain elements of indigenous folk songs, such as sparse acoustic accompaniment, a strong melodic flow, or rhetorical lyrics, then it was deemed folk in spirit if not in actuality.

Thus, during the folk revival of 1959–64, 'folk' became a question of idiom, ideology, and consciousness. It spoke to an ideal way of life based on nostalgic notions of community, self-reliance, and simplicity. It was music produced by urban, middle-class youth who sought a connection with an imagined past of rural poverty and a kind of back-to-the-land aesthetic. Its ideological underpinnings were restorative, not subversive, meaning that it was looking for cultural rather than political answers to a pervasive aura of disillusionment and lack of fulfilment (Cantwell 1996, 326). At once progressive and traditional, it sought to transform national values through the affirmation of a romantic vision of spiritual and moral virtuosity. Again, the old themes of feminization appear to have been marshalled to help give shape and focus to the revival. The popularity of folk music, with subtle protest songs like 'Where Have All the Flowers Gone' or rural ballads like 'Tom Dooley' rising to the top of the charts, served as a conduit for personalist beliefs such as social responsibility and the dignity of persons. While more commonly associated with leftist movements ranging from opposition to war to civil rights, folk music shared with personalism deep roots in charismatic religiosity. It was that religious underpinning which grounded folk music in feminizing tendencies of nostalgia and tradition.

Religious music, in particular Protestant hymns and African American spirituals, had provided the backbone for folk music as early as the 1930s. However, the stridently leftist ideologies of the folksingers in the populist movement disparaged the more overt religious messages. They rewrote lyrics to well-known melodies or even produced anti-religious parodies, which frequently failed to resonate with the rural communities they were seeking to convert politically (Denisoff 1983, 57). By contrast, the adaptation of religious music during the postwar revival was not so ideologically charged. With the rise of the civil rights movement, which became the rallying point for personalists and the new wave of folksingers, the hymns of rural African American culture were an integral aspect of any protest venture. There seems to have been no corresponding effort to despiritualize the movement as there had been during the thirties with the labour protests (Farrell 1997, 7). As Herberg had argued, religion became the crucial signifier of cultural identity at a time when class, race, and ethnicity were slowly being homogenized, in theory if not in practice. The use of traditional religious music from the African American communities in the Southern states helped to foster an ennobling image of black culture, which in turn eased the anxieties of those unsure of what civil rights might do to society. It almost goes without saying that the religious music adapted here had little relationship to traditional, triumphalist Catholicism – a point driven home in the film *Lilies of the Field* when Homer teaches the nuns to sing 'Amen' instead of their complicated, dirge-like chant. Despite the active involvement of priests, sisters, and lay volunteers, Catholicism had yet to articulate its own cultural response to the social activism in personalist-oriented movements. This would be dramatically rectified with the convening of the Second Vatican Council and the development of a modern doctrine based on notions of pastoralism and ecumenism.

One of the main priorities of John XXIII in bringing the council together in 1962 was to reform the liturgy to be more in keeping with cultural trends and the everyday lives of lay Catholics. This was not a new initiative, but a response to a grassroots movement that had begun early in the century. Pius XII had allowed for some minor variations on such fundamental church principles as Latin, Gregorian chant, and the cultivation of an art music tradition. By 1962 the level of experimentation by religious and the laity alike had become such that his successor, John XXIII, realized that only a full-scale overhaul of Catholic life could give the Vatican a chance to maintain its relevance in the modern world. To that end, the Second Vatican Council was convened and triumphalism was openly denounced in favour of a new spirit of pastoralism and *aggiornamento* (O'Dea 1968, 166). The most benign interpretation of *aggiornamento* involved the need to update certain aspects of religious life and community work. However, by the time that Vatican II was under way the idea of modernization became its own doctrine, supplanting the traditional notion of total submission to clerical authority as the only means of salvation (Quiñonez and Turner 1992, 12). John XXIII envisioned reawakening an image of the Catholic Church as a shepherd minding its flock, with all the peaceful, nostalgic connotations such an image conjured. The goal may seem obvious to some now, but at the time the idea that the priest was accountable and the liturgy had to be relevant to the congregation was nothing short of revolutionary. The very emphasis on cultural and geographic specificity left open to interpretation the extent of the reforms, but it was clear that music would be a key component in the experiment and could potentially signify the new pastoralism to the outside world.

At first glance it would seem that the old rules that gave precedent to male voices and Gregorian chant were to remain intact. However, in *Sacrosanctum Concilium*, the Vatican II document on sacred music and the liturgy, the use of the vernacular was promoted for all aspects of liturgical and extraliturgical singing (Paul VI 1963, VI:113). As well, regulations governing the use of instruments were loosened. No longer were there dictates against 'lascivious' or 'profane' instruments like guitars. Instead there was only the ambiguously phrased caution that 'the instruments are suitable, or can be made suitable, for sacred use; that they accord with the dignity of the temple, and that they truly contribute to the edification of the faithful' (VI:120). The open-ended suggestion that any instrument could be 'made suitable' for sacred music, coupled with prior exhortations to use the vernacular and to adapt local musical cultures, left enormous room for experimentation. With the release of *Inter Mirifica*, the Vatican II decree on the mass media, many religious felt they had received a new mandate for expanded cultural outreach far beyond the simple goals of the choral groups just a few years earlier. For one thing, the choral groups were very careful to distinguish between liturgical and extra- or non-liturgical music. They also did not try to produce their own original music or make any claims about a new religious music tradition. Now the Vatican was urging religious to become adept in the mass-media industries and to look to popular culture for new idioms that could be adapted for religious purposes. At the same time, they were applying similar principles to the cornerstone of Catholic life, the liturgy, and encouraging the development of modern music.

The timing of these papal pronouncements coincided with a major breakthrough in Catholic music around the world. In December 1963 an unpretentious folk song rose to the top of the pop charts. The unlikely artist was a shy novice from Belgium, Soeur Luc-Gabrielle, who was dubbed The Singing Nun when she crossed the Atlantic. Her fleeting success in the music industry speaks not only to the changes underway in the Catholic Church but also to the popularity of folk music and its related discourses of authenticity and personal expression. She helped to set in motion a major revolution in music in the Catholic Church and became the precursor of the new nun: young, creative, and earnest. Tragically, her fleeting success came at the cost of her vocation and, eventually, her life.

In November 1963, towards the end of the first session of Vatican II and the life of President John F. Kennedy, Americans had yet another reason to discover the new image of Catholicism. Appearing in the lower regions of both the *Cash Box* and *Billboard* singles chart was a simple chanson entitled 'Dominique.' There was no face to attach to the sweet soprano, no major public appearances or interviews in music magazines. In fact, the singer was identified only as The Singing Nun. This was a very different song from the bubbly pop hits then in vogue, such as Bobby Vinton's 'Blue Velvet' or 'Sugar Shack' by Jimmy Gilmour and the Fireballs, that dealt with themes of innocent teen desire. 'Dominique' entered the *Cash Box* Singles Chart on 2 November 1963 at number one hundred and rose steadily for sixteen weeks. It shot to number one the week after Kennedy was assassinated and remained there for five weeks, until just after Christmas. It was at the top of the *Billboard* charts for four weeks beginning 7 December 1963 and finished the year as the twentieth best-selling single. It took Beatlemania to unseat 'Dominique,' as 'I Want to Hold Your Hand' claimed the top spot on the charts. Eventually it dropped off the charts on 8 February 1964, after twelve weeks (Hoffman 1983; Whitburn 1992). During her brief success, The Singing Nun captured the imagination of a restless public that was thirsty for spirituality. Listeners soon learned that the mysterious voice belonged to a Belgian novice in her thirties named Soeur Luc-Gabrielle, who had never been outside her country and did not even speak English. She had entered the Dominican convent in Fichermont and brought along her guitar, which she called Sister Adele – much to the surprise of the other sisters, who never would have dreamed of bringing such a personal object with them. As a young, sincere Catholic sister she seemed to be the epitome of the Vatican II spirit. Her lilting voice and simple guitar accompaniment were as pure as anything Joan Baez had recorded, minus the hard political edge that mitigated the popularity of the folk music revival. There was even a touch of mystery and exoticism about this anonymous foreign sister, harking back to the major media attention garnered for *The Nun's Story* and Audrey Hepburn's role as another Belgian named Sister Luke. Thus, without even trying, The Singing Nun became a harbinger of the progressive musical movement about to occur in the Catholic Church and a symbol of the new pastoralism that was just being conceived by the Vatican.

Her intention in recording her songs was not to become an international singing star, but to have a few records on hand to give to young girls who came to the Dominican convent in Fichermont for youth retreats. The girls loved the songs of Soeur Luc-Gabrielle and asked for sheet music or tapes so that they could learn them at home. Thinking that a recording could generate a small amount of funds for the convent's missionary activities, the mother superior approached Philips, the Dutch-based multinational record label, and asked for some help. It is unclear why Philips acted so shrewdly – some might say in bad faith – to negotiate a contract in which they retained the vast majority of the profits and offered little protection for the artist. The convent would be the sole beneficiary of any royalties, at a rate of 3 per cent of 90 per cent of gross sales in Belgium and only 1.5 per cent of 90 per cent of international sales. Nothing would be given directly to Soeur Luc-Gabrielle, in keeping with her vow of poverty (Delaporte 1996, 38). In return, the convent received assurances that their young novice's face would not appear on any promotional materials and her name would be concealed from the press. A Philips executive coined the name Soeur Sourire (Sister Smile) and explained why it was so appropriate: 'Why Sister Smile? Because, in agreement with her superiors, we thought that it was better for a young novice to remain anonymous. This charming name, which we are happy to give her, reflects the freshness, the simplicity and faith that enlightens every song of SISTER SMILE' (36). Thus, Philips was faced with creating a publicity campaign without the asset of an artist to introduce to the musical press. Yet this was 1963, when the whole world was captivated by the new image of modern Catholicism being promoted by the kindly old pope and his ecumenical council. The idea of a nun – even an anonymous one – adopting folk music to sing of her devotion to Saint Dominic not only fit neatly into the spirit of Vatican II, but also merged imperceptibly into popular music radio formats and play lists.

The album design was carefully considered to meet this balance of piety and authenticity and retain Soeur Luc-Gabrielle's anonymity. It was listed as part of the Connoisseur Collection and given the full artistic treatment. A fable on the life of Soeur Sourire and her faithful companion, her guitar Soeur Adele, was printed on heavy paper and illustrated with original line drawings by F. Strobelm, who also did the cover art. The story and music lyrics, translated into English, were made into an attractive large-format brochure and glued into the gate-

Soeur Luc-Gabrielle ('The Singing Nun') on *The Ed Sullivan Show.*

fold. The total package was almost like a vocation book with an inspirational musical soundtrack. The story spoke of excitement and
adventure in the convent but also of the joys that would come to girls
with a purity of mission and a simple spirit, like Soeur Sourire:

> The young novice enthusiastically embraced convent life and this life
> gave back warmth and love, direction, purpose. After mass in the crisp
> early mornings, Soeur Sourire and her companion nuns would spade and
> rake and hoe in the flower and vegetable gardens surrounding the con-
> vent. Whether a stately tulip or a shy violet, a capricious daisy, or a pert,

humble cactus, each green leaf knew the tender care of Soeur Sourire. 'Who knows,' she asked a lush red rose, twinkling with morning dew, 'who knows what you, Adele, my guitar, and I might do together.'

The result was an album that suggested intimacy and spiritual fulfil-ment but that possessed neither an actual image of the artist nor any direct references to Catholicism or religious duty. It seemed to have tapped into a sense of yearning in audiences, who embraced the single 'Dominique' despite its French lyrics and scrambled to remake the image of Soeur Sourire into an idealized American folksinger – Joan Baez with a wimple.

The single was selling an average of one hundred thousand copies a week in America during its peak in November and December 1963. Before it even hit number one it had already sold more than half a mil-lion copies, and the full-length album was enjoying brisk sales as well. Philips spoke of a follow-up album with the same prestige packaging, and there was talk that The Singing Nun could become the top-selling recording artist of the year ('Singing Nun Goes On' 1963, 4). What's more, the song was breaking first in major urban centres, not small con-servative markets, and receiving airplay on a wide range of radio for-mats, from Top 40 to FM to middle-of-the-road. One Chicago station devoted an entire half-hour to debut the album and claimed that, 'the listener response to the "Singing Nun" [w]as the biggest reaction we've ever had to any record. When the station played it four times in the 7–noon segment, the switchboard lit up each time' ('Singing Nun Has Chi Talking' 1963, 1). Under pressure from Philips, Fichermont even-tually released a photo of Luc-Gabrielle with her guitar, which was run in major magazines, including *Life* and *Time*. They also agreed to per-form two songs taped at the convent for *The Ed Sullivan Show* after the host personally visited the convent and assured the mother superior that 'my taste was unquestionable' ('Singing Sister' 1963, 51).

The album was well on its way to becoming the biggest seller in his-tory and, as some executives suggested, reviving a moribund recording industry. The *Saturday Evening Post* explained:

'Business was dead,' one record-company executive recalls. 'Then along came this singing nun. You should call her the swinging nun. Who in the world would have expected it? Look, I'm not a Catholic, I was brought up to believe that when you saw a nun, it meant bad luck. But this chick's no bad luck, believe me. She's dragging the customers back into the stores. She's reviving the whole industry. It's a miracle.' (Aronowitz 1964, 68)

Her success was also credited with helping boost the sales for the less ambitious Singing Sisters of Mount St Mary and the Jesus and Mary Choral Group (Shepard 1963, 39). The Singing Nun was changing the face of Catholicism in a country that had previously viewed nuns with a mixture of curiosity and loathing. Since she herself went to great efforts to shield her identity, the mass media could reinvent her according to their own ideal image of a folk-singing nun. The Singing Nun became a kind of tabula rasa on which to draw a picture of pietistic zeal, feminine moral righteousness, and sincere cultural expression in a distinctly American context.

Beginning early in 1964 MGM initiated plans to produce a fictional musical biography of The Singing Nun. They turned to Father Leo Lunders, who had been such a strong supporter of *The Nun's Story* a few years earlier, to convince the rather media-weary sisters at Fichermont to assist them. Just as with the earlier film, there were delicate negotiations with the sisters to find a balance between dramatic appeal and religious accuracy. Among the agreements was that neither the convent nor Soeur Luc-Gabrielle be identified by name, nor would there be an appearance by any of the sisters in the movie. In fact, both the film and any advertising would have to include a disclaimer that this was not the life story of Soeur Sourire but a fictitious account inspired by her. They were allowed to use the Dominican habit and were to observe strict accuracy in any scenes of convent life. Finally, the sisters made it a condition of their cooperation that the movie include a 'spiritual dimension' and especially stress the missionary ideal (*The Singing Nun* [TSN] MPAA File). The resulting film, released in 1966, was about an independent young woman named Sister Ann who had enjoyed a vibrant life as a student in Paris before joining the convent. There she befriends a young motherless boy named Dominic and begins to write songs for him and the other children at the convent school. The local priest decides to have her songs recorded and arranges a meeting at Philips, where who should be her producer but her ex-boyfriend from Paris. Of course, Sister Ann's vocation is completely secure and her encounter with Robert does not ignite any sexual tension, but only inspires her old

flame to produce more music with a spiritual edge. With her astonish-
ing success Sister Ann feels caught up in a whirlwind and longs to
return to the peaceful life of the convent. After helping Dominic's family get a fresh start in the country, she gives his older sister her guitar,
named Brother John, and heads off to the missions in Africa, content at
last.

The film was a critical and box-office bomb. For one thing, the producers had been extremely keen to cast Debbie Reynolds in the lead
role. After her successful star turn in *The Unsinkable Molly Brown*, the
producers argued that 'this girl at the moment is bigger than anyone in
Hollywood. We must have her in our picture' (King Collection).
Unfortunately for them, by 1964 Reynolds was thirty-two years old,
long past being a girl. Her age was exacerbated not only by the unflattering habit but also by casting teen heart-throb Chad Everett to play
her pining ex-boyfriend, Robert. Another major problem was the
incredibly unflattering image of Sister Ann as a carping, critical, and
self-righteous bully. Her harsh attacks on the teenage girls who visit the
convent for their Saturday evening dances was hardly in keeping with
the image of smiling, self-effacing, and compassionate sisters that the
film insisted it wanted. The character was described thus amongst
MGM executives:

SISTER ANN (Debbie Reynolds): an ebullient, zesty, exuberant, mature
young woman who has taken her final vows. She is full of joy and happiness, she is somewhat aggressive without being offensive, she is a girl who
though orphaned had the benefit of a good Catholic education and training, a product of the Conservatory of Music, had a romance with a boy,
had taken a drink, had gone to dances, had a knowledge of swinging
music, a girl who had touched the world but had not been touched by the
seamier side of life, a girl of character who would never be pushed around,
nor would she ever push anyone around. (King Collection)

This description sounds strikingly similar to the ideal all-American girl
advocated by vocation books. Perhaps that is why the producers looked
to Reynolds, a sweetheart star. However, here she played Sister Ann as
a shrill, prurient busybody, helping to start a backlash against nuns in
films. One reviewer stated, 'As for all that sweetness and light I yearned
for, it's laid on here so thickly that I'm going to demand a bit of rape in

my next Nun-film' (Shipman 1966, 57). Other reviews were perhaps not quite as graphic, but they were equally dismissive. There was also a sad irony to the happy ending of the movie since by 1966 Soeur Luc-Gabrielle had left the convent and was desperately seeking credibility as a bona fide folksinger.

At the end of 1966 the former Soeur Sourire, now Jeanine Deckers, spoke candidly to the press about her decision to leave the religious life and her eagerness to cross the Atlantic to promote her latest recording. 'I wanted to be closer to people, and I found no matter how hard I tried that my nun's habit was a barrier, a shell that made communication difficult,' she told the *New York Times* ('Singing Nun Sets U.S.-Canada Tour' 1966, 173). Her difficulties with the austerity of the convent resonated with similar stories that were slowly starting to seep out in magazines such as the *Saturday Evening Post* (1966) and *Harper's* (1965). She released a new album that, in keeping with her more mature and independent persona, was promised to be more hard-hitting and contemporary. It failed to register on the American charts, and her new record company, Hébra, was forced to acknowledge that the public were more interested in the persona of Soeur Sourire as the eternally buoyant singing nun than in the artist Jeanine Deckers (Delaporte 1996, 77). This was made evident in a copycat recording released probably in 1965 or 1966 in which a faux Singing Nun sings an English version of 'Dominique.' It solidified the relationship between the feminine face of Catholic piety and the personalism of the folk music revival, creating a uniquely American image of the Belgian sister.

The Crown Records recording was entitled *Dominique from the 'Singing Nun'* and included no spiritually inflected illustrations on the back cover but only advertisements for other records on the label. On the front was a picture of a model in a white habit with a guitar hanging across her back. This was definitely not Luc-Gabrielle, who was short, plump, and near-sighted. The Singing Nun on this album was tall, thin, and gorgeous. Besides 'Dominique,' the song selections were a mix of traditional African-American hymns that had recently been popularized by the civil rights movement, a couple of Christmas carols, and the antiwar protest song by Pete Seeger 'Where Have All the Flowers Gone.' There were no other original compositions by Luc-Gabrielle, nor did she even receive a writing credit (to be fair, neither did Seeger). The album was an obvious attempt to cash in on the popularity both of Soeur Sourire and the folk music revival generally. Through its musical selections and the buoyant image of a beautiful young sister on the cover, the album spoke to the convergence of the feminizing image of the Catholic Church with the burgeoning strains of authenticity and integrity fostered in folk music and the personalist movement, even as it was exploiting all three. In effect the media had invented a Singing Nun for itself that suited the trends and styles circulating in popular culture at that time. The real-life singing nun was extraneous.

Having been turned into kitsch, Jeanine Deckers was never able to shake off the image of The Singing Nun and struggled for the rest of her life to find a niche for her music and her spirituality. Her initial forays into contemporary psychology while attending university, coupled with a new and passionate relationship with a young woman named Annie Pecher, forced her to re-evaluate her vocation. Like so many women during these early years of *aggiornamento*, exposure to a world beyond the convent that was caught up in a fervour for authentic personal experience left her feeling that the religious life was 'static and passé' (Delaporte 1996, 66). Only Annie made her feel happy and as if she belonged. By the time the film was released, they had found an apartment together and Soeur Luc-Gabrielle had returned to being Jeanine Deckers. With the end of her career as a religious, she forfeited her right to the name Soeur Sourire and ceased to be a star (75). As a laywoman, she continued to record, although she never had another hit. She and Annie tried various attempts to launch their own missionary efforts, but also to little success. She fought with Fichermont to recoup some of her royalties, but the money had already been spent in the missions. Philips was equally ungraciously tight-fisted, even though they had earned huge profits at her expense. Since she was no longer a religious, the Belgian government went after her for back taxes on those profits that she had never received for 'Dominique.' By 1985, Deckers was hopelessly in debt and deeply depressed over her failed singing career and her vocation. She and Annie took fatal overdoses of sedatives and died together in April of that year.

Despite all the jokes at her expense over the years, the legacy of Luc-Gabrielle ultimately lies not in her image, but her music. She inspired Catholics around the world to experiment with folk music and produce their own original songs that would best express the new sense of personal authenticity fostered by Vatican II. The popularity of 'Dominique' helped convince other sisters to aim for more than the small musical ventures of the choral groups. They began producing their own original tunes and looked to popular music for inspiration in arrangements and tempos. By the mid-sixties Catholics were eagerly embracing folk music, not only for unofficial gatherings, but also for incorporation directly into the liturgy. In one sense they were somewhat behind the times since the folk music revival had all but sputtered out by 1965. Yet in terms of revitalizing Catholicism, their experiments in music were considered revolutionary and sparked some of the most contentious debates about the identity of American Catholicism in the post-conciliar era.

While it may seem hard to conceive today, some have claimed that the popularization of sacred music was the most controversial issue facing Catholics in the sixties after birth control (Dinges 1987, 138). The reason reflects back on the arguments of Herberg before the council had even begun, that religious affiliation was the sole repository for people's sense of cultural heritage and tradition. In short, Catholic identity was in flux, and one of the few things that could be distinguished as uniquely Catholic was the high pomp and mysticism of the liturgy. With the council's relaxed guidelines, some feared that the Catholic mass was being watered down to resemble Protestant church services and that the boundaries of religion were blurring (145–7; Greeley 1971, 112; Ahlstrom 1978, 23). These conservative voices were a frustrated but highly vocal minority. Against them were many seeking out new meaning systems for religious devotion that were responsive to contemporary social issues and cultural differences. For the sisters and priests who accompanied civil rights and antiwar protestors, their exposure to folk protest music and African American spirituals awakened them to new possibilities in expanding their community outreach and becoming more integrated into everyday society. To them, folk music expressed the communality of ideals between social justice activists and Catholic reformists. They adopted not only the musical styles, but also the ideologies of authenticity and personal integrity and attempted to create a new framework for American Catholicism from that point of convergence.

It may seem ironic that Catholics, who were at the vanguard of the anti-Communist movement in the fifties, should embrace the music of their enemies just ten years later. However, the folk music revival had altered the meaning and purpose of the genre away from its overtly political roots and instead promoted the ideal of folk as any heartfelt expression performed with simplicity. It was this definition that Catholic music reformers embraced. As one priest explained, 'When someone among us (and there are more such people than we moderns tend to believe) expresses a mature, deeply felt human reaction to some common human experience by welding together a simple, singable melody and strong, simple, singable words, he has written a folk song, and a good one' (Reilly 1963, 9). The idea that folk music could be adapted to meet Catholic liturgical concerns had not been conceived until the end of the Second Vatican Council. Yet there were indications by reformers that, at its core, folk music had a spiritual depth that went beyond the issues of the day. In a ten-page photo-essay on folk music published just before the end of the council, the Catholic magazine *Ramparts* was among the first to claim a religious dimension to the music and the movement that inspired it:

> There is a deep thing at work in all of this. The Reality behind the American dream and the truth behind its mythology is being attacked relentlessly by a generation that takes nothing for granted from its elders ... This is the New Morality and these are the New Moralists who are revising the priorities of the entire society. They are simplistic and evangelical and military visionaries. They say the virtues are Love and Truth and Beauty and the ultimate sins are to hurt another human, to break trust and not to love. (Gleason 1965, 47–8)

While the enthusiastic support of the younger generation and their music was one thing, it remained to be seen if Catholic musicians could rise to the occasion and produce their own folk music. By 1965 the first stirrings in musical experimentation had set about to challenge the centuries-old supremacy of Gregorian chant and the turgid definitions of sacred music that had dominated the Catholic liturgy up until this time. At the forefront of this latest cultural revolution was a young missionary sister who had just completed her degree in music and was looking for ways to take her education further.

When Sister Miriam Therese Winter was assigned the role of musical director in her congregation, the Medical Mission Sisters, she was surprised and more than a little disappointed. She had joined them in

1955 with the desire to become a doctor and travel the world. However, because she was the only member available with any musical training (she had taken piano lessons as a child), the job fell to her. In those days, a sister did not question her assignment, and so even though her superior did ask her, Winter felt obliged to agree. The Medical Mission Sisters were already on the vanguard of Catholic reforms and had made many changes to their own services, including hymns from Protestant churches and the use of English in some parts of the mass. Yet by the time of the Second Vatican Council, the congregation felt they had gone as far as they could and needed to designate a leader to take charge of their musical and liturgical practices.

In 1964 Winter graduated from Catholic University with a specialty in organ music and Gregorian chant. Upon her return she experimented with English versions of the chant and presented them to the liturgical commission, since nothing could be included in the liturgy that had not received official approval from diocesan authorities. The priest in charge was shocked that a woman would be writing original chants in the vernacular on her own initiative but reluctantly approved her first efforts. He decided soon after that it was inappropriate for her to proceed. Vernacular chant was deemed too important an exercise to be in the hands of one nun and was better left to the experts in Rome. While he may have felt the issue was now closed, he instead moved Winter into another direction with her music. She abandoned the organ in favour of the guitar and began to compose her own songs inspired by the music she was hearing out on the streets of her congregation's missions.

The evolution of Winter's music coincided with the most contentious period in the modernization of the religious life for women. All around her were the changes that had begun with the Call for Renewal and been pushed to new levels with the Second Vatican Council. Her initial intent was to give the traditional texts and themes of Sunday liturgy a contemporary setting. The songs were so well received that someone suggested they be recorded. However, Winter saw what the media had done to young Luc-Gabrielle and feared for her own sense of identity and spirituality. She did not want to be placed in the spotlight to become yet another 'sweet nun singing.' The image was simply not right, but at the same time it was liberating, even exhilarating. She told me that the early phase of experimentation was, in her own words, 'agony for me.' As with so many other progressively minded and well-educated sisters, Winter was trying to figure out her place in the new matrix of religious meaning and purpose. On a more personal level, she also wanted to understand the steps that had led her to become a musician and how that fit into her original vocation to be a missionary. Some of the first songs she wrote spoke deeply of her spiritual struggles and provide a strong antidote to the saccharine-coated image of The Singing Nun. The debut album by the Medical Mission Sisters, *Joy Is Like the Rain*, was a striking example of that anxiety, in which sentimental images of singing sisters striding across open fields clashed with anguished lyrics over the trials of faith. When contrasted with the album by the Singing Sisters, which was simply entitled *Joy!* and held no uncertainty about the fulfilment of the religious life, Winter's contribution to Catholic folk music was a sign of more troubling times ahead for sisters. Released in 1965, the album's liner notes offered up an image of an unperturbed young sister to whom music sprang forth naturally: 'With her guitar, alone in the fields, on the hill, she simply sang her songs.' Yet the actual lyrics were far from simple. The title song opened with the verse

> I saw rain-drops on my window
> Joy is like the rain
> Laughter runs across my pain
> Slips away and comes again
> Joy is like the rain.

Other songs such as 'Howl, My Soul' or 'It's a Long Road to Freedom' echoed these thoughts of pain and spiritual longing. In the latter song, the final verse went

> I walked one morning with my King
> And all my winters turned to spring
> Yet every moment held its sting.

The album was released on a new label based in New York City called Avant Garde, which wanted to specialize in new music with a social message. The Medical Mission Sisters were the first artists to be signed by them, an important signifier for both. For the congregation, they were reaching out to new audiences by not going with a Catholic-run publishing house and by strategically aligning themselves with the folk music movement in New York, more specifically Greenwich Village. For Avant Garde, by signing a religious group to their label they were capitalizing on the rising interest in ecumenism and sparking media attention with yet another example of the new nuns in action. The album went gold in the United States and elsewhere in the world. It was carried to missionary outposts across the developing world, not only to the Catholic stations, but to those of other denominations as well. Winter herself was voted into the American Society of Composers, Authors and Publishers (ASCAP) in 1967 and has been named to the Popular Awards list annually since 1968 (Paulos 1998, 30).

Other albums followed, the most interesting of which was *RSVP: Music for Militants (and Others Who Care)*, released in 1970. Its promotional package billed it as 'music for militants, for those who build and all who tear apart.' The picture of Winter was nothing like the veiled virgin in the field from her first album. Instead, here was an attractive and stylish young woman whose only outward sign of her vows was a small crucifix pin on her plain dress. The album was dedicated to 'all who hunger and thirst for justice' and pulled no punches in confronting the complexities of faith in troubled times. The opening song, 'Lord, Have Mercy on Your People,' included some of the angriest lyrics in folk music, certainly defying any attempts to trivialize this as the work of another sickly-sweet singing nun:

Down in the ghetto the blood flows free.
There is rebellion in the university.
Who is the guilty, is it they or is it we?
Lord, have mercy on your people.
Lord, have mercy.
Christ, have mercy.
Lord, have mercy on your people.
Are we concerned? Well, I think we're not!
The rich get richer while the poor just rot!
Who dares to be indifferent condemns his own lot!
Lord, have mercy on your people.
Lord, have mercy.
Christ, have mercy.
Lord, have mercy on your people.
Children grow old in the prime of youth.

Sister Miriam Therese Winter gives a more realistic image of the new nun on the cover of her album *RSVP* (1970).

Hippiness or happiness the search is for truth.
But don't close the carnival 'cause you can't stand our booth.
Lord, have mercy on your people.
Lord, have mercy.
Christ, have mercy.
Lord, have mercy on your people.

Winter had not set out to broaden the definition of missionary work in her congregation, yet such was the case as her musical efforts came to be recognized for their healing power between different cultures and communities. Because the focus of her ministry was not abroad but at home, she wanted to raise awareness of the crises going on in the streets of America. To that end she agreed to participate in a landmark ecumenical concert organized by Avant Garde Records at Carnegie Hall in 1967. The goal was to bring religious folk music out of the churches and into the streets and, subsequently, the sounds of the streets into the churches. The ecumenical concert was called 'Praise the Lord in Many Voices' and featured six contemporary religious performances from Catholic, Protestant, and Jewish traditions. The artists included Winter, jazz pianist Mary Lou Williams, the New York Philharmonic's composer-in-residence, David Amram, and *America*'s music critic, the Rev. C.J. McNaspy, as emcee. The sold-out affair was intended as an informal occasion to explore different musical idioms, from the Caribbean-inflected folk songs of Winter, to the jazz styling of Williams, and even a full electric rock and roll band. The concert opened with the premier performance of Winter's 'Mass of a Pilgrim People.' Its syncopated rhythms and driving drumbeat were indicative of just how much Catholic church music had already changed. As Winter suggested to the press, the goal was to 'make a big noise to the Lord' in a way that brought fun and excitement back to religion and appealed to the younger generation especially:

All right, now we are over the hump with the English – we know the language. Now we have to break down the barrier between church and life, show that there is no separation, that it's all one thing. The arts can open the door – if we give people the kind of music that they'll want to go on singing when they get home from church. (MMS Archives)

With the ecumenical concert, the lines were clearly demarcated between the sacralists, who argued for retaining the sacred traditions of Gregorian chant, and the reformers, who wished to reflect a new kind of pastoralism that was attuned to the everyday lives and spiritual needs of Catholics in the wake of Vatican II.

The debates over Catholic folk music were deeply divisive. One month after the concert the Vatican tried to place restrictions on the use of popular musical idioms by passing a general ban on any instruments that 'by common opinion or use, suitable for secular music only, are to be altogether prohibited from every liturgical celebration and from popular devotions' ('Vatican Limits Pop Music' 1967, 36). Such an edict sounded more likely to come from Pius XII than from the post-conciliar Pope Paul VI. It appeared that the Vatican was caught off guard by people's expectations for reforms in so many areas of Catholic life. Thus, by the late sixties Catholic officials were spending more time reeling in reforms than encouraging them.

Just as their efforts to tighten the restraints on Catholic sisters were having little effect, so too were admonishments against popular music. Rather than claim that they were looking to modernize the liturgy, some pastoralists in favour of popular music argued instead that they were the true traditionalists, referring back to the medieval ages, when local folk songs were first adapted by the Catholic Church and subsequently turned into Gregorian chant. Their arguments were historically dubious and served the political agenda of the contemporary situation more than any theological goals. Nonetheless, they suggest the intensity of the debate over popular music and how its resolution was at the core of the identity crisis that had taken hold of many Catholics (Jeffrey 1992, 78). For their part, sacralists did not have much to say about the benefits of retaining the high-art principles of sacred music, except that, as one scholar suggested, 'It may be unpleasurable to have to face Gregorian chant, but we should endure it' (Bomm 1969, 168). Thus it was that popular music went to the heart of the conflict in American Catholic life, where the old order of discipline, unity, and hierarchy was being supplanted by personalist values of individual expression and spiritual honesty. For the sisters who were searching for new ways to articulate their vocation and make their spiritual work more purposeful to society, popular music became an effective tool. Symbolically, it aligned them with the protest movements that were percolating on the streets. On a more pragmatic level, it gave sisters a vital form of communication that they could use to promote alliances between themselves and the urban ghetto communities they were entering.

Musical outreach programs were initiated by these sisters as part of ambitious plans to become active witnesses in poor urban neighbourhoods. Summer in the City took place in New York, while Project Pied Piper was directed from Alverno College in Wisconsin, home of Sisters Mary Joel Reed and Mary Austin Doherty from the National Organization for Women. And there were many other programs that were given no formal names, but were efforts by sisters to bring popular music into their work as a way to bridge the cultural and economic divides between the convent and the ghetto. This kind of music education bore little resemblance to the formal training earlier promoted by the Sister Formation Conference, but it evoked the same kind of spirit in likening song to prayer. As one sister argued, echoing the romantic ideologies of folk music, 'Music is power; music is creation, expression, unity. Music belongs to man; it helps him to live and to express his life in a new way' ('Urban Music Education' 1969, 40).

The sisters not only taught the new religious folk songs to the children in the ghettos; they also tried to learn more about different musical cultures as a first step in integrating with the community. What they may not have been prepared for once the music did its job were the shocking revelations about social inequality in America. Sheltered in their female and solidly middle-class institutions, sisters had been lulled into believing that all was good in America; it just needed a bit of tweaking. Confronted with the harsh realities of life in the urban slums, they began to question the belief that through the integration of a particularly progressive, personalist American idealism, Catholicism would find the new pastoralism it was seeking. Their own doubts gave strength to a rising reactionary stance by the Vatican to curtail renewal and to help end a period when Americanism was seen to be the salvation of the church worldwide. The main target of this reaction was women religious, the same group who had been thrust forward not too long ago. However, sisters who had embraced social activism were more than ready for the challenge. They redoubled their efforts not only to open the church up to harsh social realities, but also to make their own society accountable to their spiritual, personalist principles of human dignity and autonomy.

Programs like Summer in the City were intended to augment more politically assertive initiatives by sisters with easily digestible strategies like folk music. In that way, they served dual functions. On the one hand, they were like a calling card to marginalized communities, helping sisters to gain trust. On the other, the delicate soprano voices helped to mitigate any accusations of unfeminine or unpious behaviour and neutralize to a degree criticisms of their awakening political consciousness. At the same time as women like Winter were singing out their frustrations, they were also moving aggressively into the social ferment of their times. Sisters marched with the yippies at the Chicago riots of 1968 and did their evenings in jail along with the rest. Angelica Seng and other nuns embarrassed the Chicago diocese further by staging protests against segregation at Catholic universities. In the *Saturday Evening Post* profile 'The New Nuns' (Novak 1966), they were pictured down in the ghettos playing with children from relocated Appalachian farming families, further cementing their link to a folk sentimentality. Thus, the experiments in folk music undertaken by sisters were both a sign of deeper and more critical engagement in the world as well as a move to bring optimism to their activism and dispel fears over their innovations. As one member of the Summer in the City project who was working deep in New York's Harlem stated,

> Just as many tones can blend into a beautiful melody, so have people through *Summer in the City* united in their search for what is mutually precious in their lives. The discovery of these riches in others confirms that it is *people* who make life in the cities good, rich, and beautiful. As a caption of *Full Circle* [a Catholic poetry journal of the time] reads: 'I sing from the deepest part of you,' so music has touched the well-springs of people in New York's streets, placing hope, joy, and trust where fear and hesitation had been. ('Urban Music Education' 1969, 16)

The role of popular music in the early days of urban experimentation after Vatican II suggests that sisters were not quite ready to become fully politicized. They were still seeking relatively simple cultural answers to pressing socio-economic problems of poverty and racial inequality. Indeed, the sisters who discussed their programs at the Urban Music Education Symposium in 1969 were unqualifiedly positive about popular music's benefits in relieving tensions in the ghetto and sparking feelings of community. Like so many other aspects of popular culture, the experiments with music were part of a long line of efforts to modernize the religious life and merge the best of Catholic spirituality with the most liberating aspects of progressive American nationalism. However, once the guitars and tambourines were put away and sisters looked around they saw the near insurmountability of their task and began to question the effectiveness of their doggedly upbeat tactics. By the late sixties many sisters were becoming increasingly more countercultural in their outlook and were searching for new strategies to combat the social inequalities they were only now realizing. Some turned to feminism and tried to claim allegiance with the radical efforts of the generation of feminists who came after Friedan and the National Organization for Women. Perhaps they were surprised to discover that their experiences were not welcome by these younger feminists, who saw the religious life as an old-fashioned and repressive throwback that had no place in a movement caught up in a swirl of sexual and identity politics. It seemed as if the early enthusiasm of the mass media in highlighting the contemporary sister had backfired by creating the impression that they were ebullient, feisty, but ultimately ineffectual women. This problem with stereotyping had begun with The Singing Nun, but it was brought to new levels with the launch of a frivolous family sitcom, *The Flying Nun*. Thus, by the end of the decade there was a growing chasm between the real lives of sisters and the media portrayals of the convent, which would widen much further before it could ever begin to be corrected.

6

Gidget Joins a Convent:
Television Confronts the New Nuns

By the late sixties sisters were at the peak of their radical experimentation. They were removing their habits, closing down the large institutions, and relocating in small groups to urban, ecumenical ministries rather than only serving a Catholic subculture. They were also refashioning the role of the Catholic Church in the everyday lives of its members through their participation in liturgical reforms and the introduction of popular music. Yet the sentimental image of sisters that some hoped had reached its apogee with The Singing Nun could not be shaken. With the debut of the family sitcom *The Flying Nun* the sickly sweet virgin image appeared to have triumphed. In many ways *The Flying Nun*, which aired from September 1967 to September 1970 on ABC, was a step out of time. Its positive image of a traditional religious congregation unperturbed by the fervent debates over reforms sweeping across convents may not have been an accurate reflection of the religious life in the late sixties. Nonetheless, it does stand as a mediating point between the systems of representation begun in the fifties and the newer, more politicized image of sisters evident in B-movies like *Change of Habit*. At the same time the strategic use of the nun continued to operate as a stand-in for a host of other issues unrelated to religious life. In the case of *The Flying Nun*, the central relationship between a spunky young novice, played by Gidget alumna Sally Field, and her stern superior, played by veteran Broadway actress Madeleine Sherwood, spoke to a broad set of ongoing conflicts between a younger generation of independent women and their older, more traditional mentors.

The producers of *The Flying Nun* capitalized on the intense interest in the convent to provide a picture of two generations of independent-minded women trying to come to terms with each other in a way that indirectly addressed the growing radicalism of the women's movement. At the same time, it also managed to steer clear of much of the controversy surrounding convent reforms while still promoting an image of intelligent, vibrant sisters. With both elements watered down for a family-oriented television audience, the religious premise of The Flying Nun acted as a kind of pacifier. In other words, ambivalent feelings about femininity and women's independence were displaced, appearing in a context that was at once familiar but not directly relevant. Thus, conflicts that were meant to reflect ongoing problems in society were deflected onto the well-known crises facing the Catholic Church, especially the convent. The fact that the show was set in a missionary outpost in Puerto Rico helped to further defuse any possibility for direct critique of American values or civic unrest.

The Flying Nun reflected the changes taking place in the Catholic Church and the increasingly radical message of women's liberation in the unlikely premise of a diminutive novice sent to a Puerto Rican mission who discovers that she can fly. Once again, the conjoining of religious and gender issues, which were becoming increasingly complex by the late sixties, were mediated through the figure of the nun. The show was responsive to public interest in the religious life, which appeared to offer an alternative model of femininity by striking a balance between independence and demureness in women. The general format of sitcoms, particularly in the late sixties, incorporated an open-ended narrative structure in which the peace of a community – a family, a workplace, or, in this case, a convent – would be disrupted by some conflict that would ultimately be resolved with little lasting effect on the characters. The change-resistant structure of sitcoms provided opportunities for the exploration of some of the more radical elements not only of convent reforms but also of the counterculture within a stabilizing context of social conservatism and traditional gender roles.

Sally Field played Sister Bertrille, a young and exuberant novice who is on her first missionary assignment at the Convent San Tanco, in San Juan, Puerto Rico. Her superior, Mother Plácido, is a stern but loving nun who is schooled in the old ways but is willing to make certain small adjustments for her younger nuns. She is assisted by the kind-hearted Sister Jacqueline, who also acts as the narrator for the show. Other nuns include Sister Sixto, a Puerto Rican native prone to malapropism, and Sister Ana, a placidly devout novice. Among their many friends in the town is the notorious playboy gambler Carlos Ramirez. He is charmed by Sister Bertrille and becomes the convent's most dedicated benefactor. He is also the only person outside the convent who is aware that Bertrille can fly. Bertrille's ability to fly is determined to be due to a combination of her winged coronet and voluminous habit, exceptional wind patterns in San Tanco, and Bertrille's own compact size. Thus, it is not an innate power within Bertrille but is made possible through a string of external factors related to her decision to become a missionary nun. Unfortunately, that explanation does not make her bizarre talent any more agreeable to Mother Plácido. Yet Bertrille is not banned from flying but is allowed to make the decision to fly a matter of personal conscience. Mother Plácido's disapproving yet conciliatory attitude is a device to keep the flying a part of the plot. It was also a first step in depicting an up-to-date version of the religious life, in keeping with the philosophy of the new nuns.

The man behind *The Flying Nun* was Harry Ackerman, who was then enjoying success with his sitcom *Bewitched*. He was approached by veteran television producer Max Wylie with an offer to turn an obscure children's book called *The Fifteenth Pelican* into a television show. Wylie argued that, between the box-office success of films like *The Sound of Music*, the musical success of The Singing Nun, the liberalizing of the Catholic Church, and its renewed interest in working with the mass media, the time was ripe for a convent-based sitcom. The beauty of the story of Sister Bertrille, he claimed, was that she was 'a nun with sex appeal' for whom the possibilities were endless – especially if she was paired with a more strait-laced mother superior (Whitney 1968, 22). In the book Sister Bertrille was a young American sister sent to the mission Convent San Tanco in Puerto Rico to eventually take over as superior from the ageing Spanish Sister Servant Plácido. The story's conflict was not generational but nationalistic. Sister Bertrille was praised for her all-American good looks and health, which lent an 'invisible sparkle and twinkle in the air about her whole blue-clad person that was pure American. This comes, some theorists say, from vitamins, ice skating, braces on the teeth, dancing lessons, and liberal doses of free air' (Ríos 1965, 11).

By changing the central conflict between the two lead characters to a

Sister Bertrille (Sally Field) learns how to fly in *The Flying Nun*.

generation gap, the sitcom not only played to a growing concern of the late sixties, but it also signalled that the long-standing problem of Catholic integration into American culture was finally resolved. The ethnic biases against Catholics, which were still prevalent at the beginning of the decade and evident in films such as *Lilies of the Field*, were no longer major concern. If anything, sisters were increasingly viewed as among the more progressive and experimental groups in society, and the media began to pay close attention to their reforms and their relationship with groups in the civil rights, peace, and even feminist movements. Beginning soon after the close of the Second Vatican Council, the media signalled a change in the image of sisters. The earliest indication of this new direction was the cover story on *Harper's* magazine entitled 'The American Nun: Poor, Chaste and Restive' in August of 1965. It was the first time that the religious life was publicly accused of an oppressive structure and overwhelming routinization by sisters. At the same time, the article praised those sisters who were forging a path of reform and looking for substantial change rather than small modifications. From that article the image of the new nun – confident, assertive, critical, and young – began to overtake the old image of the sweetly industrious, duty-bound virgin crone.

The introduction of the new nun was not simply a case of supplanting one image with another. The romantic image of nuns from vocation books and films like *The Nun's Story*, which predominated in the fifties and early sixties, still found resonance in the late sixties. However, it became increasingly more troubling to both sisters and lay audiences. Before, films had depicted sisters as heroic and confidently chaste women. Yet, by the late sixties, once the influence of Catholic regulatory agencies such as the Legion of Decency was diminished, films like *Change of Habit* were exploring sisters' conflicts with church authority as well as their sublimated sexuality. Thus, their identity as women as much as religious became an integral part of the dramatic tension. The early efforts by sisters to promote a positive and non-critical image of themselves in vocation books and popular music were also undergoing significant changes. Books targeted at youth audiences were slowly being replaced by anthologies for adult readers that discussed the need to obliterate the old ways of Catholicism that strictly enforced celibacy, poverty, and obedience through strategies of repression and infantilization. As one sister complained in *The New Nuns*:

Her 'education to reality' is a study in naïveté. Worse than that. Her care-fully controlled environment, so reminiscent of a germ-free laboratory, suggests a subtle, albeit a piously motivated, manipulation. For everything seems to be arranged to 'protect' her vocation and to assure the 'right' decision ... officially 'religious' people, insofar as they institutionalize a protectivism which blocks the development of real freedom to choose, do not really believe and do not truly love. (Schaldenbrand 1967, 81)

Despite some changes to nuns' images in film, music, and magazines, there was still a lingering nostalgia for the traditional religious life. Not everyone was happy to see sisters out on the streets in regular clothes or at the front of protest marches. According to one poll, 44 per cent of Catholics disapproved of any religious involvement in the civil rights movement (Cogley 1965, 48). The debate over the extent of reforms began in earnest in 1967 when Archbishop John Francis Cardinal McIntyre censured the Immaculate Heart of Mary congregation in Los Angeles (IHMs) for not wearing the habit and refusing to acknowledge his authority over them. Their celebrated battle and others spilled into the media, framed as older versus younger sisters. *Harper's* magazine reported that 'Within each separate community of nuns, efforts to mod-ernize are accompanied by strong ideological differences. And within each convent, the gap between the older and younger generations is a pronounced one' (Wakin and Scheuer 1965, 35). Ironically, the prob-lem of a generation gap was due in part to the earliest initiatives of sis-ters to reform the religious life. In keeping with the goals of the Sister Formation Conference, as young sisters joined they were quickly sent to universities and training centres across the country. No longer shielded from the world during the crucial early years of discernment, young sis-ters could not help but bring to their congregations the new sense of political activism and self-awareness that was being championed on campuses (Wittberg 1989, 531). Furthermore, as the sexual ferment rippling across the country found its focus on campus, not even vowed celibates were safe.

It was at university that Soeur Luc-Gabrielle had met and fallen in love with Annie Pecher, and she was not unique in that regard. For some, the need to explore their sexuality overpowered their religious commitment. For others who elected to remain in their vows, a painful, introspective period of self-evaluation often led to hard questions about the church's attitude towards sex. This unforeseen crisis coincided with a volatile debate within the hierarchy over birth control. Too controversial to be included properly in the Second Vatican Council, the protracted and emotionally fraught battle took years to resolve, ultimately resulting in an entrenchment of conservative Catholic values. In the end it was seen less as a debate over sexuality per se, but as Catholicism's last bold stand against a tidal wave of modernity that put individual happiness ahead of family or communal duty. Nor were Catholic leaders alone in trying to return liberal progressivism to early models of civic duty and heroic sacrifice over such things as personal discovery. Even within the ranks of the reborn feminist movement, a split between liberal moderates and younger, radical women fuelled by the sexual revolution threatened the movement.

For some nuns, their sexual crisis forced them to re-evaluate every aspect of their lives until, as one lesbian nun acknowledged years later, 'I read myself into the women's movement. Then there was light' (Brady 1989, 100). While some joined up with the radicals and began public fights about formerly private issues such as sexual and reproductive freedom, their moral integrity as spokespeople was questioned in ways it had never been before in the early years of civil rights or peace marches. Their status as virgins marked them in society and undermined their claims to full personhood. It didn't help that clerical leaders were now joining forces with Hollywood to present a rather ridiculous portrait of the new nuns straight out of the old vocation books. Instead of representing a complex, albeit contained, image of feminine independence, The Flying Nun retreated into naïve stereotypes that helped to turn audiences further away from depictions of contemporary nuns struggling over their social and sexual identity. In their place were calcified images of women religious out of step with their times.

A simple codification of the crisis facing the convent into generational issues and accusations of hedonism fit neatly into the larger crisis facing American culture. A burgeoning youth culture, which was at the foreground of the protest movements and women's liberation, was challenging the old system of American pride in scientific and technical progress and disrupting traditional conventions of gender and age. The Flying Nun helped to offset the criticisms levelled at both church and society by creating an entertaining fiction about a confident, exuberant young woman who was experiencing something of the world while not straying too far from the conventional assignment to the domestic private sphere. Any question about her own sense of independence was neatly resolved by giving her the ability to soar like a bird, but only if she wore the traditional habit of a nun. In this way, the convent reasserted its long-standing position as a privileged symbolic space for the representation of independent, yet traditional, women.

The Flying Nun was the most obvious and unapologetic signal that the media was done with complex images of the religious life and were recasting it as a symbol that would not emphasize feminine independence, but compliance with limiting social structures. In the sixties it was difficult to find television shows that depicted smart, sexy, and independent women. Offbeat dramas such as *Honey West* (ABC 1965–6) and the British import *The Avengers* (ABC 1966–9), with their coolly sensual female characters, helped define this new woman of the sexual revolution and foreground cultural representations of women's liberation centred on the body and sexuality (Luckett 1999, 296). These were in many ways muted responses to the challenges put forward first by Helen Gurley Brown in *Sex and the Single Girl* (1962) and Betty Friedan in *The Feminine Mystique* (1963). While the former celebrated the working girl and her economic independence, which led in turn to sexual freedom, the latter offered the first cogent critique of media stereotypes of women, especially the housewife. Yet, for the most part, television preferred to keep a lid on these growing movements of feminine sexual and economic liberation by keeping their heroines young, innocent, and fresh-faced.

Ilana Nash argues in her study of *Gidget*, which starred Sally Field in the sitcom version, that teen girl characters were transitional figures in the rise of second-wave feminism because they represented a compromise position between demands for greater economic, political, and sexual liberation for women and the anxiety that these changes were creating in society (2002, 343). The response in popular culture was to focus on girls' sexual and consumer power while presenting them as giddy, impulsive, and generally needing firm guidance, preferably from a father figure. Thus, their independence was depicted in containable ways that would provide innocent titillation without undermining existing social conventions (344). Susan Douglas sums up such portrayals in one word: perky. By this she means that sitcom girls were assertive but not aggressive, cute without being sexy, and walked a tightrope between tomboyishness and proper ladylike behaviour, depending on what suited the moment (1994, 108). This was in direct contrast to the 'cool' persona favoured by college girls (Greene 1964, 24). As Luckett points out, teen girl sitcoms such as *Gidget* (ABC 1965–6) and *The Patty Duke Show* (ABC 1963–6) negotiated a space in which girls were at the centre of their own universe, while never forgetting their inevitable destiny to submit to the patriarchal order (1997, 102). For those women who needed some kind of temporary outlet from the stultifying routine of feminine submissiveness, television's answer was to offer heroines with magical abilities and then place them in situations where they would have to choose the feminine mystique over these fantastic feminine powers.

The off-the-wall premise of *The Flying Nun* actually fit well with sitcom conventions that featured women characters who possessed some kind of alien force. *Bewitched*, about a young witch who marries a mortal and chooses to live the life of a suburban housewife, and *I Dream of Jeannie*, the adventures of a beautiful but naïve genie and her astronaut 'master,' were the two most popular fantastic family sitcoms of the era. The element common to these dramas, according to Lynn Spigel, was an idyllic and highly conformist community that was subjected to outlandish and inexplicable happenings which caused a great deal of anxiety for a time but whose effects were ultimately temporary before social order was inevitably restored (1991, 214). It was not inconsequential that these outbursts were caused by women. Plots tended to revolve around domestic turmoil or the threat of the domestic realm to encroach upon the patriarch's place in the world of business and politics. The antics of the female leads upset conventional notions of the private sphere and women's passive role within it. However, it was only a momentary destabilization, since each episode required that the woman in question restrain her powers and recapitulate to the domestic order, leaving it ultimately unscathed. In effect, these fantastic sitcoms offered a chance for women to momentarily transgress social conventions and allow some of the more radical elements of the counterculture into their lives, but not in any way that would have lasting repercussions. Instead, they served as valuable outlets for audiences' fears and anxieties over the cataclysmic changes in society, but only as a fantasy that would provide temporary release before re-affirming the moral correctness of family values and feminine acquiescence (Hamamoto 1989, 62).

While *The Flying Nun* did not occur in the suburbs, it was set in the preferred alternative location for feminine containment: the convent. This allowed the lead character to share experiences more in keeping with young, single girls than with housewives and to explore the generation gap for women while bracketing its most obvious burning issues, sexual freedom and self-exploration. When it debuted in September 1967, *The Flying Nun* was placed in ABC's Thursday night line-up of fantastic and feminine programming. It was the lead-in to the popular sitcom *Bewitched*, followed by *That Girl* and *Peyton Place*. This line-up was a likely attempt at counter-programming against the other two networks' male-oriented detective and western shows on that evening: NBC with *Daniel Boone*, *Ironside*, and *Dragnet*, and CBS with *Cimarron Strip* (Brooks and Marsh 1995, 1188). ABC's programming strategy to attract more women viewers was accomplished through the apparent connection between the fantastic and the feminine. It suggests that the idea of temporary escape from a banal existence was especially resonant for women. However, it would be too simple to offer an argument about resistance in women's cultural practices to explain the contradictions inherent in *The Flying Nun* and the need for a supernatural gimmick to overcome the limits of its feminine-driven premise. Such an analysis may help to explain women's ability to find pleasure in otherwise limiting or oppressive representations of their lives, but it does not go far in explaining the social conditions of women that influenced those representations in popular culture.

What is necessary here is to make tangible connections between the status of women in society and the role that the convent played in mediating discourses about women's expected roles and relations during the highly volatile period of the late sixties. As Spigel notes, sitcoms often borrowed heavily from other media that offered more critical perspectives on public issues and then muted that critique through such conventions as humour, simple resolutions, and unaffected characterizations (1991, 214). In the case of *The Flying Nun*, it would appear that the heightened interest in the reform movement in the convent and the phenomenon of the new nun provided a unique cover for the exploration of larger issues of gender and generations that were coming to the forefront. So much of the new nuns' attitude was influenced by the youth-oriented counterculture of antiwar, free speech, and civil rights protests that were just beginning to incorporate questions of gender equality. The generation gap among sisters that was identified in *Harper's* was not unique to the convent. It was also a major factor in the increasingly divisive feminist movement. In the late sixties a disjuncture was occurring between young women caught up in countercultural activities and the older and professionally established group of women – including two sisters – who sided with Friedan's more domesticated brand of feminism. The development of an alternative form of second-wave feminism diversified the women's movement by emphasizing identity issues over policy and challenging the middle-class, heterosexist biases of the National Organization for Women (NOW). It also incorporated a personalist ethos of cooperative, collective organizing.

It is not hard to imagine the intertwining of the younger brand of feminism with personalism in the sixties, since so many of the founding principles of personalism were rooted in feminized ideals and language. In particular, the belief that political action should be informed by personal values such as compassion, cooperation, and community had its roots in nineteenth-century reform movements that espoused women's values as morally and spiritually superior. While feminine and spiritual ideals were given precedence in the radical social action movements, the actual leaders and decision makers of the movements were almost always men. Women's roles within the personalist-based movements for civil rights, antiwar, or other social justice causes were circumscribed by notions of women's cultural identity as the nurturers and caregivers in society. It was this problem of confronting injustices within organizations which perpetuated gender stereotypes that helped awaken the radical women's movement.

It wasn't only in the social arena of protests and demonstrations that young women began to assert themselves. Advertising and the mass media were more and more ready to address women directly as an important and lucrative market. This consumer power eased imperceptibly into an enhanced political consciousness of autonomy and individuality. As Radner has suggested, the new mantra of the radical women's liberation movement reflected those consumerist roots (1999, 34). The view that the personal is political can be characterized as both a socialist concern to bring women's productive and reproductive capacities into the public arena and as a reconfiguration of personalist concerns over the dignity of persons. However, it also shows the slip-page from personalism to individualism, where the fulfilment of per-sonal desires became central to definitions of freedom and equality. As economic power tied in closely to political and cultural power, the line between consumer and citizen blurred. The result was a reconceptual-ization of feminism through questions of identity, personal authority, and pleasure, and the unleashing of feminine erotic power (22). While this shift redrew the boundaries of feminist politics, it also served a stra-tegic purpose in bringing feminism into the mainstream of popular cul-ture. As Barbara Ehrenreich argues, the sexual undertones of the newly radicalized women's movement contradicted criticisms of frigidity or libidinal disorder and helped make feminism 'cool' (Ehrenreich, Hess, and Jacobs 1986, 72). Redefining personhood along the lines of individ-ual gratification led to a rejection of the heavily bureaucratic type of organizing favoured by NOW. Consciousness-raising groups, small meetings, and local activism were championed over national network-ing and lobbying. The goal was to heighten individual awareness and, through that, ignite a force that would shake up the establishment from the ground up. Social change was to come through personal enlighten-ment, not the other way around.

There was something to this more radical form of organizing that was attractive to many religious sisters, despite, or even because of, its sex-ual underpinnings. They were certainly not immune to forces of erotic exploration and the pleasures of the self. Even if the Vatican was attempting to shut down public debate, the reform movement had gone too far to simply stop because the bishops told them to. The questions raised by nuns' initial forays into religious sexual-psychology were exac-erbated by massive structural changes to nearly every aspect of the reli-gious life and their rejection of doctrines that claimed eternal and unwavering adherence. However, even as their experiments adopted a more radical tone, their acceptance by the younger generation of femi-nists was not readily forthcoming. As fewer young women entered the convent, and even more were walking out, the sense of a generation gap in the women's movement was mirrored in the convent, resulting in two competing images of nuns. Simultaneously, sisters were being cele-brated for their courageous challenges to church authority while the religious life was increasingly depicted as being out of sync with the needs of the younger generation of women. The sexualized, slightly naughty nuns such as Sister George in *Where Angels Go, Trouble Follows* or the trio in *Change of Habit* were early signs of a stereotype that would explode in the seventies, especially with the arrival of European soft-core porn features set in convents. In direct competition were the reactionary and nostalgic images of unabashed piety and virginity offered up by *The Sound of Music*, The Singing Nun, and the newest addition, *The Flying Nun*.

What was missing from the Hollywood versions was an image of sisters as mature, politically aware, and even radical women who were navigating their own unique way through the debris of the counterculture without rejecting their identity as consecrated celibates. However, it did exist to a certain extent in the news. Religious communities like the Immaculate Heart of Mary congregation in Los Angeles transformed their staid religious festival, Mary's Day, into a hippie-inflected happening, complete with sisters bedecked in ribbons, flowers, and beads participating in poetry readings and open-air dancing. As Sister Corita Kent explained in *Newsweek*, happenings expressed to her 'a genuine effort to integrate the arts in a multimedia celebration of God's creation' ('The Nun' 1967, 46). Their efforts were praised as a way to bring the spiritual renewal of America to fruition:

> But now, the purely masculine way of running the church no longer seems to work so well. Catholics seeking new ways to be Christians no longer find the old patterns of much help in creating a more vibrant religious life. Love, freedom and experiment are their bywords, but this message of renewal seldom is loudly proclaimed in priests' rectories or bishops' chanceries. Instead, it is a growing legion of nuns who seem eager to sound the call. (45)

By the end of the decade sisters even had their own feminist coalition working alongside the more broadly based Conference of Major Superiors of Women. The National Coalition of American Nuns was described by *Newsweek* as a 'staunchly militant group' working to improve the status of women in the Catholic Church. As its founder, Sister Margaret Ellen Traxler, said, 'It's a part of the human rights movement. If women in society have second-class citizenship, women in the church have third-class' ('Battling for Nuns' Rights' 1969, 81).

Sisters were utilizing the media to publicize their affinity with new social movements by aligning themselves with the youth culture and women's liberation of the late sixties on social and spiritual, if not sexual, terms. However, through their invocations to personalism they attempted to mitigate this thorny issue by acknowledging the need for experimentation with identity and self-awareness in creative ways that had more to do with a re-evaluation of love than sex. Unfortunately, the critical outlook evident in cover stories such as *Newsweek*'s was all but absent from *The Flying Nun*. Sister Bertrille was supposed to embody the vivacity of the new nun. However, her willingness to forego those principles to appease the more traditional Mother Plácido was not in keeping with sisters' real efforts to step up the pace of reform. The contradictory state of sisters in the late sixties resulted in a great deal of cultural confusion that formed the nucleus for the premise of *The Flying Nun*. By placing a show about a group of independent, single women in a convent, it also helped to subvert any questioning of women's liberation and maintain the focus on religiously inflected moral themes rather than radical social or sexual issues.

The compromised image of the religious life in *The Flying Nun* came not from sisters but from their clerical leaders. There were many Catholic officials who were keen to establish a relationship with television executives, in keeping with their interpretation of the Second Vatican Council. They turned to television to represent their modified vision of reform, as counter to the sisters on the magazine covers. By emphasizing the role of social communication in religion, the members of the Second Vatican Council made a clear gesture that they were ending a long history of closed-door relations between the Catholic hierarchy and the rest of the world. No longer relying on a triumphalist belief in institutions and absolute authority, new importance was given to the mass media as a key strategy in building dialogue not only with Catholic audiences, but also between other religions and even secular cultures. Furthermore, with its emphasis on social rather than interpersonal communication, the Vatican privileged the mass media that 'touch man's spirit and which have opened up new avenues of easy communication of all kinds of news, of ideas and orientations' (Flannery 1975, 283). This new attitude of respect and openness between the Catholic Church and the mass media finally put an end to the Legion of Decency in America. In 1965 it was replaced by two advisory agencies, the National Catholic Office for Motion Pictures (NCOMP) and the

National Catholic Office for Radio and Television (NCORT). The fact that broadcast media gained their own agency and were not considered subsidiaries of film, which had been a major concern of the Vatican's since the thirties, was a sign that church officials were recognizing the unique abilities of television to assist the Catholic Church in its desire to enter into a broader relationship with regular lay society.

Before production could go too far on *The Flying Nun* there had to be in place the support and cooperation of the National Catholic Office of Radio and Television. Rosalind Wyman, head of public affairs for the Screen Gems production company, which had purchased the rights to the fledgling sitcom, rightfully reasoned that gaining clerical support first would make any negotiations with NCORT much easier. It would also be a way to test the waters to ensure that no protests would arise at a later date, which might prove costly and embarrassing. Her strategy was, as she put it, to prove that '*The Flying Nun* was no "Going My Way" and that instead it brought the Church up-to-date' (Whitney 1968, 24). She first approached Cardinal McIntyre of the Los Angeles diocese. Surprisingly, she met little resistance. After some initial meetings with him and his staff, the only issues raised were that Sister Bertrille be identified as a novice since no vowed nun would ever act so frivolously, and that there be no sexual tension between any of the nuns and the handsome casino owner, Carlos. One other concern expressed by the diocese's vocation director, Sister Michael Marie, was that the mother superior be toned down and not act so rigid and authoritarian: 'American superiors aren't like the cold, stern superior Madeleine Sherwood was playing at first, and I didn't want her to be too authoritarian. Authority is in enough jeopardy today' (Humphrey 1967, 32). With McIntyre's support, two other high-ranking officials – the even more conservative archbishop of New York, John Francis Cardinal Spellman, and Archbishop Philip Matthew Hannan of the staunchly Catholic New Orleans diocese – endorsed the show. The National Catholic Office of Radio and Television then was able to offer its full cooperation, and Sister Michael Marie signed on as technical advisor.

Ironically, it seems therefore that the only people not concerned about negative public reaction to a comedy about nuns were religious advisors. Charles Reilly, the Executive Director of NCORT at the time, marvelled at the hesitancy of television executives: '[NCORT] looked upon it as an excellent recruiting poster and could thus afford to be lenient. "The show is positioning nuns as human beings ... Only the studio, the agencies and the sponsors were worried. I guess they thought Catholics might stop buying toothpaste'" (Whitney 1968, 24). His jovial tone suggested that the entire history of the dreaded Legion of Decency – which in its heyday probably could have stopped Catholics from buying toothpaste if it had wanted to – was now being swept under the carpet. However, it took some time to convince entertainment producers of this new spirit of cooperation. CBS, Warner's, and MGM all passed on the premise. They stated that they saw no humour in it and only 'large religious obstructions.' Even the show's first writer, Bernard Slade, was loath to involve himself in such a tricky situation. As he put it, 'I shuddered. The modern nun had some appeal, but this was something else. We would have to make her resemble an everyday human being' (Whitney 1968, 22–3).

By contrast, NCORT was only too happy to assist on the show. In keeping with the new spirit of cooperation and mutual respect between Catholic officials and entertainment producers, there was no attempt to gain a controlling interest. Along with Sister Michael Marie, their role was to read the scripts and make suggestions about the portrayal of the religious life to improve its accuracy. This task ranged from training the actresses in the subtle techniques of walking, sitting, and eating like a nun, to more direct changes to scripts, which NCORT referred to as damage control. For example, one script called for a bishop and his wife to visit the Convent San Tanco. While marriage was allowable in the Anglican Church – this was likely the reason for the confusion – clerical celibacy was still an unquestioned rule of Catholicism (Wolff 1991, 75). However, for the most part the involvement of NCORT was limited to smaller technical matters that would improve the overall aura of authenticity in the doctrinal sense of the word, as opposed to its personalist meaning, and continue a traditional attitude of respect and deference towards nuns.

With Catholic officials enthusiastically onside, the producers could now turn to the far more pressing concern of making the show popular with audiences other than religious advisors. After all those negotiations, Catholicism was put on the back-burner of *The Flying Nun*, in favour of more broad-based episodes dealing with the ongoing generational conflicts between perky Sister Bertrille and conservative Mother Plácido. It seems that the premise of the sitcom was important not so much for providing an opportunity to explore the life of the new nuns. Instead, it was seen as an effective vehicle for providing a protective environment from which to portray the conflicts facing idealistic young women as they butted heads with older women who were also looking for ways to improve their status in society. Perhaps that is why the producers felt that it was so urgent that Sally Field, the irrepressible teenager from *Gidget*, play the role of Bertrille. It would certainly explain why the producers took such pains to draw parallels between the two characters and the actress who portrayed them both. Field's responses were simultaneously defensive while acknowledging that her own lack of sexual dynamism kept her pinned to these sorts of roles. As she complained in the press, 'In the motion picture "The Way West," I played a teen-ager who becomes an unwed mother. Nobody yet has asked me if she is the real Sally Field' (Field 1967, B6).

Eventually, even Field had to agree that her star persona was far from the image of sexually liberated countercultural feminism. When asked in another interview if she missed 'the pot and LSD which seems to be part of the heritage of your generation,' she only frowned and said that she would be more likely to be trying out for sororities and school plays on campus than indulging in such hedonistic activities (de Roos 1967, 18). And though she was an adult living on her own in Los Angeles, that wasn't so she could become a swinging single girl à la Helen Gurley Brown, but because she loved to 'play house' and decorate. Brown's dreamy reveries of girls in pink silk Capri pants lounging on overstuffed pillows and reading Proust in their own apartments, waiting expectantly for their lovers to arrive, was nowhere near the carefully constructed image of Field as the all-American girl star. As her own mother said, this state of independent singledom was a mere stopgap to prepare her daughter for inevitable marriage and motherhood. She said, 'I think it is important for a woman to taste independence between the time of her dependence on her family and dependence on her husband' (de Roos 1967, 18).

This asexual image was fairly typical of conservative, domestic ideals for women, which upheld that the move from dependent daughter to dependent wife was simply a matter of learning basic home economics and improving your decorating skills (Ehrenreich, Hess, and Jacobs 1986, 26). Yet, it wouldn't help the popularity of the show if Field were totally out to lunch on the new wave of feminist consciousness. Nonetheless, her knowledge seemed to be much more in keeping with the concerns of the liberal, middle-class form of feminism than the radical movement. She insisted that she had grown up considerably since her Gidget days, when her youth and naïveté had left her scrambling to understand the business of stardom: "'I don't know anything," I'd say. "I'll do anything you guys say." Now I stand up for equal rights' (de Roos 1967, 17). With a salary of four thousand dollars per week on *The Flying Nun*, Field 'missed the last years of rebellion,' said her mother, 'instead she had to become a citizen with responsibilities' (18). In keeping with her state of controlled, asexual independence, the public was assured that Field was placed on a tight budget by her business manager, to whom she had to justify every purchase, from groceries to a new dress (19).

This link between consumption and sexuality was not coincidental. As Radner suggests, the liberated woman was no longer merely an object of consumer culture but an active agent in her own social and sexual construction through consumption. Her pursuit of pleasure, championed by Brown, was financed by her own ambitions, and demonstrated most explicitly through her refusal of domestic dependence both sexually and economically (1999, 9). The opening up of the girl market in beauty, fashion, and popular culture was a major economic indicator of erotic power, as Gael Greene noted in her study, *Sex and the College Girl*:

> With a buying power that packs an impressive wallop, the teenager is the pet of manufacturers, who woo her with sex and encourage her to spend $25m a year on deodorants, $20m on lipstick, $9m on home permanents. In her 30AA bra and Jackie Kennedy hairdo, she is a living, fire-breathing *femme fatale* at 14. There is no time to be a child. She is quickly an adolescent and a teenager, a strange interim plateau that is fraught with paradox and goes on forever. (1964, 42)

That sense of open-endedness and lack of boundaries created opportunities for young women to experiment with their newfound sexual and economic freedom and threatened to upset the careful balance of gender roles demanded by heterosexual domestic order. *The Flying Nun* was one attempt at restoring traditional values by offering a limited sense of independence that came at the cost of both sexual and consumer power. Sally Field's star persona and her previous incarnation as the ultimate perky teenager, Gidget, was therefore crucial to this underlying message by linking the convent to girl culture more generally.

Field argued that the main difference between Gidget and Bertrille was that the former character was merely 'a seeker after her own desires and pleasures' while the nun's dedication to others highlighted her maturity. For her own case, her desire to become a 'really good actress' could seem as indulgent as Gidget's 'passion for the hero-of-the-week,' but it was really much more in keeping with Bertrille's vocation to contribute to society by bringing happiness and enjoyment to others (Field 1967, B6). As the show progressed, this link between Field, Gidget, and Bertrille became stronger in order to solidify a representation of appropriate femininity that could still be cool even if it was virginal. It was a defensive mode that Gloria Steinem had first recognized five years before the show went on the air, and one that was genuinely needed to counteract the apparent demand that liberation be proven in the bedroom more so than the boardroom:

> In the fine old American tradition of conformity, society has begun to make it as rough for virgins and women content to be housewives as it once did for those who had affairs before marriage and worked afterward. Chaste girls feel 'out of it' and women are apologetic for being 'only housewives.' The whole situation is as ludicrous and in need of remedy as the one that put a scarlet 'A' on Hester. (Steinem 1962, 156)

As the show progressed, it inserted more references to Bertrille's old life before entering the convent in order to confirm for audiences that this was, indeed, a 'normal' girl. A visiting friend tells the sisters that Bertrille was voted Miss Far Out at her high school. She becomes well known in San Tanco for her folk songs and is offered her own variety television series, in an obvious nod to the now infamous story of The Singing Nun. Her infectious style even converts Mother Plácido to at least some aspects of modernization. During an outdoor concert at which Sister Jacqueline, Sister Bertrille, and Mother Plácido are to sing a hymn, it is the Reverend Mother who puts a stop to the dirge-like accompaniment of the organist and calls forth (seemingly from the heavens, since there is no band in sight) an electric-folk ensemble. With all three sisters now grooving to the music, the audience wakes up and claps along joyously.

Perhaps the most overt reference to the youth culture and its relationship to the convent was in the episode 'The Reconversion of Sister Shapiro.' At first the episode appears to be an attempt to demonstrate the new ecumenism when a young Jewish girl decides she wants to become a nun. In fact, it was an effort to give a broader picture of the pre-convent Bertrille. In home movies Bertrille shows the infatuated child how she had enjoyed all the fun of a normal teenage girl, including fashionable clothes, rock and roll music, and owning her own car, before deciding to join a convent. The most interesting aspect of these scenes was that some of the shots seem to be outtakes from Field's old series, *Gidget*. Although it had already been established in the series that Bertrille had grown up in New York and gone to university in Chicago, in the home movies she is a ponytailed surfer tomboy from California. This direct link between the teen-surfer Gidget and the devout yet unconventional Sister Bertrille solidified a sense of natural progression for independent and idealistic young women. It took the least confrontational aspects of the popular images of young women and placed them in a traditional context. Thus, the convent offered an effective middle ground for young women like Gidget, Bertrille, and even the real-life Field, who embraced some aspects of feminism but did not feel comfortable with the extreme elements of the counterculture. That was great for some women, but it didn't do much for the convent, which was fast being viewed as an institution in decline. In the more religious-themed episodes, there was a half-hearted attempt to deal with contemporary issues facing nuns. Still, the resolution always seemed to lie in a return to traditional values.

In the pilot episode, when Bertrille lands in San Tanco, she blithely informs the sisters that she has just been released from prison after taking part in a free-speech rally. Apparently oblivious to the shock effect of such a statement, she then proposes a number of changes to the convent in an effort to make it more modern and accessible. The orphaned children who attend the convent school are freed from the classroom in favour of long walks along the beach and through the town while Bertrille sings a chirpy little song. Discovering that the convent is in dire financial straits, she organizes fund drives, outdoor concerts, and garage sales with the dual purpose of raising money and reacquainting the townspeople with the sisters. She even sneaks into the local disco and enjoys a brief dance before accosting Carlos, the owner, to request a major donation. Throughout all this the superior of the convent, Mother Plácido, is conveniently absent. Although the older and more experienced sisters are quickly charmed by their perky new novice, they know that her innovations will not likely be as appreciated by the Reverend Mother and try to prepare her for the first meeting. In a conversation that alludes directly to the changes in the convent, Sister Jacqueline warns Bertrille:

> SISTER JACQUELINE: Sister Bertrille, you must understand that when the Reverend Mother entered the order, profession was reached by discipline – discipline which destroyed all traces of self will or rebelliousness. [sigh] At least that was the idea. I suppose what I'm trying to say is that her ideas are rather traditional.
> SISTER BERTRILLE: Oh but Sister, times are changing so fast!
> SISTER JACQUELINE: I know. And the Reverend Mother tries very hard to understand. But for her sometimes it's difficult.

For the dignified and reserved Mother Plácido, the forthright activism of her newest novice is indeed often difficult to bear. However, she soon learns to make some small allowances for Sister Bertrille in order to preserve an overall air of pious femininity.

While religion generally operated as a kind of backdrop against which other aspects of everyday life took precedence in the plots, in one particular episode the problem of modified habits received special attention. 'The New Habit' was one of the few episodes in which Bertrille's ability to fly was an integral part of the story, rather than an incidental moment of inspired lunacy. It foregrounded the fact that it was only by virtue of her religious vocation that Sister Bertrille could fly, and only because of the relaxed controls of the modern convent that she was able to use her gift. As Sister Jacqueline puts it, only as a missionary nun in San Tanco could Sister Bertrille 'fly emotionally, and when the wind was right, fly literally as well.' Yet, by way of providing a balance, it was also made clear in one episode that if the modernizing went too far she would lose her special ability.

In 'The New Habit' Mother Plácido is told by the Superior General to finally do away with the old-fashioned habits and change to more fashionable, up-to-date outfits. The result is a powder blue combination of drop-waisted dresses and matching cloche hats. At first Bertrille is delighted with the prospect of wearing a pretty dress again and not looking so out of place when she goes about in public. Her excitement is short-lived, however, after she discovers that without the old habit, and especially the elaborate coronet, she can no longer fly. Once the news spreads, the other sisters also become upset and the whole convent plunges into despair. When their friend and patron, Carlos Ramirez, realizes the situation and sees how desperately unhappy Bertrille is, he decides to make it so the convent will have to return to the old ways. He interrupts a visit by the Superior General with some trivial excuse as a pretext to show off his latest girlfriend's new dress, a much sexier version of the new habit. The girlfriend says that she has designed it herself and expects it to become all the rage on the island. Obviously shocked and uncomfortable, the Superior General rescinds her order to modernize, allowing the sisters to return to the old habit and giving Bertrille the chance to fly once again. This episode was indicative of the kind of overriding theme at work in *The Flying Nun*; namely, that the best kind of freedom was earned through acceptance of at least some of the old-fashioned, traditional ways. In the socially conservative medium of the television sitcom, the balance between traditional and progressive values tipped decidedly in favour of the former. However, for sisters struggling for new definitions of their way of life there was little chance of turning back. Thus, *The Flying Nun* stands as a final gesture to a dying image of the religious life: one based upon a vision of easy integration of some socially progressive values into a traditional framework to offer a controlled level of feminine independence.

The irony of *The Flying Nun* is that while it enjoyed some ratings success during its three years on ABC, enrolment in the convent was setting new levels of decline every year. According to the Official Catholic Directory, the number of sisters dropped 10 per cent, from 176,671 to 160,931, in the three years between 1967 and 1970. Meanwhile, the age gap between members was rising steadily. In 1960 almost half of the sisters in America were between the ages of twenty and forty. By 1967 they composed only 27 per cent of the sister population, which was only going to get older without new recruits. By the time *The Flying Nun* went off the air, only 10 per cent of sisters were in the twenty-to-forty-year-old age group. Furthermore, the era of large entering classes was also over. In a survey of 287 congregations, 27 per cent had no new entrants in 1970 compared with only 4 per cent in 1965, the last year of the Second Vatican Council. Over half had less than ten new entrants. In 1965 the numbers had been reversed with 52 per cent of the congregations having at least ten new entrants (Ebaugh 1977, 69–71). It would seem, then, that the hope of the National Catholic Office for Radio and Television that the show would encourage youthful vocations did not materialize. Ultimately, *The Flying Nun* had little to do directly with the state of the religious life. Rather, it used the convent as a setting for telling cautionary tales about the counterculture and feminine independence through the popular trope of the generation gap.

Margaret Miles makes a distinction between a popular culture in which religious elements are intended for devotional purposes and one that incorporates religious themes and scenarios in order to provide a context for a wider exploration of human relationships (1996, 46). Clearly, *The Flying Nun* belongs to the latter category, but that is not to say that it avoided the topic of religion altogether. The convent setting allowed for some exploration of the issues facing sisters. However, the show simplified these issues with quick resolutions that usually involved Bertrille happily compromising her radical ideals to meet the demands of the religious life. In return, she was rewarded with exciting adventures, meaningful work, and even the supernatural ability to soar like a bird. There was no need to worry, for example, that Sister Bertrille might begin to question her vocation, as so many others were doing when faced with the kind of traditional authority structures represented by Mother Plácido. Nor was there a chance that the radical political movements in which she participated before coming to the Convent San Tanco would reach her again and pull her away from her sense of religious commitment. And there was certainly no chance that Carlos would sweep her away to his yacht with the other bikini bimbos. The fact that the media took pains to assure the audience that not even the actress playing Bertrille was susceptible to the kinds of excesses available to young women deepened that sense of security.

In effect, then, *The Flying Nun* acted as a privileged symbolic space where perplexing questions about the role of gender and religion in American culture could meet. Week after week it tried to show how each could improve upon the other when the right balance of modern idealism and romantic traditionalism was struck. It was a valiant effort, but ultimately the message fell on deaf ears. When *The Flying Nun* went off the air, it was almost immediately relegated to the level of kitsch. Even Field realized this and tried to distance herself from Bertrille by aligning herself more clearly with Gidget, a girl she had accused of self-ishness and pleasure-seeking not so long ago:

> You see, Gidget was really just an extension of me. What Gidget did riding waves and dating was what I would have been doing anyway. But that convent and that flying – that was a weird experience. You live more of your life on the stage in a series than you do on your own. I was bringing this extremely aggressive unnatural girl home with me. (Smith 1970)

Later in her career, she disowned the role, claiming it left her feeling 'mentally ill to the point of distraction' (Rovin 1985, 33). Like so much of nostalgia, *The Flying Nun* depicted a fictional era that never really was. Representations of nuns in popular culture became increasingly less grounded in the reality of sisters' lives. Instead, they began to be stereotyped according to how others would like them to be. The long, slow road towards the dustbins of cultural waste had begun.

Conclusion:
The Return of the New Nuns

At the close of the sixties, the tone of the counterculture shifted from the heartfelt – some might say naïve – optimism of personalism to more radical and oppositional stances against authority structures in society. Many sisters were still willing to join hands with the people in the streets, but their role within the Catholic Church made them suspect. While they had appeared revolutionary just a few years earlier, they were now disdained for being too sentimental and not going far enough. Even sisters felt as if they were putting popularity ahead of integrity with their cosy relationship to the media. Judith Tate put it this way:

> For the time, people are a bit fascinated by the 'new nun.' We like the attention and the approval. When some persons or groups challenge us or question us about our values, we do not like to answer in a way that may shatter our image or result in disapproval. Integrity may be more difficult for us than we would have suspected. In our eagerness to maintain approval, we may forego witness. (1970, 34)

Her statement goes to the heart of a key issue addressed here, namely, the relationship between social identity and cultural representations of women religious. The experiences of reform-minded sisters and their struggles to help shape their image in the media suggest a broader range of alternatives available to women in the postwar era than has been previously acknowledged. However, these roles did not come without compromise, nor could they be claimed as a radical rejection of the doctrines of femininity circumscribing women's lives in the formative years of second-wave feminism. They are nonetheless important because they demonstrate how difficult it can be for women to strike a balance between intellectual, professional, spiritual, and sexual independence when these gender identities are so often appropriated and exploited to serve other means.

Considering the kinds of heated battles that went on between sisters and the clergy as well as the media, it is hard to dismiss otherwise fluffy fare such as *The Flying Nun* or *The Trouble with Angels*. Instead, they alert us to a complex field of social relations that linked the representation of independent women with contemporary debates about religious authority. At first, the interest in sisters appeared to be gaining in popular culture while obliquely hinting at new forms of containable feminine independence. Ultimately, however, the images led to a stereotyping and trivializing of their accomplishments as foils for more radical notions of liberation. The religious authority that permeated their habits protected them for a time from critical scrutiny. As institutional religion came under fire for its assumed depersonalizing structures, the habit ceased to be a sign of moral inviolability and became instead an icon of repression. Furthermore, by changing into lay clothes and foregoing visibility, sisters themselves were in effect alienated from that popular image until the habit began to speak louder than the person. Eventually, nuns became little more than kitsch icons, the punchlines to not very funny jokes.

The reduction of nuns to the level of smug jokes and gag items is, therefore, worth exploring not simply because it fails to recognize the very real determination and commitment of sisters. More importantly, it provides insight into the complex network of relations and tensions that went into defining independent womanhood in popular culture. That sisters have been all but written out of cultural studies of the postwar era, despite their obviously strong presence, calls into question the easy narratives of old-school liberal feminists, swinging sex kittens, and avant-garde radicals, and the absence of other options. It also reinserts religion into the analysis, and not just as some antiquated throwback struggling for authority in a secularized society. Instead, the sheer force of influence by nuns is only one example of how religious tropes, relations, and ideals were incorporated into everyday life to infuse it with a sense of spiritual belonging and purposefulness. By entwining an alternative discourse of femininity and feminism with a recasting of religion in both its institutional and intuitive forms, the figure of the nun reimagines the past in ways that directly engage with our practices in the present.

Representations and meanings are never fixed in time even when they are historicized, as the shifts from Sister Angela of *Heaven Knows, Mr Allison* to Sister Michelle of *Change of Habit* make so clear. While there are obvious comparisons between them, the earlier Sister Angela could be hailed as a step forward for women while Sister Michelle can only be seen as a retreat backward. It is for this reason that the social context in which these popular-cultural texts emerged is so critical to understanding the role of nuns beyond their obvious religious and gender significance. The strategy of unification between past and present, therefore, is not a matter of universalizing nun's meanings. In fact, it isn't really about nuns at all, in the end. It is about discourses and doctrines of femininity and how they are applied not just to women but to places, practices, and objects. In a unique and highly specified way, the brief period of fascination with nuns in the fifties and sixties created lasting links between gender and religion that extend well beyond the convent. They can be seen in the obliquely spiritual television shows that began to crop up at the turn of the millennium, such as *Touched by an Angel* or *Joan of Arcadia*, or in social movements that try to halt their spread, like the Promise Keepers. Wherever they are, it remains that the feminization of religion, articulated so clearly in the postwar new nun, has not come about without a great deal of ambivalence. The reluctance to acknowledge it in positive ways is indicative of the double bind of femininity as both a doctrine curtailing women's erotic power in public space and as a discourse of devaluation for a wide range of social systems and structures.

By recognizing these strategies of gender distinction across institutions and identities, the way in which the nun served a contradictory role in popular culture becomes clearer. On the one hand, she was a reserved, docile, and submissive woman who kept her sexuality in check. On the other, she was an exotic and extremely desirable creature who demonstrated a level of self-reliance and adventurism unprecedented for women. While such casting worked as long as women's sexuality remained fastened to their maternal possibility, as the sixties advanced, the idea of pleasure as a practice of identity took hold and challenged such chasteness as repression (Radner 1999, 2). Given the negative attitude towards sex in the church, it was some time before sisters could formulate an understanding of celibacy as an active state of sexual independence and not just an imposition on the part of a repressive, patriarchal institution.

The breakthrough really didn't come until 1985, when the Naiad Press, an independent women's press, published *Lesbian Nuns: Breaking Silence*. Although many of the stories reiterated an image of sexual hostility in the convent, the mere fact of speaking in public about these issues finally forced open the last locked door of the convent. Later work by Sister Jeannine Gramick (1989) and Sister Sandra Schneiders (2001) furthered the debate by focusing on those who eventually reconciled their sexual identity as lesbians and as celibates in order to remain in the religious life. Their examinations recognize sexuality and consecrated celibacy as dual concerns, acknowledging that this vow is the least understood and yet the most visible sign of the religious today. Without the habit or the veil, and also without the trained obsequiousness to signal obedience and humility, it cannot be denied that the word 'virgin' is usually the first thing that tends to pop into people's minds when they think of nuns. This exposes nuns to sniggering, prurient intrusions on their lives and motivations as religious. Yet their representations against a highly sexualized culture offer exciting new lines of inquiry for feminist media and cultural studies.

Of course, the argument is just as simply made that it is unjust to force women into choosing between their intellectual and sexual fulfilment, to suggest that a life of the mind cannot be had without disparaging the needs of the body. However, I want to aim for something more messy and complex than this. The path to emancipation from the restricting conventions of masculine/feminine, mind/body that imposed chastity on those who spurned maternity is not so easily cleared by merely inserting sexuality for personal pleasure or desire. Nor can nuns be treated as outcasts of feminism because of their celibacy. As Radner acknowledges in her examination of the swinging single girl of the sixties, sexuality was a major trope in the consumerist appropriation of feminine independence as narcissistic individualism (1999, 22). Susan Douglas also criticizes the individualist, consumer impulse that reduces the discourses of feminist liberation to one of sexual narcissism (2000, 267). That is not to dismiss the sexual revolution as unimportant or damaging to women, as some may try to do. Even Schneiders slides into a rather self-serving argument about the potential of the nun's celibacy to bear witness against a 'rampantly narcissistic and hedonistic culture' (2001, 131). Rather, it is to suggest that sexuality can be understood as something much more than sexual availability. It is a form of personal praxis available to everyone and expressed by sisters in a strategically different way, not dependent on media-influenced promiscuity but on personal moral consciousness.

Sisters like Mary Aloysius Schaldenbrand raised the issue of celibacy and sexuality in the sixties not to do away with the vow, but to make it a more active and meaningful aspect of the religious life. She complained that for a young postulant 'her opportunities to experience directly a wide range of attitudes, values and life styles are minimal – this girl notably lacks the experiential conditions of arriving at real freedom to choose sexual renunciation' (1967, 81). The idea of simply relieving sisters of that vow was not seriously considered in the postwar era despite the intense revamping of almost every other aspect of the life. The vows of obedience and poverty were significantly reappraised to give sisters more authority over their spiritual fulfilment and sense of personal identity. However, with the exception of the repeal on 'personal friendships,' the celibacy issue was left virtually untouched (Wittberg 1994, 249). Once the religious life lost its pre-eminent status in the church, and as issues of sexual and reproductive freedom became central to second-wave feminism, sisters were left on the defensive. As one commentator put it, 'it is clear that the atmosphere of sexual fulfilment as a necessary ingredient for maturity and personality growth has left the celibate vocation almost in need of a "singles lib" movement' (250). Nonetheless, the nun's status as a celibate in a swirl of sexy images suggests alternative conceptions of female desire and pleasure that include a spiritual as well as a sexual dimension, rather than pitting these dimensions against each other.

Examining popular culture means exploring the fields of desire, pleasure, identity, and personal fulfilment. This becomes uniquely challenging when the subject is nuns. While they were originally represented as affirmative models of limited independence for women, by the end of the sixties that affirmation had turned into anxiety as religious conservatives railed against their apparently libertine ways while radical feminists spurned them for their veiled virginity. Thus, nuns were no longer participants in an incipient feminism but were regarded as beacons of an imagined past in which the private sphere of feminine passivity was

untroubled by political questions of gender equity and sexual independence. With their image thoroughly commodifed by the mass media
they became little more than ungrounded signifiers for a culture struggling against the tides of time to remain relevant and pertinent. In
other words, they signified not social desire but its lack (Straw 2000,
180). During a brief period of heightened fascination nuns stood for a
host of competing and complex social desires: for greater spiritual
authenticity, meaningful feminine heroics, or a public sense of personalism carried out through social justice activism. Yet, today, the mean-
ingfulness of nuns derives more from their undesirability, their cultural
obsoleteness, which was forged in part by misguided accusations concerning their sexual absence.

Radner and others have made important inroads into the complex
relationship between sexuality and consumption in the creation of a
new kind of individual during the postwar era. As she explains, a
woman's ability to be both agent and object of her desirability, in terms
of her own pleasure rather than on relational terms as a wife and
mother, placed economic and erotic power on the same continuum
(1999, 9). Helen Gurley Brown made such connections explicit by
insisting that the single girl be financially as well as sexually independent, as shrewd with her money as she was with her body. Nuns were
therefore doubly denied as outsiders to the consumer and sexual society.
While they worked hard and were no doubt models of feminine profes-
sionalization, the effort was not for themselves but always, necessarily,
for others. Ultimately, therefore, the place of the nun in popular culture
is at least as concerned with questions of consumption as sexuality. A
new form of citizenship based on consumer power could not be claimed
by nuns, who are vowed to poverty. No matter how hard they tried to
revamp personalism in a way that would afford them entrance into this
new culture of the self, they could not overcome the inherent contradictions. Their sexual 'repression' was the most obvious external sign of
this lack. They therefore could not be defined as agents but became
only objects of consumption through their sexual exploitation in popular culture.

In the seventies many sisters stepped up their political activism and
developed a sense of identity that was in opposition not only to traditional images of women in the Catholic Church but also to mainstream
popular culture more generally. They began to speak out even louder on

controversial topics such as abortion and nuclear disarmament, and they took a leading role in the worldwide movement to abolish the death penalty. Unfortunately, their lack of visibility through their aban-donment of the habit, depleted ranks, crumbling institutions, and rising median age all contributed to a major image problem. As Soeur Luc-Gabrielle had discovered years before, it was the icon of veiled, virtuous virginity that audiences flocked to, not the complicated women behind them. When all their media spokeswomen had left the religious life – some quietly, like M. Charles Borromeo, others in a hail of publicity, like Jacqueline Grennan – the media gave up on the new nuns and reverted back to old stereotypes.

In effect, the image of the new nun, rather than pointing to a refresh-ing new direction in the representation of sisters that was grounded in the reality of their daily lives, became a prisoner of its own devices. The new nun broke apart into three competing but ultimately mutually reinforcing stereotypes. As *The Flying Nun* shows, there was the impos-sibly cute and cuddly nun, so incredibly naïve about her sexual and consumer power that to renounce it was of little consequence. These nice or ninny nuns played off the nasty nun, an older, meaner version who held tight to the rules of feminine conformity. Every random image of a tight-lipped sister indiscriminately whacking people with a ruler reinforces this stereotype. Meanwhile, up through the middle came the naughty nun, a highly sexualized image of a young, beautiful woman whose unbridled passions inevitably rip through her habit. This was not a particularly new image; pornographic depictions of the convent had circulated since the Middle Ages and were revived during the nativist period in the early nineteenth century. However, this latest revival came from film and achieved unprecedented levels of explicitness. Pier Paolo Pasolini's *Il Decamerone*, released in 1970, included the tale 'Masetto and the Nuns,' in which a gardener becomes the sex toy of the convent inhabitants. This critically hailed but controversial film was a forerunner to a tidal wave of naughty nun porn that achieved cult status through quick production and underground distribution (Fentone 2000, 11). Such 'Decameroni' films merged soft-core sex with smarmy dialogue and smug anticlericalism into a distinct genre of naughty nun 'sinema' (11)

Given the prevalence of nun porn, it is interesting to note that the most enduring portrait of the new nun from the postwar era is found in

The Sound of Music. Not a nun film in the truest sense of the term, this self-consciously innocent version of pious virginity gained a new camp identity through a brief trend in interactive singalong screenings. The idea was forged at the 1999 London Gay and Lesbian Film Festival, after organizers heard about a seniors' home that distributed sheet music so residents could join in while they watched their favourite musicals. *Singalong Sound of Music* became a runaway hit and an instant spectacle, mutating to include costume parades, warm-up acts, and free giveaways for participants. There were also revised lyrics to some of the songs, parodying the naïveté of the film and its sickly sweet sentimentalism by adding a lusty dose of sexual innuendo (Tunnacliffe 2001). Organizers noted that the audience was overwhelmingly female and explained that by the fact that the musical is generally considered a feminine genre. However, given that this was not a straightforward revival of the film but a very deliberate ironic appropriation, its success as a queer cultural event suggests that it is not the antithesis of nun porn but its more accessible 'other.' As Stacy Wolf argues, the role of Maria and her relationship with the nuns opens *The Sound of Music* to a lesbian rereading that insists on its gender transgressiveness even as it conforms to dominant discourses of heterosexual domesticity (1996, 51). Since her object of analysis is not the film but the original Broadway production starring Mary Martin, her conclusions do not necessarily fit. However, once that film is reinterpreted as a live performance in which audience-players knowingly add double entendres and broadly wink at its queer possibilities, such a reading becomes much more intriguing. In the end, the ideal 'nice nun' is made an object of consumption through which sexual identities can be played out on her innocent – that is, unknowing and passive – body. Once again, the definition of the nun as lacking desirability as an active agent in her sexual identity makes her a blank text on which others can write their own sexual and gender pleasures.

Focusing on the issue of sexuality helps to explain why the image of the nun mutated into porn or parody. However, it does not offer any reason as to why nuns were singled out in the fifties and sixties in the first place. Their religiosity cannot be relegated to a cultural afterthought, an inconsequential coincidence of their proto-feminist appeal. Rather, the kind of religious temperament that nuns embodied resonated with new directions in personalist and anti-institutional spirituality. Questions of order, discipline, and hierarchy gave way to concerns about belonging, togetherness, and compassion. In other words, religious values metamorphosed into spirituality, the latter being more nebulous and more in keeping with strategies of personal affirmation and identity construction than corporate affiliation and allegiance. The linking of these new values with femininity was not particularly innovative but had its roots in nineteenth-century Protestant domesticity. What was different was that the focal point for this gender ideology of religion had shifted onto Catholicism and was represented by the figure of the nun. This transmutation of religious values to the illusory and conciliatory realm in effect privatized religion. Rather than being regarded as a structural network of organizing principles to govern daily life, religious beliefs became a locus for a different kind of desirability and desiring focused on the full spiritual realization of the person.

Ironically, such a reduction in authority actually improved the status of Catholics. Until the fifties they had been treated almost as a visible minority, voluntarily segregated from the rest of society. Some Catholics tried valiantly to deny that their church was a monolithic entity with direct and imperious control over its members. Yet it was not until the issue of religion as a whole was relegated to the back burners of society that they could overcome centuries of suspicion and prejudice. Even critics such as Paul Blanshard (1958) were quick to distinguish between institutional hierarchies and personal convictions when it came to religious devotion. While the former were to be closely monitored, the latter were recognized as an integral aspect to liberal values of individual freedom and personal conscience. The privatization of religion not only subsumed religious identity as a minor element to a person's public character, but it also linked religious issues with the status of women. By linking values such as compassion and nurturing to religious devotion, religion was feminized and reverted to the domain of women, alongside domesticity and maternalism. As the most recognizable figure of feminine faith, the nun became the archetype of modern Catholicism as much as she was also the figurehead for pre-feminist independence.

It was the religious identity of sisters that had first given them the courage to face the public. They believed that theirs was a higher calling, a supernatural commitment that left them both of the world and above it. By the mid-sixties, such an eternal conception of the religious life was under serious fire. While some sisters felt pulled by their religious commitment to become witnesses to social injustice, feminist consciousness came much later to them. There were small inklings of feminism in the sixties through the involvement of some sisters in the National Organization for Women and the establishment of feminist-based associations like the National Coalition of American Nuns in 1968. By the seventies, sisters were finding ways to merge religious and feminist concerns into such intellectual and political projects as feminist liberation theology and women's ordination. Their increasingly combative stance vis-à-vis the Catholic hierarchy, as well as business and government, further debilitated their image in the media as they ceased to fit either the sexually radical image of feminism or the socially conservative image of religious faith.

Part of my project here is to correct the idea that nuns represent a lack of desirability, either spiritual or sexual. Such conceptions in popular culture work through an appropriation of nuns not in order to deal directly with issues of the religious life for women, but to fulfil other agendas. At the beginning of second-wave feminism, nuns had represented an unarticulated sense of spiritualized yearning in their most romantic portrayal; in the early stages of so-called third-wave feminism, they now stand as caricatures of repression against the liberated woman. In a gender regime that emphasizes individuality and identity performance through consumption, the nun is an easy target. Hence, in a film like *Sister Act*, to cite one of many contemporary examples, a Las Vegas showgirl must teach a congregation of fully habited and cloistered nuns how to reconnect with society by learning to let loose and shimmy their way through Motown classics. Interestingly, in this film it is the all-male hierarchy that ultimately has to step in and convince the nuns to let it all hang out. Thus, not only are the nuns depicted as opposite to sexually confident women, but that very confidence is apparently to be bestowed by patriarchal authority. The pope unwittingly sides with a woman who exploits her sexuality for money rather than with those who adhere to the doctrines of pious chastity. In that sense, then, the casual dismissal of nuns for their lack of sexuality can be seen as a subtle way of reinforcing femininity's relationship to the body in popular culture and actually cutting off opportunities for a greater independence and sense of selfhood beyond the confines of heterosexual desirability.

In the midst of all these sexually explicit or kitschy nostalgia representations of nuns in contemporary popular culture, a few small exam-

Susan Sarandon's Oscar-winning performance as Sister Helen Prejean in *Dead Man Walking*.

ples stand out. When Tim Robbins and Susan Sarandon brought Sister Helen Prejean's disturbing book about her death-row ministry to the screen, it sparked a flurry of media interest that resembled the early days of the 'new nuns.' *Dead Man Walking* (1995) was a major critical hit, earning Sarandon a Best Actress Oscar. The publicity for the film made sure to include Prejean, having her attend interviews alongside the stars and explain her work and her way of life. Oprah Winfrey featured all of them and led a discussion on Prejean's campaign to eradicate the death penalty. *60 Minutes* also profiled her, as did other media outlets. Many sisters point to this film as finally a positive and realistic portrayal of their lives today. However, the film disappoints in that the focus is on the nun's relationship to the death-row inmate, while very little of her life as a religious is shown. A few flashbacks to her Catholic childhood, filled with white veils and rosaries, actually undermine the image, especially since her sister-companion receives little attention in the film and her whole community is mere backdrop, rather than an active, motivating force in her life. The resolute focus on the heroic individual mimics the contradictory image of the new nun from such postwar films as *The Nun's Story*. Still, this film does offer something far more complex and compelling than the usual fare of stereotypical nasty-naughty-or-nice nuns that predominate today.

Other characters have arisen that sympathetically and complexly represent the reality of nuns' lives. Rita Moreno's role as Sister Peter Marie, the in-house psychiatrist in the HBO prison drama *Oz* (1997–2003), was the major female lead in an otherwise dominantly masculine series. Her struggle with her vows in the midst of such violence and anger was frequently depicted in complex but sympathetic ways, such as when she temporarily let her guard down and almost allowed herself to be seduced by a serial killer. There was also Sister Mary Maureen in the high-profile but short-lived television series *Nothing Sacred* (1997), which had Father Andrew Greeley as a technical advisor. She was explicitly feminist, fighting for causes such as women's ordination, but the show failed to garner an audience and clerical protests hastened its early cancellation. None of these add up to a sustained cultural moment similar to what happened in the fifties and sixties. Yet they do present an alternative to the more prevalent images that rely on outmoded stereotypes.

The stereotypical nun, with her flowing garments and ornamental rosaries, is a viscerally arresting image, filled with icons, symbols, and signifiers of an evocative, romantic, but also antiquated sense of religiosity and femininity. This is a highly institutionalized and corporatized version that reinforces a culture of containment around women's sexual, spiritual, and intellectual potential by deflecting it onto idealized versions of pious femininity and the promise of higher rewards in another life. It is also, interestingly enough, the most popular and accepted version across the social and political spectrum. That conservatives and radicals alike embrace this image – either as an exemplar or as a bad joke – suggests something of the confusion that sisters present to standardized conventions of feminine emancipation as sexual liberation. Their fluid and complicated image challenges stereotypes and breaks down barriers between sexuality and spirituality. The insertion of their history into contemporary popular culture denaturalizes our easy stereotyping and forces us to confront their ideological underpinnings (Spigel 2001, 22). These are women who broke away from institutionalism and sought different forms of identity construction through their national, sexual, racial, class, or other cultural systems. They stand as a challenge to the repressive tendencies of the Catholic Church from within, and societal expectations on women from without, demonstrating a desire to bear 'witness to integrity,' as Anita Caspary phrases it (2003). More importantly, however, they force a reappraisal of femininity and feminism beyond a body politics of desire and pleasure, and into the realm of spiritual and intellectual fortitude.

Works Cited

Ahlstrom, Sydney E. 1978. 'National Trauma and Changing Religious Values.' *Daedalus* 107 (1): 13–29.

Aronowitz, Alfred G. 1964. 'The Swinging Nuns.' *Saturday Evening Post*, 4 January, 66–7.

Augustine, Sister Mary. 1959. 'Sister Sez ...' *Daily Bulletin*, 4 June.

– 1958. 'Cross My Heart: *The Nun's Story* Just That!' *Marist Mission*, June, 24–8.

Austine, Sister Mary. 1964. 'The Ad Said "Generous Souls."' In *Convent Life: Roman Catholic Religious Orders for Women in North America*, ed. Joan M. Lexau, 31–43. New York: Dial.

An Awakening of Black Nun Power. 1968. *Ebony*, October, 44–50.

'Battling for Nuns' Rights.' 1969. *Newsweek*. 8 September, 80–1.

Beane, Marjorie Noterman. 1993. *From Framework to Freedom: A History of the Sister Formation Conference*. Lanham, MA: University Press of America.

Berg, Roland H. 1955. 'A Sister from Maryknoll Becomes a Doctor.' *Look*, 15 November, 79–86.

'Bernie Becomes a Nun.' 1954. *Cosmopolitan*. December, 118–27.

Berman, Russell. 1995. 'Three Comments on Future Perspectives on German Cultural History.' *New German Critique* 65: 115–24.

Best, Marjorie. Collection. *The Nun's Story* Estimating Script, Folder 70. Margaret Herrick Library, Los Angeles.

'Birth Control: The Pill and the Church.' 1964. *Newsweek*, 6 July 51–5.

Blackwelder, Julia Kirk. 1997. *Now Hiring: The Feminization of Work in the United States, 1900–1995*. College Station: Texas A & M University Press.

Blanshard, Paul. 1958. *American Freedom and Catholic Power*. 2nd ed. Boston: Beacon.

Bomm, Right Reverend Urbanus. 1969. 'Gregorian Chant and Liturgical Singing in the Vernacular.' In *Sacred Music and Liturgy Reform after Vatican II*, ed.
Johannes Overath, 163–8. Rome: Consociato Internationalis Musicae Sacrae.

Borromeo, Sister M. Charles, ed. 1967. *The New Nuns*. New York: New American Library.

– 1965. *The Changing Sister*. Notre Dame, IN: Fides.

Brady, Sister Eileen. 1989. 'Speaking My Truth.' In *Homosexuality in the Priesthood and the Religious Life*, ed. Jeannine Gramick, 96–100. New York: Crossroad.

Breines, Wini. 1992. *Young, White and Miserable: Growing Up Female in the
Fifties*. Boston: Beacon.

Brooks, Tim, and Earle Marsh. 1995. *The Complete Directory to Prime Time
Network and Cable TV Shows*. 6th ed. New York: Ballentine.

Brown, Helen Gurley. 1962. *Sex and the Single Girl*. New York: Bernard Geis
Associates.

Cantwell, Robert. 1996. *When We Were Good: The Folk Revival*. Cambridge:
Harvard University Press.

Carlen, Claudia. 1981. *The Papal Encyclicals, 1939–1958*. Vol. 4. Ann Arbor,
MI: Pierian.

Caspary, Anita. 2003. *Witness to Integrity: The Crisis of the Immaculate Heart
Community of California*. Collegeville, MN: Liturgical.

Change of Habit [COH] Clippings File. 1969. Margaret Herrick Library, Los
Angeles.

Chase, Mary Ellen. 1956. 'An Enthralling Narrative of a Profound Experience.'
New York Herald Tribune, 9 September, sec. 1.

Cogley, John. 1966. 'Religion: A Conversation with "the New Nun."' *New York
Times*, 13 March, E7.

– 1965. 'The Clergy Heeds a New Call.' *New York Times Magazine*, 2 May,
42–54.

Coughlan, Robert. 1956. 'Changing Roles in Modern Marriage.' *Life*, 24
December, 108–18.

Could I Measure Up? Seattle: Sisters of Charity of Providence, 1957.

Crowther, Bosley. 1965. 'The Sound of Music.' *New York Times*, 3 March.
Retrieved from Movie Review Query Engine <http://www.rnrqe.com/
lookup?sound+of+music>. Accessed 30 November 2003.

– 1963. 'The Negro in Films.' *New York Times*, 6 October, 1+.

Curb, Rosemary Keefe, and Nancy Manahan, eds. 1985. *Lesbian Nuns: Breaking
Silence*. New York: Warner.

de Certeau, Michel. 1988. *The Writing of History*. Trans. Tom Conley. New York: Columbia University Press.

Delaporte, Florence. 1996. *Soeur Sourire: Brûlée aux feux de la rampe*. Paris: Plon.

del Ray, Maria. 1956. *Bernie Becomes a Nun*. New York: Farrar, Straus and Cudahy.

Denisoff, R. Serge. 1983. *Sing a Song of Social Significance*. 2nd ed. Bowling Green, OH: Bowling Green University Popular Press.

de Roos, Robert. 1967. 'Her Feet Are on the Ground.' *TV Guide*, 30 September, 16–19.

DeTurk, David A., and A. Poulin Jr. 1967. *The American Folk Scene: Dimensions of the Folksong Revival*. New York: Dell.

Dinges, William D. 1987. 'Ritual Conflict as Social Conflict: Liturgical Reform in the Roman Catholic Church.' *Sociological Analysis* 48 (2): 138–57.

Dion, Philip E. 1965. *Sister's Vow of Chastity*. New York: Joseph E. Wagner.

Dominican Sisters of Hope (DSH) Archives. Newburgh, NY.

Dominique from the 'Singing Nun.' 1965(?). Crown Records CST 522.

Dorcy, Sister Mary Jean. 1964. 'Some Call It Madness, Some Call It Love.' In *Convent Life: Roman Catholic Religious Orders for Women in North America*, ed. Joan M. Lexau, 44–70. New York: Dial.

Douglas, Ann. 1977. *The Feminization of American Culture*. New York: Anchor.

Douglas, Susan J. 2000. 'Narcissism as Liberation.' In *The Gender and Consumer Culture Reader*, ed. Jennifer Scanlon, 267–82. New York: New York University Press.

– 1994. *Where the Girls Are: Growing Up Female with the Mass Media*. New York: Times.

Ebaugh, Helen Rose Fuchs. 1977. *Out of the Cloister: A Study of Organizational Dilemmas*. Austin: University of Texas Press.

Eby, Judith Ann. 2000. 'A Little Squabble among Nuns? The Sister Formation Crisis and the Patterns of Authority and Obedience among American Women Religious, 1954–1971.' Phd Dissertation, Saint Louis University.

Ehrenreich, Barbara, Elizabeth Hess, and Gloria Jacobs. 1986. *Re-Making Love: The Feminization of Sex*. New York: Anchor.

Ellis, John Tracy. 1969. *American Catholicism*. 2nd ed. Chicago: University of Chicago Press.

Epstein, Cynthia Fuchs. 1970. *Woman's Place: Options and Limits in Professional Careers*. Berkeley: University of California Press.

Evans, Sara. 1980. *Personal Politics: The Roots of Women's Liberation in the Civil Rights Movement and the New Left.* New York: Vintage.

Ewens, Mary. 1989. 'Women in the Convent.' In *American Catholic Women: A Historical Exploration*, ed. Karen Kennelly, 17–47. New York: Macmillan.

Face to Face with a Girl Who Is Becoming a Nun. 1966. *Seventeen*, June, 117+.

Faherty, William B. 1964. 'The Secular Institute.' In *Convent Life: Roman Catholic Religious Orders for Women in North America*, ed. Joan M. Lexau, 169–73. New York: Dial.

Farrell, James J. 1997. *The Spirit of the Sixties: The Making of Postwar Radicalism.* New York: Routledge.

Fentone, Steve. 2000. *AntiCristo: The Bible of Nasty Nun Sinema and Culture.* Guildford, Surrey: Fab.

Field, Sally. 1967. Untitled. *Citizen-News*, 16 November, B6.

Fisher, James T. 1989. *The Catholic Counterculture in America, 1933–1962.* Chapel Hill: University of North Carolina Press.

Flannery, Austin P., ed. 1975. *Documents of Vatican II.* Grand Rapids, MI: Eerdmans.

Forbes, Bruce David, and Jeffrey H. Mahan, eds. 2000. *Religion and Popular Culture in America.* Berkeley: University of California Press.

Francis, Sister Mary. 1957. *A Right to Be Merry.* London: Sheed & Ward.

Frederic, Sister M. Catherine. 1954 ... *And Spare Me Not in the Making.* Milwaukee, WI: Bruce.

Freeman, Jo. 1975. *The Politics of Women's Liberation.* New York: David McKay.

Fremantle, Anne. 1956. 'Adventures of a Dedicated One.' *New York Times Book Review*, 9 September, 1+.

French, Brandon. 1978. *On the Verge of Revolt: Women in American Films of the Fifties.* New York: Frederick Ungar.

Friedan, Betty. 1985. *'It Changed My Life': Writings on the Women's Movement.* New York: Norton.

– 1963. *The Feminine Mystique.* New York: Dell.

Gallen, Reverend Joseph F. 1955. 'Statements of the Holy See on the Education and Formation of Sisters.' *Sister-Formation Bulletin* 1 (4): 23–4.

Gardiner, Harold C. 1959. '"The Nun's Story" – A Symposium.' *America*, 27 June, 468–71.

– 1957. 'Reactions to *The Nun's Story*.' *America*, 26 January, 482–3.

– 1956a. 'Enchanting Revolutionary.' *America*, 16 September, 568–9.

– 1956b. 'Story on *The Nun's Story*.' *America*, 8 December, 300–1.

Geraghty, Christine. 1996. 'Reflections on History in Teaching Cultural Studies.' *Cultural Studies* 10 (2): 345–53.

Gilbert, Sister Mary [Madeline DeFrees]. 1954. *The Springs of Silence*. Kingswood: World's Work.

Gill, Brendan. 1965. 'The Current Cinema.' *New Yorker*, 6 March, 94–6.

'A Girl Sets Out to Be a Nun.' 1963. *Life*, 15 March, 66–79.

Gleason, Ralph J. 1965. 'The Times They Are a Changin'.' *Ramparts*, April, 36–48.

Glisky, Joan. 1997. 'The Official IHM Stance on Friendship, 1845–1960.' In *Building Sisterhood: A Femininst History of the Sisters, Servants of the Immaculate Heart of Mary*, ed. Sisters, Servants of the Immaculate Heart of Mary, Monroe, Michigan, 153–72. Syracuse, NY: Syracuse University Press.

Goffman, Erving. 1961. *Asylums: Essays on the Social Situation of Mental Patients and Other Inmates*. Garden City, NY: Anchor.

Gramick, Jeannine, ed. 1989. *Homosexuality in the Priesthood and the Religious Life*. New York: Crossroad.

Greeley, Andrew. 1971. *Come Blow Your Mind with Me*. Garden City, NY: Doubleday.

Greene, Gael. 1964. *Sex and the College Girl*. New York: Dial.

Griffin, Mary. 1975. *The Courage to Choose: An American Nun's Story*. Boston: Little, Brown.

Hamamoto, Darrell Y. 1989. *Nervous Laughter: Television Situation Comedy and Liberal Democratic Ideology*. New York: Praeger.

Haralovich, Mary Beth. 1992. 'Sitcoms and Suburbs: Positioning the 1950s Homemaker.' In *Private Screenings: Television and the Female Consumer*, ed. Lynn Spigel and Denise Mann, 111–42. Minneapolis: University of Minnesota Press.

Heaven Knows, Mr Allison (HKMA) Clippings File. 1957. Margaret Herrick Library, Los Angeles.

Heaven Knows, Mr Allison (HKMA) MPAA File. 1957. Margaret Herrick Library, Los Angeles.

Hennessy, Rosemary, and Chrys Ingraham. 1997. 'Introduction: Reclaiming Anticapitalist Feminism.' In *Materialist Feminism: A Reader in Class, Difference and Women's Lives*, ed. Rosemary Hennessy and Chrys Ingraham, 1–14. New York: Routledge.

Herberg, Will. 1964. 'Religion in a Secularized Society: Some Aspects of America's Three-Religion Pluralism.' In *Religion, Culture and Society: A Reader in the Sociology of Religion*, ed. Louis Schneider, 591–600. New York: Wiley.

– 1960. *Protestant-Catholic-Jew: An Essay in American Religious Sociology*. Rev.
ed. New York: Anchor.

Her Prince Charming. n.d. Seattle: Sisters of Charity of Providence.

Hoffman, Frank. 1983. *The 'Cash Box' Singles Charts, 1950–1981*. Metuchen,
NJ: Scarecrow.

Hoover, Stewart M. 1997. 'Media and the Construction of the Religious Public
Sphere.' In *Rethinking Media, Religion and Culture*, ed. Stewart M. Hoover and
Knut Lundby, 283–97. London: Sage.

Hubbell, Albert. 1956. 'The Dedicated Life.' *New Yorker*, 29 September, 138–44.

Hudnut-Beumler, James. 1994. *Looking for God in the Suburbs: The Religion of the
American Dream and Its Critics, 1945–1965*. New Brunswick, NJ: Rutgers
University Press.

Hulme, Kathryn. 1956. *The Nun's Story*. Boston: Little, Brown.

Humphrey, Hal. 1967. 'A Flying Nun Receives Advice.' *Los Angeles Times*,
27 November, 32.

'Immaculate Heart Rebels.' 1970. *Time*, 16 February, 49–50.

Inness, Sherrie. 1997. 'Girl Scouts, Camp Fire Girls, and Woodcraft Girls:
The Ideology of Girls' Scouting Novels, 1910–1935.' In *Nancy Drew and
Company: Culture, Gender, and Girls' Series*, ed. Sherrie Inness, 89–100.
Bowling Green, OH: Bowling Green State University Popular Press.

Janosik, MaryAnn. 1997. 'Madonnas in Our Midst: Representations of Women
Religious in Hollywood Film.' *US Catholic Historian* 15 (3): 75–98.

Jeffrey, Peter. 1992. *Re-envisioning Past Musical Cultures: Ethnomusicology in the
Study of Gregorian Chant*. Chicago: University of Chicago Press.

Judith, Sister. 1956. 'Vocation Survey.' *Sister Formation Bulletin* 3 (2): 1–7.

Kael, Pauline. 1970. *Kiss Kiss Bang Bang*. London: Calder and Boyars.

Kaiser, Robert Blair. 1967a. 'The Nuns that Quit.' *Ladies' Home Journal*, April,
82–3, 136–40.

– 1967b. 'Jacqueline Grennan: Ex-Nun.' *Look*, 30 May, 106–10.

Keyser, Les, and Barbara Keyser. 1984. *Hollywood and the Catholic Church: The
Image of Roman Catholicism in American Movies*. Chicago: Loyola University
Press.

King, Henry. Collection. *The Singing Nun*. Folder 38. Margaret Herrick Library,
Los Angeles.

Kolmer, Elizabeth, ASC. 1984. *Religious Women in the United States: A Survey of
the Influential Literature from 1950 to 1983*. Wilmington, DE: Michael Glazier.

'Laborare est orare.' 1955. *Time*, 11 April, 76–84.

LaCapra, Dominick. 1983. *Rethinking Intellectual History: Texts, Contexts, Language*. Ithaca, NY: Cornell University Press.

'Letter from Rome.' 1952. *New Yorker*, 4 October, 123–5.

Levine, Milton I., and Maya Pines. 1961. 'Sex: The Problem Colleges Evade.' *Harper's*, October, 129–32.

Lexau, Joan M., ed. 1964. *Convent Life: Roman Catholic Religious Orders for Women in North America*. New York: Dial.

Lilies of the Field (LOTF) MPAA File. 1963. Margaret Herrick Library, Los Angeles.

Lilies of the Field (LOTF) Production Book. 1963. Margaret Herrick Library, Los Angeles.

Luckett, Moya. 1999. 'Sensuous Women and Single Girls.' In *Swinging Single: Representing Sexuality in the 1960s*, ed. Hilary Radner and Moya Luckett, 277–98. Minneapolis: University of Minnesota Press.

– 1997. 'Girl Watchers: Patty Duke and Teen TV.' In *The Revolution Wasn't Televised: Sixties Television and Social Conflict*, ed. Lynn Spigel and Michael Curtin, 95–116. New York: Routledge.

Lury, Celia. 1995. 'The Rights and Wrongs of Culture: Issues of Theory and Methodology.' In *Feminist Cultural Theory: Process and Production*, ed. Beverly Skeggs, 33–45. Manchester: Manchester University Press.

Malits, Sister M. Elena. 1965. 'The Meaning of Virginity in Religious Life.' In *The Changing Sister*, ed. Sister M. Charles Borromeo, 89–126. Notre Dame, IN: Fides.

Marist Missionary Sisters Archives. Waltham, MA.

Maryanna, Sister. 1964. *With Love and Laughter*. Garden City, NY: Image.

Maureen, Sister Mary. 1967. *Your Calling as a Nun: A Sense of Mission*. New York: Richards Rosen.

McAllister, Robert J. 1969. *Conflict in Community*. Collegeville, MN: St John's University Press.

McCracken, Grant. 1988. *Culture and Consumption: New Approaches to the Symbolic Character of Consumer Goods and Activities*. Bloomington: Indiana University Press.

McDannell, Colleen. 1995a. *Material Christianity: Religion and Popular Culture in America*. New Haven, CT: Yale University Press.

– 1995b. 'Catholic Domesticity, 1860–1960.' In *Religion and American Culture: A Reader*, ed. David G. Hackett, 291–314. London: Routledge.

McGoldrick, Desmond F. 1963. *The Martyrdom of Change: Simple Talks to*

Postulant Sisters on the Religious Mentality and Ideal. Pittsburgh, PA: Duquesne University Press.

McLeer, Anne. 2002. 'Practical Perfection?: The Nanny Negotiates Gender, Class and Family Contradictions in 1960s Popular Culture.' *NWSA Journal* 14 (2): 80–101.

McNamara, Jo Ann Kay. 1996. *Sisters in Arms: Catholic Nuns through Two Millennia.* Cambridge: Harvard University Press.

Medical Mission Sisters. 1970. *RSVP: Music for Militants and Others Who Care.* Avant Garde Records Inc.

– 1966. *Joy Is Like the Rain.* Avant Garde Records Inc. AVS 101.

Medical Mission Sisters Archives. Philadelphia, PA.

Miles, Margaret R. 1996. *Seeing and Believing: Religion and Value in the Movies.* Boston: Beacon.

Mission Helpers of the Sacred Heart. 1954. *Vital Steps to Chastity.* Prepared by a Committee of Sisters of the Mission Helpers of the Sacred Heart for Teachers of Religion. Archdiocese of Baltimore.

Moffatt, John E. 1960. *Step This Way, Sister: Reflections for Nuns, Young and – Less Young.* New York: Farrar, Straus and Cudahy.

– 1958. *By the Way, Sister … Obiter Dicta for Nuns.* New York: Farrar, Straus and Cudahy.

'The Morals Revolution on the US Campus.' 1964. *Newsweek*, 6 April, 52–9.

Nash, Ilana. 2002. ' "Nowhere Else to Go": *Gidget* and the Construction of Adolescent Femininity.' *Feminist Media Studies* 2 (3): 341–56.

Neal, Sister Marie Augusta. 1990. *From Nuns to Sisters: An Expanding Vocation.* Mystic, CT: Twenty-Third Publications.

– 1984. *Catholic Sisters in Transition: From the 1960s to the 1980s.* Wilmington, DE: Michael Glazier.

– 1965. 'Sociology and Community Change.' In *The Changing Sister*, ed. Sister M. Charles Borromeo, 9–45. Notre Dame, IN: Fides.

'A New Look at the American Woman.' 1956. *Look*, 16 October, 35–54.

Nielsen Media Research. 1968. *Summary of Program Audience Estimates.* New York: Nielsen Media Research.

Novak, Michael. 1966. 'The New Nuns.' *Saturday Evening Post*, 30 July, 21–7, 66–72.

'The Nun: A Joyous Revolution.' 1967. *Newsweek*, 25 December, 45–8.

The Nun's Story (TNS) MPAA File. 1959. Margaret Herrick Library, Los Angeles.

The Nun's Story (TNS) Clippings File. Margaret Herrick Library, Los Angeles.

'Nuns Take on TV.' 1955. *Life*, 29 August, 53–4.

Oakley, J. Ronald. 1986. *God's Country: America in the Fifties*. New York: Dembner.

Oberg, Sister Jennifer. 1967. 'Margaret Mead Looks at the Modern Sister.' In *The New Nuns*, ed. Sister M. Charles Borromeo, 66–70. New York: New American Library.

O'Brien, David J. 1972. *The Renewal of American Catholicism*. New York: Oxford University Press.

O'Dea, Thomas F. 1968. *The Catholic Crisis*. Boston: Beacon.

Ong, Walter J., SJ. 1961. *Frontiers in American Catholicism: Essays on Ideology and Culture*. New York: Macmillan.

Orsi, Robert A. 1997. ' "Mildred, Is It Fun To Be a Cripple?" The Culture of Suffering in Mid-Twentieth-Century American Catholicism.' In *Catholic Lives, Contemporary America*, ed. Thomas J. Ferraro, 19–64. Durham, NC: Duke University Press.

Parsons, Sister Francis Loyola, and Sister Thomas Clare Dunleavy. 1967. 'Renewing Religious Power Structures.' In *The New Nuns*, ed. Sister M. Charles Borromeo, 133–41. New York: New American Library.

Paul VI. 1963. *Sacrosanctum Concilium – The Constitution on the Sacred Liturgy*. 4 December. <http://www.christusrex.org/www1/CDHN/v8.html>. Accessed 30 Nov. 2004.

Paulos, Dan. 1998. 'How I Have Longed.' *Christianity and the Arts* (Fall): 29–30.

Pius X. *Motu Proprio on Sacred Music*. 22 November 1903. <http://www.unavoce.org/intersollicitudines.htm>. Accessed 30 November 2003.

'The Pope and the Pill.' 1965. *Newsweek*, 12 April, 66.

'Priests and Nuns: Going Their Way.' 1970. *Time*, 23 February, 51–8.

Proctor, Kay. 1957. ' "Mr. Allison" Wins "Extra-Glowing" Class.' *Los Angeles Examiner*, 15 March, 2+.

Quiñonez, Lora Ann, and Mary Daniel Turner. 1992. *The Transformation of American Catholic Sisters*. Philadelphia: Temple University Press.

Radner, Hilary. 1999. 'Introduction: Queering the Girl.' In *Swinging Single: Representing Sexuality in the 1960s*, ed. Hilary Radner and Moya Luckett, 1–35. Minneapolis: University of Minnesota Press.

Radway, Janice. 1984. *Reading the Romance: Women, Patriarchy and Popular Literature*. Chapel Hill: University of North Carolina Press.

Rand, Lorraine. 1971. 'Masculinity or Femininity? Differentiating Career-Oriented and Homemaking-Oriented College Freshman Women.' In *The*

Professional Woman, ed. Athena Theodore, 156–66. Cambridge, MA: Schenkman.

Raphaela, Sister. 1989. 'Home By Way of Roundabout.' In *Homosexuality in the Priesthood and the Religious Life*, ed. Jeannine Gramick, 76–88. New York: Crossroad.

Reilly, Cyril A. 1963. 'The Lively Art of Folk Music.' *Today* (February): 8–11.

Religious of Jesus and Mary (RJM) Archives. Mount Rainier, MD.

Review of *The Sound of Music*. 1965. *America*, 13 March, 374–5.

Review of *The Sound of Music*. 1966. *Esquire*, August, 20–1.

Review of *Where Angels Go, Trouble Follows*. 1968. *Motion Picture Herald*, 10 April, 79.

Riesman, David, with Nathan Glazer and Reuel Denney. 1969. *The Lonely Crowd: A Study of the Changing American Character*. Abridged edition with a 1969 preface. New Haven: Yale University Press.

– 1951. 'Freud, Religion and Science.' *American Scholar* 20 (3): 267–76.

Ríos, Tere. 1965. *The Fifteenth Pelican*. Garden City, NY: Doubleday.

Robinson, Gertrude Joch. 1983. 'The Media and Social Change: Thirty Years of Magazine Coverage of Women and Work (1950–1977).' *Atlantis* 8 (2): 87–111.

Rousset, Suzy. 1955. 'Medical Aspects.' In *Religious Life versus Chastity*, ed. Lancelot C. Sheppard, 194–203. London: Blackfriars.

Rovin, Jeff. 1985. 'Sally Field: There's a Part of Me That's Just Coming to Life.' *Ladies Home Journal*, July, 26+.

'Ruritanian Reich.' 1965. *Newsweek*, 15 March, 100.

Samuels, Gertrude. 1951. 'Why Twenty Million Women Work.' *New York Times Magazine*, 9 September, 13+.

Sanders, Marion K. 1960. 'A Proposition for Women.' *Harper's*, September, 41+.

Schaldenbrand, Sister Mary Aloysious. 1967. 'Freud and Sisters.' In *The New Nuns*, ed. Sister M. Charles Borromeo, 71–82. New York: New American Library.

– 1965. 'Personal Fulfilment and Apostolic Effectiveness.' In *The Changing Sister*, ed. M. Charles Borromeo, 127–74. Notre Dame, ID: Fides.

Schneiders, Sandra M. 2001. *Selling All: Commitment, Consecrated Celibacy and Community in Catholic Religious Life*. New York: Paulist.

'The Second Sexual Revolution.' 1964. *Time*, 24 January, 54–9.

Seng, Sister M. Angelica. 1965. 'The Sister in the New City.' In *The Changing Sister*, ed. Sister M. Charles Borromeo, 229–62. Notre Dame, IN: Fides.

Shea, Sister Mary Berchmans. 1967. 'Protest Movements and Convent Life.' In

The New Nuns, ed. Sister M. Charles Borromeo, 59–65. New York: New American Library.

Shepard, Richard F. 1963. 'Singing Nuns Hit Record Jackpot.' *New York Times*, 7 November, 39.

Shipman, David. 1966. Review of *The Singing Nun*. *Films and Filming* (June): 57.

'Singing Nun Goes On; Dominates Disk Sales.' 1963. *Billboard*, 30 November, 4.

' "Singing Nun" Has Chi Talking.' 1963. *Billboard*, 16 November, 1+.

The Singing Nun (*TSN*) MPAA File. 1966. Margaret Herrick Library, Los Angeles.

'Singing Nun Sets U.S.-Canada Tour.' 1966. *New York Times*, 4 December, 173.

'Singing Sister.' 1963. *Newsweek*, 23 December, 51.

Singing Sisters of Saint Dominic. 1964. *Joy!* XSV85781.

Skinner, Cornelia Otis. 1956. 'Women Are Misguided.' *Life*, 24 December, 72–6.

Skinner, James M. 1993. *The Cross and the Cinema: The Legion of Decency and the National Catholic Office of Motion Pictures, 1933–1970*. Westport, CT: Praeger.

Smith, Cecil. 1970. 'What to Do with a Grounded Nun?' *Los Angeles Herald-Examiner*, 26 November.

Smith, Dorothy E. 1990. *Texts, Facts and Femininity: Exploring the Relations of Ruling*. New York: Routledge.

Smith, Sophia. Collection. Fiftieth Anniversary, 1966. Planned Parenthood Federation of America Archives, Series II. Box 24.

Soeur Sourire. 196X?. *The Singing Nun, Her Joy Her Songs*. Philips PCC 209.

– *The Singing Nun*. 1963. Philips PCC 203.

'Speaking of Pictures.' 1952. *Life*, 15 December, 16–17.

Spigel, Lynn. 2001. *Welcome to the Dreamhouse: Popular Media and Postwar Suburbs*. Durham, NC: Duke University Press.

– 1991. 'From Domestic Space to Outer Space: The 1960s Fantastic Family Sitcom.' In *Close Encounters: Film, Feminism and Science Fiction*, ed. Constance Penley, Elisabeth Lyon, Lynn Spigel and Janet Bergstrom, 205–36. Minneapolis: University of Minnesota Press.

– 1989. 'The Domestic Economy of Television Viewing in Postwar America.' *Critical Studies in Mass Communication* 6 (4): 337–54.

'Spree for Sister Marie.' 1961. *Look*, 5 December, 85–90.

Star, Jack. 1963. 'Trouble Ahead for the Catholic Schools / The Vanishing Nun.' *Look*, 22 October, 37–40.

Steinem, Gloria. 1962. 'The Moral Disarmament of Betty Coed.' *Esquire*, September, 97, 153–57.

Straw, Will. 2000. 'Exhausted Commodities: The Material Culture of Music.' *Canadian Journal of Communication* 25 (1): 175–85.

Suenens, Leon Joseph Cardinal. 1962. *The Nun in the World: New Dimensions in the Modern Apostolate*. Westminster, UK: Newman.

Tate, Judith. 1970. *Religious Women in the Modern World*. New York: Herder and Herder.

– 1966. *Sisters for the World*. New York: Herder and Herder.

'Time For a Change.' 1967. *Time*, 28 April, 62.

The Trouble with Angels (TTWA) Clippings File. 1966. Margaret Herrick Library, Los Angeles.

The Trouble with Angels (TTWA) MPAA File. 1966. Margaret Herrick Library, Los Angeles.

Tunnacliffe, Catharine. 2001. 'The Hills Are Alive with the Sound of Heckling.' *Eye Weekly*, 22 February. <http://www.eye.net/eye/issue/issue_02.22.01/film/sound.html>. Accessed 30 November 2003.

'Ultimatum to Nuns.' 1968. *Time*, 21 June, 63.

Urban Music Education. 1969. *Musart*. September-October, 13+.

Valentine, Sister Mary Hester. 1968. *The Post-conciliar Nun*. New York: Hawthorn.

'Vatican Limits Popular Music in the Mass until it Is Suitable.' 1967. *New York Times*, 8 March, 1+.

Vickie, Sister. 1989. 'The Mirror Child.' In *Homosexuality in the Priesthood and the Religious Life*, ed. Jeannine Gramick, 101–8. New York: Crossroad.

Villet, Barbara, and Grey Villet. 1966. *Those Whom God Chooses*. New York: Viking.

Von Weidinger, A.R. 1957. 'Portrait of a Nun.' *New Yorker*, 23 February, 96–104.

Wakin, Edward, and Father Joseph F. Scheuer. 1966. *The De-Romanization of the American Catholic Church*. New York: Macmillan.

– 1965. 'The American Nun: Poor, Chaste, and Restive.' *Harper's*, August, 35+.

'Walled-in World.' 1955. *Life*, 20 June, 12–13.

Walsh, Frank. 1996. *Sin and Censorship: The Catholic Church and the Motion Picture Industry*. New Haven, CT: Yale University Press.

Welter, Barbara. 1987. 'From Maria Monk to Paul Blanshard: A Century of Protestant Anti-Catholicism.' In *Uncivil Religion: Interreligious Hostility in*

America, ed. Robert N. Bellah and Frederick E. Greenspahn, 43–71. New York: Crossroad.

'What's with the Girls?' 1961. *America*, 27 May, 359.

Whitburn, Joel. 1992. *Billboard Top 40 Hits*. 5th ed. New York: Billboard.

White, Hayden. 1978. *Tropics of Discourse: Essays in Cultural Criticism*. Baltimore: Johns Hopkins University Press.

Whitney, Dwight. 1968. '"I Didn't Want to Play a Nun."' *TV Guide*, 16 March, 21+.

Whyte, William H., Jr. 1957. *The Organization Man*. Garden City, NY: Doubleday.

Willingham, Saundra. 1968. 'Why I Quit the Convent.' *Ebony*, December, 64–74.

Wills, Gary. 1972. *Bare Ruined Choirs: Doubt, Prophecy and Radical Religion*. Garden City, NJ: Doubleday.

Wittberg, Patricia. 1994. *The Rise and Fall of Catholic Religious Orders: A Social Movement Perspective*. Albany: SUNY Press.

– 1989. 'Feminist Consciousness among American Nuns: Patterns of Ideological Diffusion.' *Women's Studies* 12 (5): 529–37.

Wolf, Stacey. 1996. 'The Queer Pleasures of Mary Martin and Broadway: The Sound of Music as a Lesbian Musical.' *Modern Drama* 39 (1): 51–68.

Wolff, Rick. 1991. 'The Flying Nun and Post-Vatican II Catholicism.' *Journal of Popular Film and Television* 19 (2): 72–80.

'Woman, Love and God.' 1956. *Life*, 24 December, 36.

'The Women Have It.' 1957. *Newsweek*, 18 March, 93+.

Wuthnow, Robert. 1994. *Producing the Sacred: An Essay on Public Religion*. Urbana: University of Illinois Press.

X, Sister. 1958. 'Love Is Forever.' In *Melody in Your Hearts*, ed. Rev. George L. Kane, 100–21. Westminster MD: Newman.

Young, Iris Marion. 1989. 'Throwing Like a Girl: A Phenomenology of Feminine Body Comportment, Motility and Spatiality.' In *The Thinking Muse*, ed. Jeffner Allen and Iris Marion Young, 51–70. Bloomington: Indiana University Press.

Zeitlin, David. 1959. 'A Lovely Audrey in Religious Role.' *Life*, 8 June, 141–5.

Zinnemann, Fred. Collection. *The Nun's Story*. Margaret Herrick Library, Los Angeles.

Credits

Index

91 (*see also* civil rights; nuns: and race, social justice activism; personalism); and sexuality, 131–2 (*see also* birth control: Catholic doctrine on; convent: sex education; *Humanae Vitae*; nuns: and sexuality; sexual revolution and religion). *See also* Catholic Church; ecumenism; liberation theology; Mariology; parochialism; pastoralism; Second Vatican Council; triumphalism; ultramontanism

CBS (Columbia Broadcasting System), 199, 205

celibacy. *See* nuns: vow of chastity; virginity

Change of Habit, 62, 66, 77, 85–94, 190, 194, 202, 216

chastity. *See* nuns: vow of chastity; virginity

Cimarron Strip, 199

civil religion, 5, 17, 25, 33, 40, 72–5, 117, 157, 166–8, 179, 222. *See also* Americanism: and Catholicism

civil rights movement, 54, 73–4, 92, 168–9. *See also* African American nuns; Americanism: and race; *Change of Habit*; *Lilies of the Field*; nuns: and race, social justice activism; personalism

CMSW. *See* Conference of Major Superiors of Women

Cold War, 131–4

Columbia Records, 158, 162–4

Conference of Major Superiors of Women (CMSW), 6, 27–9, 42, 49, 56, 74–5, 96–7, 123, 130, 160,

202. *See also* Call for Renewal; Leadership Conference of Women Religious; Sister Formation Conference

consumerism: and religion, 18, 126, 219; and gender, 5–6, 10, 12, 35, 63, 137, 200, 207, 217–20. *See also* adolescent girls: and consumerism; Americanism; girl culture; sexual revolution

convent: as asylum, 98; enrolment/population, 27, 43, 127, 211–12; metaphors of the family, 148–9, 152, 155–6; and public/private spheres, 10–11; reforms, 28, 32, 41–2, 49, 56, 87, 96, 129–30, 160, 181, 189, 194–5, 201, 223 (*see also* Call for Renewal; new nuns; nuns: modernizing the religious life); religious-run hospitals, 127; religious-run schools, 127–9; sex education in, 131–2, 142; traditional attitudes about 32, 45, 49, 87, 195, 211; training, 26, 145, 156 (*see also* nuns: vows); vocations, 43, 66–7, 115–16, 123–56; vocation crisis, 45, 127. *See also* adolescent girls: and the convent; Conference of Major Superiors of Women; Leadership Conference of Women Religious; National Coalition of American Nuns; nuns; Sister Formation Conference

Coughlan, Robert, 75

Could I Measure Up?, 141

counterculture, 73, 136, 139, 196–8, 200; nuns in, 43, 85–94, 189, 202 (*see also* new nuns). *See also* civil

activism, 41–3, 55–7, 74, 85–6, 159, 170, 187–9, 219–20; stereotypes in mass media, 29–30, 33, 44, 60–5, 74, 76, 176, 189, 194–6, 201–2, 213–16, 219–21, 223, 225–6; urban ministries, 88, 159, 185–7; and women's ordination, 223; vocations, 43, 45, 66–7, 115–16, 123–56 (*see also* adolescent girls: relationship with nuns; vocation books); vow of chastity, 39, 55, 57, 66, 83, 93, 99, 133, 148–50; vow of obedience, 27, 39, 99; vow of poverty, 172; vows, 45, 74, 145, 217–19. *See also* Call for Renewal; Conference of Major Superiors of Women; convent; Leadership Conference of Women Religious; National Coalition of American Nuns; Sister Formation Conference

Office Central Catholique du Cinéma, 109–10
Ong, Walter, 160
Open End with David Susskind, 43–4, 49, 54
Oprah Winfrey Show, The, 225
Oz, 225

parochialism, 24–5, 27, 107, 127. *See also* triumphalism; ultramontanism
particular friendships. *See* PFs
Pasolini, Pier Paulo, 220
pastoralism, 18, 167, 169, 171, 186, 187. *See also* personalism: and Catholicism; Second Vatican Council

Patty Duke Show, The, 198
Paul VI (Pope), 50, 186
Peace Corp, 56
Pecher, Annie, 178, 195
Perfectae Caritatis, 41, 44. *See also* convent: reforms; nuns: modernizing the religious life; Second Vatican Council
Perry Como Show, The, 162
personal friendships. *See* PFs
personalism, 16, 19, 39, 133, 156, 169, 178, 187; and Americanism, 166, 177; authenticity, 167–8; and Catholicism, 41, 180, 186, 189; and class, 168; and folk music, 166–8, 180; and gender, 73, 200–1; and nuns, 19, 157, 179–80, 186, 188–9, 221; and religion, 166–8, 222. *See also* Americanism: and Catholicism; civil rights; counterculture; folk music; New Left; nuns: social justice activism
Peyton Place, 199
PFs, 26, 99, 114, 149–50, 218. *See also* homosexuality; nuns: and homosexuality
Philips, 172, 174, 178. *See also* Luc-Gabrielle, Soeur; 'Dominique'
Pines, Maya, 37
Pius X (Pope), 161
Pius XI (Pope), 106
Pius XII (Pope), 27, 106, 128, 159, 161, 169, 186
Planned Parenthood Federation (PPF), 43, 48
Poitier, Sidney, 68
Poor Clares, 141
pornography, 93, 202, 220–1